M000290685

Challenges in U.S. National Security Policy

A Festschrift Honoring Edward L. (Ted) Warner

David Ochmanek, Michael Sulmeyer

EDITORS

James M. Acton, Michael Albertson, Alexei G. Arbatov,
Elbridge A. Colby, Michèle A. Flournoy, Rose E. Gottemoeller,
Andrew R. Hoehn, Christopher J. Lamb, James N. Miller,
David Ochmanek, Eugene Rumer, James A. Schear,
Walter B. Slocombe, Michael Sulmeyer, Dean A. Wilkening

CONTRIBUTORS

Funding for this book was made possible by RAND's Investment in People and Ideas program, which combines philanthropic contributions from individuals, foundations, and private-sector firms with earnings from RAND's endowment and operations to support innovative research on issues crucial to the policy debate but that reach beyond the boundaries of traditional client sponsorship.

Library of Congress Cataloging-in-Publication Data is available for this publication.

ISBN: 978-0-8330-8456-9

The RAND Corporation is a nonprofit institution that helps improve policy and decisionmaking through research and analysis. RAND's publications do not necessarily reflect the opinions of its research clients and sponsors.

Support RAND—make a tax-deductible charitable contribution at www.rand.org/giving/contribute.html

RAND® is a registered trademark.

© Copyright 2014 RAND Corporation

RAND OFFICES
SANTA MONICA, CA • WASHINGTON, DC
PITTSBURGH, PA • NEW ORLEANS, LA • JACKSON, MS
BOSTON, MA • CAMBRIDGE, UK • BRUSSELS, BE
www.rand.org

Contents

Figures and Tables

Figures

Tables

Acknowledgments

Editing this volume has been an enriching experience, presenting an unexpected opportunity to collaborate with both long-time friends and new colleagues. It is a testimony to Ted Warner's lasting influence and his relationship with former colleagues that every author we contacted about the project was quick not only to accept our invitation to join the effort but also to respond to deadlines. We thank them for following through on their commitments to this book and for their patience with us through several rounds of edits. We also thank Ted himself for his involvement in the project. He worked actively with each author to help shape their contributions, in some cases applying the rather dense editing familiar to his former subordinates. In every case, however, he struck the perfect balance between support for the work and deference to the contributors, always cognizant that he was the honoree.

A brief note on sources: This festschrift contains the candid memories of many close friends and colleagues of Ted Warner. While the authors frequently cite publicly available sources and undertook additional research to resolve questions about the historical record, they have written largely from personal recollection and without reference to archival materials. We also engaged in additional fact-checking and verification when needed.

Several individuals deserve special mention for their contribution to turning this book into reality. When we were looking for a publisher for this project, Andy Hoehn kindly secured the RAND Corporation's support. When we sought to convene an author's conference so that each author could share their ideas and benefit from the feedback of their colleagues, Kathleen Cutsforth graciously arranged for us to convene at RAND's Washington, D.C., office. And when we asked for substantive reviews of the first draft of the manuscript, Alan Vick and Jim Thomson provided thorough feedback and comments for each chapter. Each of these individuals has our sincerest thanks, and we are deeply grateful for their efforts.

While RAND has been most supportive of this effort, its primary role was as this book's publisher. This volume is not the result of a RAND study, but rather is a compilation of work by authors whose observations and arguments reflect neither the views of their employers nor those of the RAND Corporation. To that end, RAND does not necessarily endorse the perspectives presented throughout this volume.

David Ochmanek
Michael Sulmeyer
Washington D.C., 2013

Foreword

Walter B. Slocombe

Wikipedia, that totally authoritative font of knowledge, defines a *Festschrift* as

> a book honoring a respected person, ... presented during his or her lifetime. The term, borrowed from German, could be translated as *celebration publication* or *celebratory (piece of) writing*. ... Sometimes, the Latin term *liber amicorum* (literally: "book of friends") is used for a Festschrift.[1]

As applied to this book, honoring Ted Warner, Wikipedia has it right—it is a collection of papers by his friends, who have come to respect him and now join to celebrate his career, as he leaves (if only partially) the latest stage of his work.

Ted and I met more than 50 years ago, when we both participated in a student conference at the then recently opened Air Force Academy, I as a junior from Princeton University and Ted as a first classman (senior) from the U.S. Naval Academy. That the conference topic was arms control, at that time a newly fashionable academic and public policy subject, proved to be prescient, for Ted was to be centrally involved in arms control issues throughout his career, both in public office and as a scholar, an analyst, and—though he might accept the designation only with some reluctance— a powerful advocate. His commitment to reducing the nuclear danger is all the more effective because it is so firmly grounded in expertise, experience, and deep understanding of the realities of power in general and deterrence in particular.

But as the range of essays in this "Book of Friends" demonstrates, Ted's arms control work is only a part of his intellectual and practical contributions to the field of international security. The breadth of subjects covered, to each of which Ted has made, and continues to make, major contributions, highlights a unique aspect of his ability to do effective work on arms control and other defense matters: Few enough are the real experts on the technical issues of nuclear weapons and their delivery systems; on the strategies of deterrence and warfighting; or on the nature, culture, and history, and indeed the language, of Russia. Ted is an expert in all three fields. The topics of the varied contributions to this volume—reflecting Ted's early work on the bureaucratic politics of the Soviet military; his service as an assistant air attaché at the U.S. Embassy

---

[1] "Festschrift," definition, Wikipedia, February 3, 2014.

in Moscow and long experience as an analyst of the Soviet Union; his genuine intellectual and personal fellowship with several Russian counterparts; and his oversight, while serving as an assistant secretary of defense, of U.S. defense planning and strategy development and the review of U.S. defense programs to ensure that resource decisions support strategy and policy—all highlight the extraordinary spectrum of skills and perceptiveness he brings to policy issues, both as a senior policy advisor and as an analyst.

One aspect of his work that I had a special opportunity to observe and benefit from is, however, addressed only in passing in the chapters that follow. That is his role, as an assistant Secretary of Defense during the Clinton administration under secretaries Aspin, Perry, and Cohen, in the policy review of the major contingency plans for conventional warfare developed by the military commanders of the various geographic and functional U.S. combatant commands. Most of the details of these plans are still (properly) classified, but it is right that the broad outline of his contribution should be recognized, if only allusively.

When Ted came to the Office of the Secretary of Defense as the Assistant Secretary of Defense for Strategy and Requirements in 1993, the Goldwater-Nichols Act was relatively new and so was the responsibility of the Policy office to, in the words of the statute, "assist the Secretary of Defense in preparing written policy guidance for the preparation and review of contingency plans and in reviewing such plans." During the time I was first Principal Deputy and then Under Secretary of Defense for Policy, Ted had lead responsibility for this task and he (and I) took it very seriously. The review of contingency plans by Ted and his team—like their review of budgets and programs—became a significant element of the process without becoming a source of turf wars or infighting (at least, not more than was inevitable in any such effort carried out seriously). For the process, Ted combined intellectual application, recruiting a cadre of superior analysts (both civilian and military), the well-earned confidence of the Secretaries of Defense (and Under Secretaries) he served, and immense tact with a firm and demonstrated resolve not to be, or appear to be, a mere rubber stamp for the plans the military commands and the Joint Staff sent forward through Policy for the approval of the Secretary of Defense. Ted and his team managed to make the plan review process one that had real impact, assuring that plans reflected national policy, strategy, and resourcing priorities; rested on political assumptions that made sense; and could maximize the chances of achieving national, as well as strictly military, objectives. He thus made what could have been a purely formal review process a powerful instrument for true civilian policy oversight of a key aspect of U.S. defense policy, without improperly invading the professional prerogatives and expertise of the military.

One example must suffice to illustrate both the scale and the significance of the contingency plan reviews Ted led. During the 1990s, given confrontation and periodic provocations from North Korea; Iraq; and, to some degree, Iran, U.S. defense planning for major military conflict focused heavily on two regions: Northeast Asia, and

Southwest Asia. In each region, time and geography were (and remain) major factors: U.S. conventional military advantages were such that, given time, the United States could defeat any military effort by an enemy, but only after deploying very considerable additional forces to the theater and positioned for the fight. Most of these forces had to be moved literally halfway around the world. This "tyranny of time and distance" presented two dangers. First, a would-be aggressor might believe it could attain its objectives quickly, before the United States (with whatever regional and allied help was available) could have sufficient forces in place to halt its advance. Second, the attacker might believe that, having done so, it could raise the price of reversing its initial military success beyond the level the United States would be prepared to pay. That is, deterrence of the initial attack would be ineffective, and the military operations required to first halt, then roll back, and ultimately defeat the enemy would be prolonged and very costly in lives and resources.

Ted recognized that most "contingency planning" in the conventional (if not the nuclear) context is about logistics—allocating forces, getting them into place to operate effectively, and providing critically needed support to sustain their operations—not about the details of how they will be employed operationally and tactically in combat and that this is overwhelmingly true of the aspects of the contingency plans for major theater conflict that touch on issues of policy, strategy, and resources. Furthermore, he recognized that, while all plans included what were called "flexible deterrent options (FDOs)," American notions of what might deter the rulers in Pyongyang, Baghdad, or Teheran were not easy to identify. Moreover, these FDOs did not necessarily link directly to increasing the capability of the United States and its allies to apply military force effectively in theater.

Rather, and broadly speaking, the existing FDOs, which were designed to be implemented as a regional crisis deepened, but prior to the outbreak of war, were supposed to "convey resolve," i.e., help to convince the adversary that the United States would forcefully resist and thereby deter that adversary. They were also designed to rapidly send additional intelligence, surveillance, and reconnaissance assets to the region to more closely monitor the unfolding situation and to send forward units, such as port opening teams, to facilitate the reception of the massive flow of forces and materiel that would follow if war were to occur. The actual flow of forces that would be needed to fight if deterrence failed and war broke out was—certainly conceptually and, to a considerable degree, in practice—seen as a distinctly separate matter—and one that was more or less governed by an "off-on" switch, i.e., the declaration of "M (mobilization)-Day," a move that would trigger the massive, time-phased dispatch of the whole force to be committed to the war, after a decision by the President made only when conflict seemed all but certain.

Ted's insight was that a better way to both deter and be militarily effective if deterrence failed was to arrange the plans so that, as a crisis built, steps were taken early on that directly contributed to military capability in the relevant theater and that, in particular, cut into the time needed for the U.S. force buildup. So instead of FDOs that might or might not contribute directly to capability and instead of leaving the initiation of forward deployment until conflict seemed all but inevitable, the plans should explicitly be based on using the crisis period to, in effect, shorten the time needed to achieve full capability to prosecute the theater war. A simple example: If a particular sort of capability would be needed and if most of the equipment had to come by sea, the plans should envision the assets starting for the theater early in a crisis, not waiting for a later decision to start moving the whole force. Similarly, if, as would almost always be the case, relatively small logistics and other support elements had to be in place and be making preparations to receive the large reinforcements, these "door-opener" elements should be moved forward at an early stage, even as diplomatic and political efforts to avert conflict continued. The basic idea was that, instead of seeing the military buildup as something that would start only when conflict seemed virtually certain, the movement of some elements should be initiated early, precisely because doing so could help avert conflict, as well as increase U.S. capability if conflict did occur.

Of course, the notion that deterrence turned in part on capability enhancements was not original with the review process, and some of the existing FDOs would have had that effect, but to a considerable degree, the ideas that military planning should explicitly focus on early action to send a strong deterrent message by shortening overall deployment time lines and that the best deterrent of conventional aggression was visibly increasing the chances that such aggression would be promptly defeated were novel ones.

Similarly, Ted and his team realized that it was important that U.S. military actions not exacerbate the crisis or add to tensions and that force movements and preparations be geared to the actual situation at the time. So plans needed to incorporate the principle that execution of these early measures would require high-level authorization. (Indeed, another of their principles was generally to reduce automatic responses and provide for flexibility in execution.) The approach was, however, also based on the general principles that convincing the adversary that the United States was, without doing anything irreversible, making the adversary's prospect of military success far less likely and that, by dispelling the hopes of quick success, this would tend in most cases to bolster deterrence and assist in nonmilitary efforts to defuse crises the adversary's bluster had created. Further, the reality that the moves would become known—and, indeed, would usually be announced publicly—was an advantage, not a defect, for the process itself would signal both capability and resolve to adversaries, allies, and the U.S. public alike.

This effort was not simply theoretical, not simply a matter of improving paper plans. More than once during Ted's long tenure, between May 1993 and October 2000, plans that reflected his reconceptualization of how to make contingency planning mesh with crisis management were actually put into operation, in the contexts of both Korea and Iraq. When intelligence information showed signs of a possible preparation for attacks, when the adversary started making explicit threats, or (as was usually the case) both happened together and as indications of possible trouble built, small advance-preparation teams were deployed in theater; and "long-pole-in-the-tent" elements stationed outside the theater were readied and even started forward; all this while other, nonmilitary efforts to deter conflict were still in train. There can, to be sure, be no proof that these actions helped prevent what at the time looked like very serious tensions from building into conflict, but these actions, which followed from the review process Ted managed, were undertaken, and the crises were resolved.

Such appeared to be the case, for example, in October of 1994, when the rapid deployment of leading-edge FDO elements of what promised to be a massive U.S. military response to Saddam Hussein's movement within Iraq of some of his ground force divisions south toward the borders with Kuwait and Saudi Arabia, combined with high-level communication to Baghdad, helped convince the Iraqi leader to halt and reverse those threatening troop movements. Similarly, in the mid-1990s, when Pyongyang was ranting about "seas of fire" engulfing Seoul, significant air and other forces were prepared and started to move, providing important backup to the ultimately successful diplomatic efforts to restrain the North Korean nuclear program that was the fundamental source of the crisis.

Recent U.S. actions taken during the early stages of a crisis with the potential to grow into an armed conflict suggest that this basic approach continues to be a key element in U.S. military contingency planning and crisis management.

This aspect of Ted's work takes its place as another link in the remarkable list of his contributions to the nation, its defense, and its chances of living in peace.

CHAPTER ONE

The Life and Work of Ted Warner

David Ochmanek and Michael Sulmeyer

Edward L. Warner III, nicknamed Ted, was born in Detroit, Michigan, on December 4, 1940. Ted grew up in Okemos, Michigan, a very small town that was transforming into a suburb of nearby East Lansing. His father, Ed, was an executive with the Oldsmobile Division of General Motors; his mother, Dorothy, a substitute elementary school teacher. Ted was the middle child and the only son; his older sister, Anne, was born two years before him and his younger sister, Carol, six years after him.

Ted attended Okemos High School, where he graduated in 1958. He was valedictorian of his class of 55 and earned varsity letters in basketball, football, track, baseball, and golf. Ted inherited a great love of sports from his father, a former sports writer for the *Detroit Free Press*, and has remained a diehard fan of the athletic teams from the University of Michigan and the city of Detroit—the Tigers, the Red Wings, the Pistons, and even the often hapless Lions—to the present day.

During his senior year, Ted received an appointment to the U.S. Naval Academy and entered Annapolis along with roughly 1,200 other aspiring young midshipmen in June 1958. While at the Naval Academy, Ted, like all his fellow midshipmen at the time, earned his Bachelor of Science degree in Marine Engineering, there being no other academic majors offered. His experiences in taking a superb "overload" course in Russian Military History and attending a student conference on U.S. national security policy at the U.S. Military Academy at West Point, where he first learned of the concepts of nuclear deterrence and conflict escalation, as well as the potential for U.S.-Soviet arms control, kindled an intense interest in these matters that was to profoundly shape his subsequent professional life.

When Ted graduated from the Naval Academy along with 889 classmates in 1962, he elected to accept his commission as a second lieutenant in the U.S. Air Force. Bouts of seasickness while on summer cruises, combined with a strong desire to pursue graduate study in international security affairs as soon as possible after graduation, suggested that numerous tours at sea over the course of a naval career were not the right choice for him. His opportunity to switch services on graduation from the Naval Academy reflected the facts that the recently created U.S. Air Force Academy in Colorado Springs had graduated its first class in 1959, and its graduating classes over the next few years remained quite small. Thus, a limited number of graduates from Annapolis and West Point were able to seek their careers within the Air Force on graduation each year, as had been the case since the Air Force became an independent service in 1947.

Ted's first assignment was as an Air Intelligence Officer at Castle Air Force Base in Atwater, California, which was then the home of the 93rd Bomb Wing, the largest B-52 bomber and KC-135 refueling aircraft wing in the Strategic Air Command. The intelligence section, where Ted worked, provided daily intelligence briefings to the bomber and tanker crews standing alert and built the target materials for the combat mission folders that were to be used if the bomber aircrews were ordered and authorized to carry out their assigned nuclear strike missions.

The highlight of Ted's three-year tour at Castle Air Force Base was the opportunity in late October and early November of 1962 to brief the latest intelligence information to the full complement of bomber and tanker aircrews at the base every day throughout the four weeks of the Cuban Missile Crisis. These crews were all on generated alert, ready to sprint to their fueled and, in the case of the B-52s, nuclear-armed aircraft and take off in less than 30 minutes to carry out their assigned missions. While at Castle, Ted was promoted to the rank of first lieutenant in late 1964.

Ted returned to academia in the summer of 1965 when he began graduate studies in the Politics Department at Princeton University, in preparation for his assignment as an instructor, later an assistant professor, in the Political Science Department at the U.S. Air Force Academy. At Princeton, Ted's studies focused on comparative and international politics, with emphasis on the politics and defense policy of the Soviet Union. After two years of study with such distinguished professors as Cyril Black, Harry Eckstein, Klaus Knorr, Robert C. Tucker, and Richard Ullman, he passed the general examinations needed to qualify to pursue a Ph.D. in politics and was awarded a Master of Arts degree in June 1967. While attending Princeton, Ted was promoted to captain.

It was during Ted's time as a Princeton graduate student that he met his future wife, Pam, over the Thanksgiving weekend in 1966. They met on a United Airlines flight from Rochester, New York, to New York City's LaGuardia Airport. Pam was a flight attendant at the time, deadheading to New York City to meet her parents. Ted recalls that, as he boarded the nearly empty plane, he spotted a very pretty girl sitting by herself and proceeded to sit next to her. He also recalls that Pam did her best to ignore him. But as those who have known and worked with Ted can attest, ignoring Ted Warner is just not possible. And so, by the end of the trip, Ted had arranged to drive her into New York City and got her phone number. Seven months later, following a series of long-distance dates, Ted and Pam were married in Nashville, Tennessee, just before heading out to Colorado Springs, where Ted would begin the teaching phase of his career.

After two years of teaching a variety of political science courses at the Air Force Academy and spending six weeks in the summer of 1968 working on the Policy Planning Staff at the Department of State, Ted went back to Princeton for a year in 1969 and 1970 to begin work on his doctoral dissertation. In his dissertation, which was finally completed and approved in May 1975 and subsequently published, Ted applied the recently developed concept of bureaucratic politics to analyze several aspects of the roles the military played in contemporary Soviet politics. (See Chapter Two, by Michael Sulmeyer and Michael Albertson, for a discussion of this approach and its continuing relevance to the study of Russian defense policy.) After the year back at Princeton, Ted returned to the Air Force Academy faculty to teach for two-and-a-half more years while also writing the initial chapters of his dissertation.

In January 1973, Ted, Pam, and daughters Kelly and Erika moved to Reston, Virginia, where they would maintain a home until 2012. Ted began work in the Office of Strategic Research, the military intelligence element of the Central Intelligence Agency (CIA). His assignment had been arranged by Andy Marshall, formerly of the RAND Corporation, who was working on the National Security Council Staff. Marshall placed Ted with the CIA analytic staff at Langley, Virginia, as a means of encouraging the agency to use a wider range of conceptual approaches, including aspects of the bureaucratic politics paradigm, to analyze Soviet defense policy.

Ted's two-and-a-half years of work at Langley provided invaluable exposure to an impressive group of fellow intelligence analysts and to the latest intelligence information on emerging Soviet military concepts, force developments, and activities, including the participation of the Ministry of Defense in the U.S.-Soviet Strategic Arms Limitation Treaty (SALT) I strategic arms negotiations. While seconded to the CIA, Ted was promoted to major.

After a six-month stint at the Armed Forces Staff College in Norfolk, Virginia; four months of military attaché training in Rosslyn, Virginia; and a 47-week Russian language course at the Defense Language Institute in Monterey, California, Ted and his family moved to Moscow, where he served from June 1976 until June 1978 as an assistant air attaché at the U.S. embassy. During his time in Moscow, he worked closely with the embassy's political section on political-military reporting and in support of U.S. efforts to conclude the second SALT with the Soviet Union. Ted also traveled extensively throughout much of the Soviet Union with his fellow U.S. military attaches to observe Soviet military activities.

On returning to the United States in August 1978, after a very brief period working in the Plans Directorate of the Air Staff, Ted was assigned to the newly formed Staff Group of the Air Force Chief of Staff, General Lew Allen. He worked on that staff in the Pentagon for almost four years, heading the group for the last two years. This group of six officers, usually headed by a colonel, provided direct support to the Air Force Chief and Vice Chief of Staff on a wide range of issues. Ted assisted General Allen regarding strategic arms control with the Soviet Union, directly supporting his Senate testimony in support of SALT II in fall 1979 and efforts to gain approval to modernize key Air Force strategic nuclear delivery systems. The latter included involvement in the search for a survivable basing mode for the M-X (later Peacekeeper) intercontinental ballistic missile (ICBM) and the decisions to develop and ultimately deploy first the

B-1B and later the B-2A strategic bombers. Ted was promoted to lieutenant colonel in 1978 and selected for promotion to colonel in 1981.

In fall 1982, Ted turned down promotion to colonel, retired from the Air Force, and went to work in the RAND Corporation's Washington Office. Over the next ten years, his work at RAND as a senior defense analyst focused on assessments of U.S. and Soviet defense policies, including their strategic nuclear and conventional forces, arms control policy, the conventional military balance in Europe, and ways to enhance the capabilities of U.S. and NATO conventional forces that would be needed to defeat the Soviet-led Warsaw Pact. The latter effort placed particular emphasis on developing innovative operational concepts for the employment of NATO's air power. (See Chapter Three, by David Ochmanek, about Ted's work with Lt Gen [ret] Glenn Kent on end-to-end operational concepts and their application to enhancing NATO's defense capabilities in Central Europe.)

During his time at RAND, Ted had the opportunity to testify before a subcommittee of the House Armed Services Committee that was chaired by Congressman Les Aspin (D-Wisconsin), which was focused on seeking to understand changes in Soviet defense policy under Gorbachev. This interaction with Chairman Aspin and his staff led to Ted's being invited to participate as an expert advisor on Soviet defense policy during a 17-day trip in August 1989 to Germany and the Soviet Union with Chairman Aspin, his staff, and more than 20 members of the committee. This work in direct support of Chairman Aspin and his staff almost certainly played a key role in Mr. Aspin's subsequent decision in February 1993 to ask Ted to become the Assistant Secretary of Defense for Strategy and Requirements after Aspin was selected by President Clinton to serve as the Secretary of Defense.

While working in the Pentagon during his final years in the Air Force and while working at RAND throughout much of the 1980s and early 1990s, Ted taught graduate-level seminars on Soviet, later Russian, defense policy at several universities. These included George Washington University, Columbia University, and Princeton University. Several of his students in these seminars subsequently worked for him during his tenure as an assistant secretary of defense in the Office of the Under Secretary of Defense for Policy.

As the Assistant Secretary of Defense for Strategy and Requirements, Ted directly reported to Frank Wisner, the Under Secretary of Defense for Policy, and his Principal Deputy, Walt Slocombe, who later succeeded Wisner, and ultimately served under three Secretaries of Defense: Les Aspin, William Perry, and William Cohen. Many of Ted's most important efforts during President Clinton's first term were focused on the conduct of the "Bottom-Up Review" and ensuring that the decisions taken during the review were captured in key programmatic and military contingency planning documents and subsequently implemented. (See Chapters Four and Five, by Andy Hoehn and Chris Lamb, respectively, for discussions of these processes.)

The years immediately following the end of the Cold War were a busy and productive time in Ted's career. Among other things, Ted oversaw the drafting by David Ochmanek and his Strategy Office of the new U.S. National Defense Strategy, which was the cornerstone of the Bottom-Up Review. He also supervised the work of the office, headed by Sarah Sewell, that was responsible for developing and implementing peacekeeping, humanitarian assistance, and disaster relief policy during real-world contingencies in Somalia, Haiti, Bosnia, and the Congo. (See Chapter Six, by Jim Schear, on the drafting and implementation of Presidential Decision Directive 56, an interagency directive identifying things that must be done to carry out such complex contingency operations effectively, which built on the experience gained during these operations.) Ted also worked closely with Fred Frostic, his Deputy Assistant Secretary of Defense for Requirements and Plans, to direct the conduct of the ambitious and controversial Deep Attack Weapons Mix Study, which unsuccessfully sought to develop a consensus among the military services, the Joint Staff, and other offices in the Office of the Secretary of Defense (OSD) regarding the appropriate mix of precision weapons the Department of Defense (DoD) should procure in the years ahead.

Ted's portfolio expanded in November 1997 as he became the Assistant Secretary of Defense for Strategy and Threat Reduction, taking on added responsibility for all the offices that had previously reported to the Assistant Secretary of Defense for International Security Policy. Major efforts under Ted's leadership during President Clinton's second term included a key role in conducting the first-ever Quadrennial Defense Review, mandated by the Congress, which included refinement of the U.S. National Defense Strategy, this time by Michèle Flournoy and her Strategy Office; further developing defense relationships with the newly independent states that emerged following the demise of the Soviet Union, including work with the militaries in Uzbekistan and Kyrgyzstan that paved the way to very valuable cooperation with these states that directly supported U.S. military operations in Afghanistan following 9/11; working with Jim Miller's Requirements, Plans, and Counter-Proliferation Office to procure improved chemical and biological defense equipment and to conduct "Breeze" planning exercises with selected combatant commanders and their staffs to identify needed adjustments to their force training and contingency planning to take into account possible enemy use of chemical or biological weapons (see Chapter Four, by Andy Hoehn, on these planning exercises); and work on nuclear and conventional arms control, including supporting the conclusion of the Adapted Conventional Forces in Europe Treaty in 1999 and participation in ultimately unsuccessful, high-level talks with the Russians on the possible initiation of a combined negotiation seeking agreement on further reductions in U.S.-Russian strategic offensive arms and amendment of the Anti-Ballistic Missile Treaty to preserve the treaty while permitting the United States to develop and deploy a limited, nationwide ballistic missile defense to protect itself from possible small, first-generation ICBM attacks from North Korea or Iran in the years ahead.

During his nearly eight years as an assistant secretary of defense, Ted gained a reputation for being a demanding but very effective mentor for the many exceptionally talented people that worked with him in the various offices he oversaw. Among the most outstanding civilian defense officials he worked closely with and mentored were Michèle Flournoy, Jim Miller, David Ochmanek, Andy Hoehn, Sarah Sewell, Jim Schear, Kathleen Hicks, Christine Wormuth, Peter Lavoy, Barry Pavel, Deborah Rosenblum, Bob Scher, Amanda Dory, and Chris Lamb, many of whom served or are currently serving in key national security positions in the Obama administration. Ted also worked closely with and mentored many outstanding military officers assigned to his various offices and personal staff, including Charlie Martoglio, Clay Stewart, Harry Spies, Mark Gunzinger, Paula Thornhill, Chris Shepard, Chip Boyd, Mark Edwards, Doug Fraser, Terry Etnyre, Bob Butler, and Reggie Gillis.

Another key figure who directly supported Ted throughout his tenure as an assistant secretary of defense was his confidential assistant, Ceil St. Julien. Ceil unfailingly managed his demanding daily schedule, advised him regarding the state of his organization, planned and often accompanied him on his extensive domestic and international travel, and served as the unofficial photographer for the office.

Ted left DoD in October 2000 as the longest serving assistant secretary of defense in the Clinton administration. After a brief return to RAND, he spent the next eight years as a principal at Booz Allen Hamilton, consulting with the Joint Staff, the military services, and U.S. Joint Forces Command to draft or "red team" transformation road maps, as well as new joint and service operational concepts. He and his staff also worked closely with the Joint Staff and the acquisition communities in OSD and the military services to recast the nexus between the military's recently revised Joint Capabilities Integration and Development System, which identified capability shortfalls and possible changes in doctrine, training and the like to remedy these shortfalls, and the opening stages of the system development and acquisition activities managed by the defense and service acquisition executives under the DoD 5000 series of directives. Ted and his team helped his clients streamline DoD's system for setting requirements for the future development of military capabilities and translate these requirements into materiel and nonmateriel solutions designed to provide the needed military capabilities.

Ted rejoined DoD in April 2009, becoming a member of the Obama team as Secretary of Defense Robert Gates' representative to the New START negotiations and deputy head of the U.S. New START delegation. At that time, his former principal deputy, Michèle Flournoy, was the Under Secretary of Defense for Policy, and another former deputy, Jim Miller, was Michèle's Principal Deputy. Ted worked closely with Miller, who oversaw nuclear policy and missile defense matters, as well as OSD's participation in the New START negotiations. It was in this capacity that Ted hired Bridge Colby and later Mike Albertson to assist him in the negotiation with his Russian counterparts of the myriad inspection provisions in the New START agreements and in the successful effort to secure Senate ratification of the treaty. Having spent several months of 2009 and early 2010 in Geneva helping lead the New START negotiations, he returned to work in the Pentagon once Presidents Obama and Medvedev signed the treaty in Prague in April 2010 to assist the Obama administration's lengthy and challenging effort to ultimately gain Senate ratification of New START. (See Chapter Eleven, by Rose Gottemoeller, on Ted's role in the negotiation and ratification of New START.)

With the treaty ratified and entered into force in February 2011, Ted assumed a new position as the Senior Advisor to the Under Secretary of Defense (Policy) for Arms Control and Strategic Stability. Concurrently, he served as the U.S. Deputy Commissioner of the Bilateral Consultative Commission, which oversees implementation of New START. In December 2011, Ted hired Michael Sulmeyer, and the two of them spent the next two years analyzing and engaging the Russians in official and unofficial Track Two discussions regarding possible next steps in nuclear arms reduction. They also assessed the challenges associated with maintaining strategic stability with Russia and China, including ways to deal with growing, albeit limited, U.S. missile defense capabilities and the development of next-generation, long-range, rapid-response, high-precision conventional weapons, and participated in Track Two discussions with Russian and Chinese representatives regarding these matters. (See Chapter Eight, by James Acton, for discussions of the challenges to strategic stability and possible next steps in U.S.-Russian nuclear arms control.) Ted also worked with Dean Wilkening to explore the implications of limited U.S. homeland missile defenses for strategic stability with Russia. (See Chapter Nine, by Dean Wilkening, on the use of strategic force drawdown curves to assess U.S-Russian mutual deterrence and strategic stability under varying conditions.) Throughout this period, Ceil St. Julien once again provided superb support to Ted as his confidential assistant and to the U.S. delegation during the New START negotiations in Geneva.

In mid-November 2011, Ted and Pam moved from Reston, Virginia, to Gig Harbor, Washington, where they are located 40 miles from the Seattle homes of their daughters, Kelly and Erika, and their families, including four grandsons. At the end of December 2012, Ted transitioned to become an intermittent, rather than a full-time, highly qualified expert in the Office of the Under Secretary of Defense for Policy. He now works part time for the Under Secretary of Defense for Policy on strategic stability matters, including both unofficial and possibly official engagements with the Russians and the Chinese on issues of strategic stability. He also continues to serve as the U.S. Deputy Commissioner of the New START Bilateral Consultative Commission, attending periodic sessions of the commission in Geneva. Ted has also returned to work with the RAND Corporation, where he is an adjunct member of the RAND professional staff addressing a range of U.S. defense policy issues. His enthusiasm for playing golf and rooting on his beloved University of Michigan Wolverines, Detroit Tigers, Red Wings, and Lions (the Pistons, Ted has noted, are a lost cause) continues unabated.

CHAPTER TWO

Early Contributions to the Study of the Soviet Armed Forces and Bureaucratic Politics

Michael Sulmeyer and Michael Albertson

Michael Sulmeyer: *The year I worked for Ted Warner was a terrific reintroduction to life in the defense policy community, as I had just returned to Washington after eight years of graduate school. Michèle Flournoy, the Under Secretary of Defense for Policy, and Jim Miller, her Principal Deputy, suggested that I interview with Ted and that if I was successful, I would be the beneficiary of amazing experience, knowledge, and mentorship—and it most certainly was. Ted patiently spent hours each day teaching me the details of several topics of contemporary defense policy that I had never formally studied. Such topics as strategic nuclear forces, nuclear deterrence, and missile defense certainly were covered in school, but having a year-long tutorial with Ted on these topics was a once-in-a-lifetime experience. My education continued as I joined him on trips to Beijing, Moscow, and Geneva, where I observed how these topics were debated in both formal and informal discussions. Above all else, I was most impressed by his commitment to providing the most rigorous and clear analysis possible to his audience. From establishing a logical set of arguments to guide a study, through countless sessions with whiteboards, globes, and maps, to the revision of each bullet point of each slide to minimize the chances for confusion, he set a powerful example for how analysis should be conducted and presented. It is this methodology for analysis that I learned from Ted for which I am most grateful.*

Michael Albertson: *I first met Dr. Warner (I alone amongst this group perhaps will never call him Ted) when he arrived as Senior Advisor to the Under Secretary of Defense for Policy and the Secretary of Defense's Representative to the New Strategic Arms Reduction Treaty negotiations and was preparing to begin them. I was fortunate enough to work with him over the second half of the negotiations in Geneva and was delighted to accept his offer to work in his office for two years in Office of the Secretary of Defense, Policy. Working for Dr. Warner was an opportunity which completely changed the scope and course of my career, showing the horizons that were possible and demonstrating the value of an attentive mentor on one's professional development. Every day with Dr. Warner was a learning experience, either in a new subject I needed to study, a book or article I needed to read, or a new way of conceptualizing information. I cannot thank Dr. Warner enough for all of his guidance and assistance over the last several years.*

In this chapter, we reflect on Ted Warner's earliest scholarship, which examined the role of the Soviet armed forces in Soviet politics. Specifically, we show how his writings in the mid-1960s and 1970s were at the cutting edge of scholarship on the conceptual approach to the study of governmental decisionmaking that became known as "bureaucratic politics," as well as the substantive analysis of the Soviet armed forces. To this end, we rely on one of Dr. Warner's earliest writings: his 1977 publication *The Military in Contemporary Soviet Politics: An Institutional Analysis*, which itself is adapted from his doctoral dissertation with the same title.[1]

Reflecting on Dr. Warner's dissertation is not only an interesting personal and intellectual adventure, but reviewing the concepts imbedded in that dissertation serves as an important introduction to this volume. As a collection of essays written by practitioners of U.S. defense policy, the authors of every chapter in this book examine different characteristics of the institutions and bureaucracies that constitute the U.S. national security establishment. By providing the theoretical underpinning to the general study of these institutions and how they came to be a critical unit of analysis within political science, this chapter sets the stage for the application of these concepts in subsequent chapters.

This chapter proceeds in four parts. First, we review the academic trends that marked the decade in which Warner wrote his doctoral dissertation. Next, we provide a brief overview of his book to describe for the reader how he structured it and what specific issues he examined. We then offer lessons and conclusions that contemporary students of the Russian military can utilize from his study. Finally, we highlight some of the key theoretical contributions Warner's book made to the study of bureaucracies and military institutions in general.

Bureaucratic Politics and the Soviet Armed Forces in the 1960s and 1970s

A review of Warner's book shows an overriding interest in exploring and better understanding the role of the Soviet armed forces within the broader scheme of Soviet politics. To turn this interest into a scholarly research agenda, however, he needed a mechanism by which to understand the Soviet armed forces as an institution. Contemporaneously, efforts to understand the behavior of nation-states by analyzing the dynamics both within and among their component departments, ministries, and other national-level institutions were growing in popularity, with the RAND Corporation, the Brookings Institution, the John F. Kennedy School at Harvard University, and the California Institute of Technology all sponsoring research in this direction.[2]

---

[1]   Edward L. Warner III, *The Military in Contemporary Soviet Politics: An Institutional Analysis*, Praeger Publishers, New York, 1977.

[2]   Graham Allison, *Essence of Decision*, 1st ed., Boston: Little, Brown and Company, 1971, p. 278, note 2.

The years between when Ted Warner entered graduate school in the Politics Department at Princeton University in 1965 and the publication of his dissertation in 1977 were crucial ones for the development of the scholarship of the theoretical and substantive debates that informed his research. While general concepts of the nature of bureaucracies date back at least to Max Weber's writings in the 19th century, contemporary articulation and application of the theories of bureaucratic operation to account for foreign policy outcomes achieved prominence with the 1969 publication of Graham Allison's "Conceptual Models and the Cuban Missile Crisis."[3] Allison then published an expanded edition of his work in his 1971 book, *Essence of Decision*.[4]

Warner's work at this time was part of this growing body of scholarship on bureaucracy, but that scholarship was cast almost from the beginning as an alternative to a far simpler and thus more-persuasive method of understanding foreign policy outcomes: considering the state as a unitary rational actor. By personifying state action and analogizing national policies to "the purposive acts of individuals," observers greatly simplified state behavior.[5] By contrast, studies of how governmental institutions affected state behavior offered the promise of unpacking the "black box" of the machinery of governmental decisionmaking, which the traditional rational-actor model had assumed away as merely a function or reflection of rational choice.

Warner's dissertation differed from the work of Allison and other contemporaries in the crucial respect that it was not employing bureaucratic politics to explain the behavior of the Soviet Union in a particular crisis or circumstance. Rather, Warner wrote about the roles that the Soviet armed forces played in Soviet politics. Instead of only querying *whether* the armed forces exerted influence on various aspects of Soviet foreign and defense policy, he focused on *how* the armed forces exerted that influence. That distinction matters because it shifted the nature of the task from explaining how well bureaucratic politics in the Soviet case accounted for a certain outcome, to explaining how bureaucratic politics as a conceptual lens could be useful in its own right to shed much-needed light on otherwise opaque entities, such as the governing institutions of the Soviet Union. In the section that follows, we provide a brief overview of how Warner took on the task of understanding the roles the Soviet armed forces played in Soviet politics.

A Framework for Analysis

Warner began his dissertation by noting that "analysis of Soviet defense decisionmaking is a distinctly speculative undertaking" due to the intense security concerns sur-

---

[3] "Conceptual Models and the Cuban Missile Crisis," *American Political Science Review,* September 1969.

[4] Allison, 1971.

[5] Allison, 1971, p. 4.

rounding that country's military policy decisions and the resulting secrecy about these undertakings.[6] Any analytic approach must begin with a careful and systematic examination, which Warner tackled in Chapter 2, of the major players and entities within the Soviet system that determine defense policy. In detailing the roles various key individuals, military organizations, military services, and party organizations played, Warner regarded the overlap between governmental defense and party organizations in the Soviet Union as particularly important: The Soviet military was represented on virtually all the significant organs of the Soviet government and the Communist Party of the Soviet Union. Organizations Warner identified for further exploration during the course of his book would be the Military-Industrial Commission [*Voyenno-promyshlennaya kommissiya*] and the Defense Council, both Soviet governmental organizations that played crucial roles in the development of Soviet national security policy, and the Communist Party Secretary, who oversaw the defense-industrial sector of the Soviet economy.[7]

The Party Politburo, as the highest decisionmaking body in the Soviet Union, was a key institution in which this interaction between party and defense interests could be observed. Here, full or candidate Politburo members, such as the Defense Minister, or invited figures, such as the Chief of the General Staff, could register their professional views before the party elite. This institutional access, coupled with the defense professionals' overwhelming advantages over their civilian counterparts in terms of technical expertise related to military matters, led Warner to conclude in his opening that "the Soviet military is in an excellent position to wield enormous influence in those matters which concern it most—budgetary allocations for defense, weapons development and production, military doctrine, arms control, and the exercise of military capabilities in support of Soviet foreign policy."[8]

Warner identified the key difficulties associated with carrying out his research to be the lack of direct survey research data and of the ability to interview key figures in the Soviet defense policy process, the typical sources used to identify and measure institutional preferences, mores, and apparent influence in comparable studies in the West. These deficiencies forced outside analysts to rely on materials published by the Soviet military and other defense figures, such as leading weapon designers, and the public statements of its leading figures.[9] While a bounty of information was available in such publications as *Pravda* [*Truth*], *Izvestiya* [*News*], *Krasnaya Zvezda* [*Red Star*], or *Kommunist Vooruzhennykh Sil* [*Communist of the Armed Forces*], the burden was placed squarely on the shoulders of the analyst to interpret the subtle shifts in the party lines regarding defense policy as debates swirled on such topics as threat perceptions, mili-

---

[6] Warner, 1977, p. 16.

[7] Warner, 1977, p. 55.

[8] Warner, 1977, p. 55.

[9] Warner, 1977, p. 72.

tary doctrine, assigned roles and missions, and resource allocations. This visible and available information represented only a fraction of the total debate on the issue but nonetheless served as a starting point for analysis.

In his overarching survey of key topics over a roughly 20-year period, Warner identified viewpoints on several foreign policy and domestic issues. He found that the Soviet military expressed consistent opinions on the allegedly serious threats the West posed, the possibility of victory in a nuclear war, the crucial importance of sustaining priority investment in heavy industry and defense, and the desirability of achieving military-technological superiority over Western adversaries, in particular, the United States.[10] Critical differences emerged, however, in the approaches different parties favored for achieving broadly agreed goals; each service chief or outside pundit would advocate his preferred doctrinal solution or pet weapon system to achieve the desired objective. With a sizable but finite pool of resources to spend, however, the competition between the various groups outside and within the military would be fierce, leading debates to spill over into the public realm.

Warner used two case studies to test the institutional approach examining the role of the Soviet military in decisionmaking: The first was the evolution of Soviet strategic thought, and the second was on Soviet force posture, including both the size and character of the various military services and branches, as well as their major weapon systems. In both instances, Warner noted that, while high-ranking Soviet political and military leaders were often credited for major changes in strategic thought and force posture, important evidence suggested that institutions and individuals, such as military researchers, scientists, historians, and leading weapon designers, and their defense industrial management allies played an often underappreciated role in shaping the policy preferences of their superiors. These groups saw their role as vital to the defense policy decisionmaking process because their knowledge and subject-matter expertise in key technical or military science-related fields would improve the decisions of senior party officials and their closest defense advisors.

Warner discovered two methods by which these players could affect decisions made at the highest level of the Soviet defense decisionmaking. First, given their institutional access to senior officials, when their key defense interests were at stake, these players could use a direct approach to reach the decisionmakers.[11] Second, actors could use indirect methods to shape the mind sets of party leadership over the long term,

---

[10] Warner, 1977, p. 103.

[11] See, in particular, the following comment:

> There is also ample evidence that the senior military commanders and their partners in the defense production field have utilized their direct access to the political leadership both to press their requests for the development and series production of new weapons and to resist vigorously any attempts to cut back on the Soviet defense effort.

Warner, 1977, p. 269.

such as by publishing influential articles in military journals, fostering relationships between key officials and leading weapon design bureaus, and developing new and improved weapon system designs to fill gaps in Soviet military capabilities.

Warner then examined the Soviet approach to arms control to demonstrate how defense advisors, employing both direct and indirect approaches, could influence policy outcomes. Warner extensively tracked debates within the Soviet military regarding the Strategic Arms Limitations Treaty (SALT) I Agreement and the Anti-Ballistic Missile Treaty, both concluded in 1972, and the SALT II negotiations then under way to test his theories regarding the military's role in arms control. With data from these negotiations, he sketched the various communities of arms control commentators within the Soviet defense community, including military scientists and other officers on the General Staff, Ministry of Defense (MoD) spokesmen, defense commentators in such publications as *Krasnaya Zvezda*, and various uniformed military commanders, and then described how each of these institutions apparently worked to advance organization-specific interests.[12]

Although the Ministry of Foreign Affairs led (and still leads) the Soviet (Russian) delegations for bilateral and multilateral arms control negotiations, the MoD maintained significant influence in the determination of the overall Soviet negotiating positions. Because the MoD was the second major participant in bilateral and multilateral arms control negotiations, the deliberations within the MoD on its negotiating positions were critical for any arms control debate of the period. Although commonly portrayed in the open press and in Western memoirs as hostile to international arms control agreements, Warner demonstrated that the MoD and the military services within the ministry could "live quite comfortably with détente as long as arms control agreements appear[ed] likely to constrain adversary military programs without threatening their own present and projected courses of action."[13] These restraints on U.S. capabilities and programs, coupled with the need to be seen as pleasing their political leadership in the Kremlin, could shape the decision calculus of previously skeptical military and defense industrial interests, leading them to lend cautious support to further engagement and arms control negotiations.

Lessons and Observations for the Study of the Russian Armed Forces

Many of Warner's observations continue to have relevance for contemporary analysts of U.S.-Russia relations. Above all, Warner's work serves as a reminder to today's analysts of Russian national security policy that they should avoid a monolithic view of the decisionmaking processes, given the wide variety of interest groups within Russia's

---

[12] Warner, 1977, pp. 228–229.

[13] Warner, 1977, p. 222.

defense policy community. Schisms and nuances persist between serving and retired senior officers, officers within the various services, military scientists within the General Staff apparatus, outside defense commentators, and leading weapon designers. Each of these individuals and groupings pursues its unique interests by influencing and informing the broader political decisionmaking process on defense matters. While Warner highlighted the existence and described the general features of these different entities, the material available at the time was not adequate for a more detailed analysis that would explain differences between entities due to age, nationality, education, or job experience. He cautioned that "there are almost certainly a host of other differences of viewpoint and preference among Soviet military personnel concerning defense-related matters and a variety of broader domestic and foreign policy questions as well."[14]

Despite these challenges, Warner argued that these schisms were at the foundation of public, observable debates on a number of core issues. Warner believed that the central issues and questions regarding Soviet defense were "complex and inherently indeterminate in that no policy solution is demonstrably more correct than others."[15] Given the wide variety of possible solutions to these difficult issues, interested parties were driven by necessity to take their ideas outside closed sessions and into more public forums. In doing so, advocates of various defense approaches would be able to garner additional widespread and insider support for their ideas.

The Soviet effort to develop and field an intercontinental-range bomber offers a particularly vivid example of this phenomenon in operation. As Soviet documents were declassified in the early years of the post–Cold War era, historians and analysts were able to flesh out these heated internal debates in more detail. Steven J. Zaloga, in his book *Target America*, tracked the Soviets' unsuccessful attempts to develop a significant intercontinental-range bomber capability, from reverse engineering the B-29 into the Tu-4 (Bull), to the abject failure of the Mya-4 Molot (Bison), to the repeat flyovers of bombers during the Moscow parade that led Western defense attachés to believe that the Soviets had achieved a significant bomber advantage over the United States.[16] The unsatisfactory nature of the first Soviet intercontinental ballistic missile (ICBM), the R-7 (SS-6), as a military weapon led to a competition among competing missile design bureaus. Khrushchev and Leonid Brezhnev, then in his role as the Politburo member responsible for overseeing defense industry, formally approved the development of these two competing second-generation missiles on May 13, 1959. This heated competition between the R-9 (SS-7) from Sergey Korolev's OKB-1 design bureau and the R-16 (SS-8) from Mikhail Yangel's OKB-586 design bureau was documented in enormous detail, from the missile blueprints and backdoor lobbying to testing and

---

[14] Warner, 1977, p. 269.

[15] Warner, 1977, p. 270.

[16] Steven J. Zaloga, *Target America: The Soviet Union and the Strategic Arms Race, 1945–1964*, Novato, Calif.: Presidio, 1993, pp. 63–88.

insider intrigue regarding the selection.[17] The rise in the late 1970s of the Nadiradze OKB design bureau, now called the Moscow Institute of Thermal Technology, which specialized (and still specializes) in solid-fueled strategic ballistic missiles, would see further debates between competing design bureaus and officials for their favorite new-generation ICBM. These discussions would later be documented in detail by Vitaly Katayev in a series of unclassified interviews, as Dr. Acton cites in Chapter Eight, and in materials shared with David Hoffman and discussed in his superb book, *The Dead Hand*.[18] Even today, rival Russian design bureaus and defense industrial producers compete for contracts, and Russian defense interests lobby regarding the proper size and composition of the strategic nuclear forces.[19]

Interestingly for contemporary observers of the Russian military, most of the questions that Warner identified in his analysis continue to be hotly debated topics within the Moscow defense establishment today: how much money should be spent on defense, what weapon systems should be developed and procured and in what quantities, which services should be assigned which missions, how forces should be structured in the context of arms control agreements and ongoing negotiations, and what the appropriate strategies are for deterrence and waging war in the various theaters surrounding Russian territory.[20] Additionally, defense officials today continue to use the mechanisms of influence that Warner characterized as direct or indirect as they slow-roll or expedite the latest defense reform initiative, curry favor for their latest fighter aircraft or ballistic missile, or jockey for position within the defense hierarchy.

Warner's work should also dissuade current analysts of the Russian military from basing their conclusions on too little available information. To be sure, the amount of detailed data available to Warner was limited. In his conclusions, Warner noted the challenges of attempting to understand the workings inside the Soviet hierarchy, complaints that sound familiar to any modern-day Kremlinologist:

> It is readily apparent that in almost all cases, informed speculations about the domestic political interplay associated with these issues are the best we can manage. The student of Soviet politics lacks the abundance of routine reportage, investigative analysis, and the opportunity to conduct personal interviews that are so frequently available in the study of Western policy making. Denied such information, the Sovietologist must settle for analysis that points out the visible signs of political

---

[17] James E. Oberg, *Red Star in Orbit*, New York: Random House, 1981, 35–36.

[18] John G. Hines, Ellis M. Mishulovich, and John F. Shull, *Soviet Intentions 1965–1985*, Vol. I: *An Analytical Comparison of U.S.-Soviet Assessments During the Cold War*, McLean, Va.: BDM Federal, Inc., September 22, 1995, pp. vii–xi, and David Hoffman, *The Dead Hand: The Untold Story of the Cold War Arms Race and Its Dangerous Legacy*, New York: Random House, 2010, p. 24.

[19] Pavel Podvig, "New ICBM Contract Reportedly Went to Makeyev Design Bureau," Russian Strategic Nuclear Forces blog, May 14, 2011.

[20] Warner, 1977, p. 270.

conflict in Moscow, suggests the identity of various individuals and institutions involved, and hypothesizes about the likely shape of their political maneuvering.[21]

Despite the inherent secrecy of the Soviet system, especially regarding military affairs, Warner assiduously collected a wide body of information and, by employing the bureaucratic politics model, offered several conclusions. He did so by connecting the dots between the various data points to determine subtle shifts in organization or personal views during the constant debates involving Soviet defense policy. As noted above, Warner did this in a number of cases involving Soviet strategic thought and force posture, as well as Soviet thinking on arms control.

He gauged the relevance and importance of the various players, such as the central role of the MoD in defense policy:

> The Ministry of Defense appears to enjoy considerable autonomy and unrivaled expertise ... [and] is greatly assisted by the fact that, unlike most Soviet government ministries, it does not have to contend with a specialized department within the powerful central apparatus of the Party.[22]

Warner also mapped how entities inside the Soviet defense apparatus used institutional mechanisms, direct appeals, and public lobbying to pursue their interests. Outside experts and analysts also played a key role in Warner's analysis of Soviet decisionmaking, assisting insiders in achieving their preferences or altering policy to suit their own needs.

Unfortunately, this debate often had negative consequences for the attainment of policy objectives; overriding defense interests often tended to warp their policymakers' perspectives into seeing a world filled with latent threats and enemies on all sides, with the military as the only shield defending the country. Nikita Khrushchev, for one, was aware that the Soviet Armed forces had their own agenda, one at odds with the premier's emphasis on improving agriculture and the overall standard of living, with his thinking reflected in his memoirs:

> I know from experience that the leaders of the armed forces can be very persistent in claiming their share when it comes time to allocate funds. Every commander has all sorts of very convincing arguments why he should get more than anyone else. Unfortunately there's a tendency for people who run the armed forces to be greedy and self-seeking. They're always ready to throw in your face the slogan "If you try to economize on the country's defenses today, you'll pay in blood when war breaks out tomorrow." I'm not denying that these men have a huge responsibility, and I'm not impugning their moral qualities. But the fact remains that the living

---

[21] Warner, 1977, p. 271.

[22] Warner, 1977, p. 270.

standard of the country suffers when the budget is overloaded with allocations to unproductive branches of consumption. And today as yesterday, the most unproductive expenditures of all are those made on the armed forces.[23]

At Camp David, Khrushchev and President Eisenhower reminisced about how military leaders constantly approached them for money under the guise of the necessity of security.[24] As Eugene Rumer mentions in Chapter Seven, successors, such as Gorbachev, would similarly have to try to beat back demands from defense officials clamoring for more funds for conventional or nuclear forces at the same time the Politburo was attempting to invest in light industry or restructure the Soviet economic system.

When looking at current defense initiatives in Moscow, we see many of the same specters Warner raised 35 years ago in his analysis. An outward appearance of monolithic decisionmaking exists, with President Putin taking the place of the General Secretary of the Communist Party of the Soviet Union. But just under the surface lies a debate among a large number of defense interest groups seeking to foster and cultivate a security environment that supports their parochial interests.

Contributions to the Theory of Bureaucratic Politics

Ted Warner's book made important contributions to the theoretical study not only of Soviet defense policy but also of defense-related institutions more broadly. In our judgment, the most significant of these are how his study offered a rigorous test for the then newly emergent model of bureaucratic politics, its contribution to and connections with the study of civil-military relations, and its appreciation for how organizational process and bureaucratic politics could be complementary, not just competing, tools for analysis.

Testing Bureaucratic Politics with a Hard Case

By concentrating on the Soviet military, Warner tested the bureaucratic politics model with a "crucial" case. One aspect of why the Soviet military was a crucial case was the difficulty of collecting sufficiently reliable data. The previous section describes how he addressed this challenge, but the fact that he was able to conduct the analysis showed that the theoretical premises of bureaucratic politics could not only be applied but also appeared to remain valid in the context of military institutions of authoritarian communist states.

The more-substantive challenge of applying bureaucratic politics to the Soviet armed forces stemmed from the very nature of Marxist-Leninist ideology, which made

---

[23] Nikita Khrushchev, *Khrushchev Remembers*, Strobe Talbott, trans., Boston: Little, Brown and Company, 1970, p. 519.

[24] Khrushchev, 1970, pp. 519–520.

the party leadership innately suspicious of any sort of autonomy for the Soviet military due to an overriding concern about the possibility of a violent military coup. Derived from the early years of the Soviet regime, when control of former Czarist officers was essential, a "pervasive, Party-directed system of political commissars ... permeated the military structure."[25] Looking for evidence of bureaucratic autonomy that could reflect interests that diverged from those of the formal Communist Party was a tall order indeed. However, Warner showed that, even in regimes that are structurally predisposed to control and limit divergent bureaucratic interests, bureaucratic politics was still a useful framework.

Bureaucratic Politics and Civil-Military Relations

Warner argued that the Soviet military was not wholly captive to the interests of the Communist Party by providing evidence that indicated that the Soviet military had gradually co-opted the Main Political Administration, which was formally responsible for ensuring loyalty to the party among members of the armed forces. While this evidence not only justified exploration of the bureaucratic attributes of the Soviet military, it also opened the door to examining connections between bureaucratic politics and civil- (or party-) military relations.

The connection between bureaucratic politics and civil-military relations has usually been subtle. For example, Samuel Huntington's *The Soldier and the State* is often cited as the canonical work of American civil-military relations, but Warner referenced the book to describe Huntington's generalized characteristics of modern militaries—characteristics that speak to how militaries operate as bureaucratic organizations.[26] He argued that Huntington deferred providing empirical support for these characterizations until the publication of *The Common Defense*, which examined how U.S. military institutions exhibited these characteristics.[27] Warner examined many of these same characteristics in Chapter 3 of his book but in the context of the Soviet military. In so doing, he linked civil-military relations and bureaucratic politics to further describe and delineate the relationship between the party and the Soviet armed forces.

Blending Organization Theory with Bureaucratic Politics

Another important innovation Warner made was to incorporate some of Allison's work on organization theory into his discussion of bureaucratic politics in Soviet defense policy. Allison's initial framework consisted of three models or conceptual lenses. The

---

[25] Dr. Warner discussed this point in a research paper he authored when he was a graduate student at Princeton University in 1966. See Edward L. Warner III, "The Political Role of the Soviet Armed Forces," unpublished research paper, Princeton University, 1966, p. 1.

[26] Samuel P. Huntington, *The Soldier and the State: The Theory and Politics of Civil-Military Relations*, Cambridge, Mass.: Harvard University Press, 1957.

[27] Samuel P. Huntington, *The Common Defense: Strategic Programs in National Politics*, New York: Columbia University Press, 1961.

first was the previously discussed rational-actor model, with the unit of analysis being a conceptualized nation-state acting to maximize its utility. The second lens he termed "organizational process," which emphasized that governmental choices reflected outputs of large organizations operating according to standard operating procedures. "Bureaucratic politics" was his third lens, which saw policy outcomes as the results of different bargaining games played by different organizations within a government.

Although the second and third lenses both examine the machinery of government, the trend at the time was to treat them distinctly. This was not an unreasonable approach, given that organization theory could be seen to deprive individuals that led large organizations of agency; instead, they were captive to standardized processes that their organizations practiced. By contrast, the bureaucratic politics model recognized that individuals could represent their organizations in different bureaucratic struggles but that they very often shared a set of core beliefs and principles that promoted their institution's position.

In our view, Warner was one of the first to see the benefits of incorporating aspects of organization process into bureaucratic politics. Whereas Allison himself came to blur the lines between these two approaches somewhat implicitly, Ted explicitly drew on the former to provide a richer conceptualization of the latter.[28] To him, there was nothing inconsistent with the operation of influential standard operating procedures that could shape what "data" became the "facts" on which the organization would rely in the process of playing a particular bureaucratic game. In addition, the concept of satisficing—of selecting the first apparent acceptable answer, rather than searching more exhaustively for the optimal answer—which Allison originally considered in the context of organizational process, could also account for leaders' tendencies to make incremental changes in the face of large obstacles.

Conclusion

Looking back on Ted Warner's dissertation, which became his book, *The Military in Contemporary Soviet Politics*, readers find an academic study that staked out new ground not only in the substantive analysis of the Soviet military's role in politics but also in the study and application of bureaucratic politics. For contemporary students of Russian politics, the most significant lesson may be a combination of substance and theory: to be wary of explanations that treat the Russian state as a monolithic entity when projecting or accounting for decisions regarding the Russian armed forces and Russian defense policy.

---

[28] Graham T. Allison and Morton H. Halperin, "Bureaucratic Politics: A Paradigm and Some Policy Implications," in *Theory and Policy in International Relations*, supplement, *World Politics*, Vol. 24, 1972, pp. 40–79.

Although the dominant role of the Communist Party has been supplanted by President Vladimir Putin, we are reminded that, even in regimes with seemingly strong unitary leaders, governmental bureaucracies compete for influence, favor, resources, and relevance. Although we might lack complete visibility into important details of that competition, even a half-picture of that competition can yield insights into how regimes with opaque power structures arrive at decisions. Ted Warner's dissertation advanced the state of the literature at the time of its publication in 1977 by making a strong case for the continued study of such institutions as the Soviet armed forces as bureaucracies whose behavior and preferences can shape political decisions of the state as whole.

References

Allison, Graham, "Conceptual Models and the Cuban Missile Crisis," *American Political Science Review,* September 1969.

———, *Essence of Decision,* 1st ed., Boston: Little, Brown and Company, 1971.

Allison, Graham T., and Morton H. Halperin, "Bureaucratic Politics: A Paradigm and Some Policy Implications," in *Theory and Policy in International Relations,* supplement, *World Politics,* Vol. 24, 1972.

Hines, John G., Ellis M. Mishulovich, and John F. Shull, *Soviet Intentions 1965–1985,* Vol. I: *An Analytical Comparison of U.S.-Soviet Assessments During the Cold War,* BDM Federal, Inc., September 22, 1995. As of October 14, 2011:
http://www.gwu.edu/~nsarchiv/nukevault/ebb285/index.htm

Hoffman, David, *The Dead Hand: The Untold Story of the Cold War Arms Race and Its Dangerous Legacy,* New York: Random House, 2010.

Huntington, Samuel P., *The Soldier and the State: The Theory and Politics of Civil-Military Relations,* Cambridge, Mass.: Harvard University Press, 1957.

———, *The Common Defense: Strategic Programs in National Politics,* New York: Columbia University Press, 1961.

Khrushchev, Nikita, *Khrushchev Remembers,* Strobe Talbott, trans., Boston: Little, Brown and Company, 1970.

Oberg, James E., *Red Star in Orbit,* New York: Random House, 1981.

Podvig, Pavel, "New ICBM Contract Reportedly Went to Makeyev Design Bureau," Russian Strategic Nuclear Forces blog, May 14, 2011. As of June 1, 2011:
http://russianforces.org/blog/2011/05/new_icbm_contract_reportedly_w.shtml

Warner III, Edward L., "The Political Role of the Soviet Armed Forces," unpublished research paper, Princeton University, 1966.

———, *The Military in Contemporary Soviet Politics: An Institutional Analysis,* Praeger Publishers, New York, 1977.

Zaloga, Steven J., *Target America: The Soviet Union and the Strategic Arms Race, 1945–1964,* Novato, Calif.: Presidio, 1993.

CHAPTER THREE

Assessing Military Capabilities Using an "End-to-End" Conceptual Framework

David Ochmanek

I first met Captain Ted Warner in the winter/spring of 1971. He was an assistant professor of political science at the United States Air Force Academy, and I was a sophomore taking my first elective class in my major, international affairs. The class was Comparative Politics, and Ted taught it with energy and insight. For the students, it was our first exposure to contemporary political theory. Ted made the material interesting and accessible by explaining it clearly and putting it in contexts that were understandable and relevant to novices in the field.

We kept in touch over the years, and in 1985, I had the good fortune to be brought onto the staff of the RAND Corporation's Washington Office. One of my first assignments was to work with Ted to help him document his research on the "Critical Times" project, described below, which identified promising new concepts for enhancing the North Atlantic Treaty Organization's (NATO's) defense posture in Central Europe. Subsequently, we worked together on a wide range of research topics, including strategic nuclear forces, arms control, and follow-on work exploring options for improved conventional military capabilities.

In 1993, when Ted was nominated to be the Assistant Secretary of Defense for Strategy and Requirements, he asked me to join him in the Office of the Secretary Defense as the Deputy Assistant Secretary of Defense for Strategy, a newly created position. In spring 1993, my office, under Ted's supervision, drafted the new U.S. Defense Strategy, which guided the conduct of Secretary of Defense Les Aspin's ground-breaking Bottom-Up Review of the major aspects of U.S. defense policy. I continued to work for Ted in that post until 1995.

In January 1984, Ted Warner and Lt Gen (ret) Glenn Kent published "A Framework for Planning the Employment of Air Power in Theater War."[1] Ted had joined the staff of the RAND Corporation a little over a year earlier, and this report documented one of his first major research projects for RAND. This was a seminal work that spawned a number of subsequent research efforts that, collectively, changed the ways in which the U.S. defense community thought about and analyzed options and programs for

---

[1]   Edward L. Warner III and Glenn A. Kent, "A Framework for Planning the Employment of Air Power in Theater War," Santa Monica, Calif.: RAND Corporation, N-2038-AF, 1984.

modernizing the capabilities of military forces and the operating concepts to guide their employment.

Their report did two things, both of which seemed outwardly fairly simple and straightforward but were actually profoundly helpful in focusing thinking and analysis on the key dimensions of important operational problems. First, Warner and Kent identified the major roles of air forces in the U.S.-NATO operational concept for defense of NATO Europe against a large-scale, combined-arms Soviet-led Warsaw Pact invasion. This was far more insightful than yet another essay about the "roles and missions" of U.S. or NATO forces. In the report, Warner and Kent preferred to call the major components of U.S. and allied air operations "objectives." Later, they would refine their framework and call them "operational objectives." They determined that U.S. and allied air forces in a theater war in Central Europe would be called upon to achieve three major objectives:

- Gain and retain air superiority.
- Delay, disrupt, and destroy enemy follow-on forces prior to their entry into battle.
- Assist army units by proving close air support; that is, destroying or disrupting enemy maneuver units and fire support elements engaged with or in close proximity to friendly forces.

Importantly, Warner and Kent also defined the series of key operational tasks associated with each of these objectives. For example, to delay, disrupt, or destroy the enemy's follow-on forces, NATO air forces could pursue some combination of the following tasks: attacking primary lines of communication (e.g., roads and bridges), destroying or disabling enemy maneuver forces en route to the front, disrupting the enemy's battle management, destroying or disabling enemy transport assets (e.g., railroad rolling stock, wheeled tank transporters), destroying major supply concentrations, and supporting U.S. and allied "counterthrusts."[2]

Specifying the tasks associated with each objective was important to the second part of their research: identifying the range of functions—that is, the elements of a tactical-level operational concept—that must be performed to accomplish any operational task and describing how these functions must be integrated in a coherent "stream of activities" to effectively engage the target. According to Warner and Kent, there are six such functions:

- **Surveillance** is conducted throughout the theater to obtain information on enemy operations and the success of friendly forces operating against them.

---

[2]   Kent and others at RAND would further elaborate this basic framework of disaggregating a campaign strategy into its constituent operational objectives and tasks over the following ten years or so. It became known as the strategies-to-tasks approach and was eventually applied to plans for conventional operations in other theaters and to nuclear operations.

- **Assessment** entails bringing together, displaying, and analyzing surveillance data from disparate sensors. Assessment centers, where such analysis takes place, seek to locate and predict enemy activities, including determining the enemy's main force concentrations and key avenues of attack. They also seek to identify specific targets for possible attack.
- **Command** uses information from assessment centers and the mission assigned to the theater commander to inform the development of operational strategy for applying air power. Air component commanders apportion the air assets available to them among different operational objectives. They also develop plans and issue taskings to operational air units every 24 hours via the air tasking order (ATO), directing attacks and defensive operations against specific classes of targets and, in some cases, individual targets.
- In **asset generation**, U.S. Air Force wings and squadrons prepare aircraft, associated weapon systems, and air crews to carry out their assigned missions, as directed in the ATO.
- **Control** assists attack and defense assets in the timely execution of many attacks by passing the latest information about the location and disposition of targeted enemy forces in the air and on the ground. Advances in sensors, information processing, and tactical communications were, by the 1980s, enabling concepts for the real-time dynamic control of air-to-air and air-to-surface operations, analogous to the sort of dynamic control that had been used in defensive air intercept operations since the initial use of radar tracking information to guide Royal Air Force fighters during the Battle of Britain in 1940.
- In **engagement and attack**, combat platforms deliver ordnance against assigned targets.

As attacks occur, the process immediately repeats itself as sensors (sometimes the aircrew's eyes, sometimes more-acute sensors) collect information about the effects of the attacks that just occurred, feeding that information back to assessment and command centers.

In the report's summary, Kent and Warner were quick to point out that there was "nothing novel" in the identification of these six functions. In one form or another, they could all be found in U.S. Air Force doctrine manuals of the day. But the authors called attention to the importance of considering these activities as part of a coherent whole. "The value of this framework," they wrote,

> lies in the fact that it focuses attention on the process as a whole, highlighting interrelationships among the key functions and the organizations that perform them in the stream of activities that must be integrated to accomplish specific air power missions effectively.[3]

---

[3] Warner and Kent, 1984, p. v.

This was a profoundly important observation. Perhaps without fully realizing it, Warner and Kent were articulating a vision of air operations that would, in a few years' time, accompany the transformation of the air instrument and the roles that it would play on the modern battlefield. As their framework was reaching readers in the Air Force, Ted had already begun his next major research endeavor—a set of assessments he called "critical times" analyses.

"Critical Times" and the Revolution in Military Affairs

The 1980s was a period of considerable ferment in the development of U.S. military capabilities for conventional theater warfare. During the preceding decade, following the U.S. withdrawal from Vietnam, the Department of Defense had begun to turn its focus back to preparing, in concert with its NATO allies, for large-scale, conventional warfare, with special emphasis on coordinated operations for the defense of Central Europe. The United States led NATO into consideration of ways to disrupt Warsaw Pact ground forces by attacking second-echelon units under a concept called "follow-on forces attack." And the U.S. Army and Air Force jointly developed the "AirLand Battle" concept, which was also intended to present an attacking force with a wider range of military challenges than the traditional approach of focusing simply on the close battle.

These ambitious concepts were intended to offset the Warsaw Pact's very considerable numerical advantages in Central Europe. NATO's forces in the early to mid-1980s were not prepared to implement these concepts, however. They required, among other things, the ability to "see deep" and "shoot deep" into heavily defended airspace over the Warsaw Pact's operational rear areas, and NATO's forces lacked systems that would allow them to do this effectively. NATO's systems for commanding and controlling military operations were also not up to the task of handling the vast quantities of data and information that would be required once the requisite systems were fielded.

Complementing these conceptual innovations, however, the Department of Defense was developing a number of systems that later would be recognized as spawning a "revolution in military affairs." These included reconnaissance sensors and platforms that could acquire and transmit surveillance data in near real time; information processing systems to aid in the cross-correlation and display of large volumes of data at assessment centers; airborne systems designed both to conduct surveillance of enemy operations to locate potential targets in the air and on the ground and to task friendly airborne aircraft dynamically in real time to strike those targets; precision guided weapons; and low-observable ("stealth") platforms, such as the F-117 attack aircraft and the B-2 bomber. By the mid-1980s, some of these concepts were being fielded, while others were beginning to reach the testing stage, and the generous military budgets of that period facilitated their maturation and transition to production and fielding.

Although only a few of these new systems had yet been fielded, and none had been tested in combat, Soviet military theorists had taken notice of these developments. Perceptive writers, such as Marshal N. V. Ogarkov, the Chief of the General Staff; Colonel-General M. A. Gareyev, a leading Soviet military strategist; Marshal D. M. Ustinov, the Minister of Defense; and others observed that the United States was "creating new conventional weapon systems such as reconnaissance-strike complexes with great precision and range."[4] Harnessing such technologies and employing them effectively could, they judged, allow a force wielding modern, conventional weapons to achieve effects on the battlefield that were comparable to those expected from nuclear weapons.

In reviewing Soviet writings on the subject of future military operations, Ted was particularly struck by the concept of "critical time." Coined by the Soviet military theorist V. Ye. Savkin, critical time referred to the amount of time available for a military unit to achieve its assigned objective. This period defined the time available for a unit to complete what Savkin called the "control cycle" and to perform the order received. Embedded within the control cycle was the need for the unit's commanders to receive, process, and transmit information needed to govern the unit's activities.[5]

In his work assessing new means of intelligence support to NATO operations in Central Europe, Ted adapted and broadened the concept of critical time to his evaluation of operational concepts. Specifically, he determined the critical time associated with attacking key elements of the Soviet–Warsaw Pact offensive operation. For example, in its progress from its garrison in a rear area to the battle area, a Soviet ground forces division would make several road marches, generally at night, each lasting several hours. Between such road marches, the division would typically stop during the daytime and disperse in assembly areas chosen for the cover they would provide. Similarly, a mobile surface-to-air missile (SAM) system, such as the long-range SA-4, would plan to deploy in an open area and operate for a period of some hours, after which the radar and the SAM launchers would be prepared for movement, and the unit would displace to its next assigned position. If an adversary could detect, identify, locate, and attack elements of the division or the SA-4 fire unit while the units were most vulnerable, he could expect his attacks to be far more effective than if his attack assets were to conduct armed reconnaissance, simply trolling for targets of opportunity or, worse, lobbing ordnance more or less randomly into territory thought to be occupied by the enemy.

---

[4] Mary C. Fitzgerald, *Marshal Ogarkov and the New Revolution in Soviet Military Affairs*, Alexandria, Va.: Center for Naval Analyses, CRM 87-2, 1987, p. 8.

[5] V. Ye. Savkin, *The Basic Principles of Operational Art and Tactics*, Voenizdat, Moscow, 1972. Translated and published under the auspices of the United States Air Force, Washington, D.C.: U.S. Government Printing Office, 1974, pp. 185–187.

Every target or unit type has its own critical time, defined by the nature of the target and the way in which it is to be employed operationally. The vulnerable critical time for the Soviet ground force units moving to the battle would be while the unit is on the road in column formation. For the SA-4 units, it is, counterintuitively, while the unit is stationary, ready to fire.[6] The challenge for an opposing NATO force would be to orchestrate its surveillance, assessment, command, control, asset generation, engagement, and attack assets so that NATO forces could exploit these inherent vulnerabilities. Until the development of advanced electronic sensors and other elements of what the Soviets dubbed the "reconnaissance-strike complex," it was all but inconceivable that these activities could be integrated to permit attacks on enemy forces behind the front lines in a matter of a few hours.[7] By the mid- to late 1980s, in the U.S. and NATO armed forces, the requisite pieces were beginning to fall into place.

The relevance of critical times to the Warner-Kent framework was obvious: One could identify the key elements of the Soviet-led combined arms operation that would present the most lucrative targets for air attack and determine the critical times associated with each element. The challenge then was to determine whether it was possible to accomplish all the elements of the tactical-level operational concept for fulfilling the given task more quickly than the critical time window of vulnerability. As with all aspects of armed conflict, both sides could adapt: As the enemy learned of one's developing ability to exploit critical time vulnerabilities, he could adjust his tactics to try to reduce the vulnerabilities. But the goal was clear, and defining it in this way opened up new opportunities to hone the effectiveness of the new hardware that was beginning to emerge from development and testing.

Thinking "End-to-End"

In their report, Warner and Kent depicted their concept for the "end-to-end" accomplishment of an operational task as shown in Figure 3.1. Displaying it in this way emphasized the importance of connecting each of the functional activities involved in the operational concept for fulfilling a given task in a deliberate way to minimize the "seams" between them and to accelerate the process of "closing the loop" between the initial detection of a potential target and its engagement by an appropriately armed and positioned shooter. Over time, versions of this diagram were widely adopted through-

---

[6]   This is because the SA-4's radar, when in operation, creates a unique "signature" identifying it as such, and that signature can be detected and located by appropriate sensors hundreds of miles away.

[7]   In effect, the reconnaissance-strike complex would replicate for air-to-ground and long-range artillery or missile forces what radar and ground-controlled intercept had done for air defense in the 1940s, vastly increasing the efficiency and effectiveness with which a force could be employed against a set of moving targets.

Figure 3.1
Critical Functions for the Employment of Air Power in Theater War

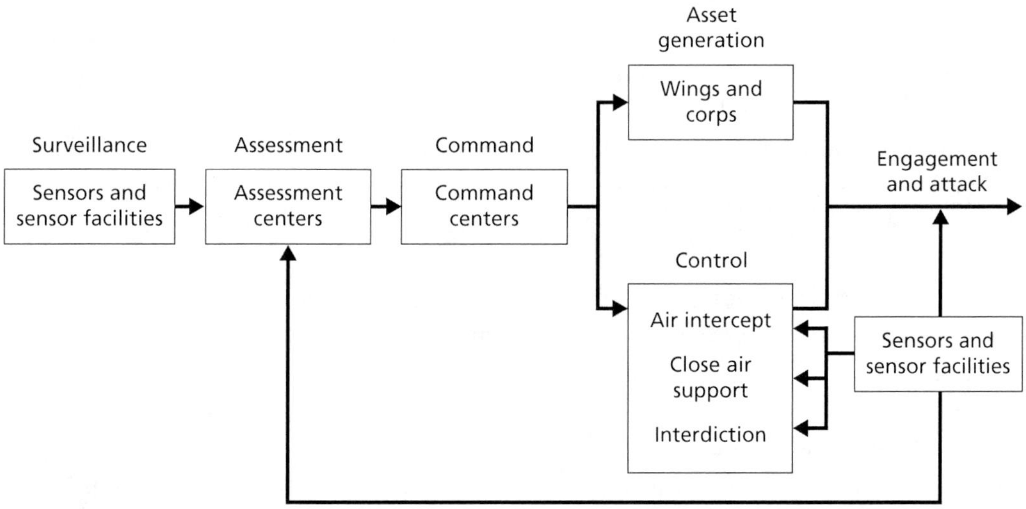

Asset
generation

Surveillance   Assessment   Command   Wings and
corps

Engagement
and attack

Sensors and   Assessment   Command
sensor facilities   centers   centers

Control

Air intercept

Close air
support   Sensors and
sensor facilities

Interdiction

SOURCE: Warner and Kent, 1984, p. 12.
RAND CP765-3.1

out the U.S. defense establishment. It became known as the "sensor-to-shooter kill chain" and, later still, the "effects chain."[8]

This proved to be a remarkably fecund set of ideas. Through the late-1980s and well into the 1990s, Warner, Kent, and others at RAND applied the framework to the development of air campaign concepts for defeating a Soviet-led, Warsaw Pact offensive in Central Europe, assessments of the conventional balance in Central Europe, NATO air defense operations, and the operation of U.S. strategic nuclear forces.[9] Versions of the framework continue to be used in assessments of concepts and capabilities for such disparate operations as power projection, urban warfare, and irregular warfare.[10] A fluent and indefatigable briefer, Ted carried the critical times and end-to-end operational concepts gospel to high-level military audiences throughout the U.S. defense community and in various NATO headquarters throughout Central Europe. They found the work useful in several ways. First, for many audiences, this was their

---

[8] As noted above, Warner and Kent referred to the sum of the parts of their kill chain as a *concept of operation*. Later, to distinguish this from larger-scale visions of a commander's intent for an overall operation, they amended the term to *concept of employment (conemp)*.

[9] The reports documenting these research efforts remain classified.

[10] See, for example, Alan J. Vick, Richard M. Moore, Bruce R. Pirnie, and John Stillion, *Aerospace Operations Against Elusive Ground Targets*, Santa Monica, Calif.: RAND Corporation, MR-1398-AF, 2001, and Alan J. Vick, John Stillion, David R. Frelinger, Joel Kvitky, Benjamin S. Lambeth, Jefferson P. Marquis, and Matthew Waxman, *Aerospace Operations in Urban Environments*, Santa Monica, Calif.: RAND Corporation, MR-1187-AF, 2002.

first exposure, in a methodical way, to many of the new systems then under development. Many people had heard of the Joint Surveillance and Target Attack Radar System (JSTARS), used to dynamically control attacks on targets moving on the ground; the Precision Location Strike System, used to precisely locate systems emitting electronic signals, such as mobile SAM radars; the Low-Altitude Navigation and Targeting Infrared for Night (LANTIRN) targeting pod, used to designate and guide laser-guided bomb attacks against selected targets; the Ground Attack Control Center, used to orchestrate air attacks within a given area; and other systems in development, but few were aware of all of them, especially those outside of their service, and fewer understood how they could be employed in combat. Ted became an agent of cross-pollination, spreading information about the coming wave of innovation in the U.S. armed forces and insights about the implications of these new capabilities for military operations.

Second, the analysis integrated both the "red" and the "blue" sides of the operational problem. It was grounded in the latest intelligence about Soviet concepts and capabilities for theater conventional military operations but was pitched mainly to operators, many of whom were not intimately familiar with the "red" side of the story. Ted was telling them how the "red" enemy apparently planned to conduct military operations and how they (the "blue" side) could orchestrate the range of intelligence, command and control, and attack assets at their disposal to counter the threat in new and more effective ways.

Third, the RAND framework provided a means for evaluating candidate concepts and systems that was operationally oriented. Because the framework depended on defining a coherent, end-to-end operational concept, it lent itself to assessing programs in ways that both operators and operational commanders readily appreciated. The focus of the briefings was not technical—sensor scan rates, data baud rates, circular error probable weapon delivery, and so forth—but, rather, operational—new and better ways to find, assign, engage, and put iron on targets. The methodology was largely qualitative, not quantitative, and it lent itself naturally to telling stories about the employment of joint forces.

Finally, by integrating the "front end" of the operational concept (surveillance, assessment, command, and control) with the "back end" (asset generation and engagement and attack), Ted's work helped operators to understand what these new sensor and information systems could do for them. And they could do a lot.

The Proof of the Pudding

In August 1990, Saddam Hussein's army invaded Kuwait. President Bush responded promptly, announcing that the United States would work actively to reverse this aggression and ordering the deployment of large-scale U.S. air, land, and maritime forces to the region as part of what would become a large, multinational coalition called Operation Desert Shield. Ready or not, modern air power was about to have its debut on the world stage during Operation Desert Storm, the war waged in early 1991 to expel Iraqi forces from Kuwait.

To be sure, most of the air forces that fought Saddam's military were not equipped with the latest gear, but the portions of the force that were made outsized contributions to the success of the joint campaign. Much of the world was fascinated by the images that were broadcast of laser-guided bombs homing in on their targets and impressed by the precision with which these and other U.S. weapons were used to dismantle key parts of Iraq's military machine. But military professionals soon became aware that other systems that received far less media attention made equally important contributions to the success of the coalition's campaign:

- The Air Force deployed its two JSTARS aircraft to the fight, even though the system was still in developmental testing. They flew parallel to the forward line of friendly troops, detecting the movement of Iraqi mechanized forces far behind the front lines at night, in all weather conditions, and in near real time. In this way, JSTARS reduced the possibility of a surprise attack by Iraqi ground forces; more than this, these surveillance and control aircraft directed coalition air forces to engage and attack enemy armored forces well before they made contact with friendly ground forces.
- U.S. aircrews developed innovative ways to use their PAVE TACK and LANTIRN pods, which were designed to mount attacks with laser-guided bombs, to detect and attack Iraqi armored vehicles hidden in the desert by sand berms and other forms of camouflage that rendered them invisible to the unaided eye. Aircrews took advantage of the fact that these armored vehicles retained heat accumulated during the day and thus could be located with the infrared sensors carried in these targeting pods late in the day and at night. These sensor detections and the laser-guided bombs they directed were the keys to the "tank plinking" that steadily eroded the armored strength and the morale of the Iraqi army hunkered down in the Kuwaiti Theater of Operations.
- Operation Desert Storm was the first large-scale U.S. military operation to harness personal computers, extensive databases, and spreadsheet programs to orchestrate daily air operations. Prior to this, command posts relied on people with grease pencils writing on Plexiglas. The change allowed the joint force air component commander to build and execute his ATO in ways that were far more flexible and responsive to changing circumstances and new information.

In short, Desert Storm provided U.S. forces the opportunity to assemble and bring to bear on the enemy the still-nascent reconnaissance-strike complex. The result, for coalition air forces, at least, was a level of sortie effectiveness that was, as Marshal

Ogarkov and others had predicted it would be, an order of magnitude greater than historical norms.[11]

The Relevance of the Framework Today

Thinking about military effects as the output of a chain of connected activities and paying heed to the importance of accomplishing those activities within a period defined by the nature of the target or task have become common practice, at least in the U.S. defense community. In fact, kill-chain analysis has influenced military thinking and planning well beyond the context of theater conventional warfare, in which Warner and Kent first applied it in the early 1980s.

One of the most challenging operational problems U.S. forces conducting counterinsurgency and stability operations have encountered in Iraq and Afghanistan over the past decade has been the need to defeat the improvised explosive devices that insurgents in both theaters have developed and employed with such profusion. Approaching the problem with a kill-chain, critical times mentality, U.S. and allied forces have brought to bear a host of surveillance and assessment assets to try to detect enemy personnel producing and attempting to emplace improvised explosive devices along roads. The forces have also developed procedures to facilitate the rapid tasking of strike assets against these targets in the short periods (often measured in minutes) during which they are vulnerable to engagement and attack. Similar approaches have borne fruit in the efforts of U.S. forces to identify, track, and target leaders of terrorist and insurgent groups globally.

Similar thinking also pervades efforts in the U.S. defense community to devise new concepts of employment for countering the sophisticated set of challenges bundled under the umbrella of anti-access and area denial capabilities, which some prospective U.S. adversaries are developing and fielding. These threats include systems for precision, long-range strike, such as medium- and intermediate-range ballistic and cruise missiles; antisatellite systems for attacking space-based assets; offensive cyber capabilities; electronic attack systems; advanced air defenses; new sensor systems; and command and control networks to integrate these forces. Nations mastering these sorts of capabilities pose threats to U.S. and allied military forces and operations that are qualitatively different from the sorts of threats that these forces have encountered in the conflicts that have occurred over the two decades since the end of the Cold War.

In response, a great deal of work is being done to identify ways in which friendly forces can disrupt and thus defeat the enemy's kill chains. For example, it will prove

---

[11] For an early analysis of significance of these innovations and their implications for force planning and strategy, see Christopher Bowie, Fred Frostic, Kevin Lewis, John Lund, David Ochmanek, and Philip Propper, *The New Calculus: Analyzing Airpower's Changing Role in Joint Theater Campaigns*, Santa Monica, Calif.: RAND Corporation, MR-149-AF, 1993.

technically challenging and expensive to employ missile defenses to shoot down ballistic missiles targeted at U.S. surface ships. These must therefore be supplemented with systems that can disrupt or deny the enemy's efforts to locate and target our ships. At the same time, we are working to ensure that our own kill chains are able to operate even when under attack by the enemy's forces. Space-based sensors and communications assets, for example, must either be hardened against direct attack or supplemented by terrestrial systems.

In short, given the complexity of the modern battlefield and our approach to military operations, it seems certain that analysts and operators will continue to develop innovative operational concepts for accomplishing important military tasks through the lens of the end-to-end, critical times approach Warner and Kent pioneered. Indeed, for many in the defense community, this may be the only way they have learned to approach such problems. It is worth remembering that it was not always so.

References

Bowie, Christopher, Fred Frostic, Kevin Lewis, John Lund, David Ochmanek, and Philip Propper, *The New Calculus: Analyzing Airpower's Changing Role in Joint Theater Campaigns*, Santa Monica, Calif.: RAND Corporation, MR-149-AF, 1993. As of January 9, 2014:
http://www.rand.org/pubs/monograph_reports/MR149.html

Fitzgerald, Mary C., *Marshal Ogarkov and the New Revolution in Soviet Military Affairs*, Alexandria, Va.: Center for Naval Analyses, CRM 87-2, 1987.

Savkin, V. Ye., *The Basic Principles of Operational Art and Tactics*, Voenizdat, Moscow, 1972. Translated and published under the auspices of the United States Air Force, Washington, D.C.: U.S. Government Printing Office, 1974.

Vick, Alan J., Richard M. Moore, Bruce R. Pirnie, and John Stillion, *Aerospace Operations Against Elusive Ground Targets*, Santa Monica, Calif.: RAND Corporation, MR-1398-AF, 2001. As of January 9, 2014:
http://www.rand.org/pubs/monograph_reports/MR1398.html

Vick, Alan J., John Stillion, David R. Frelinger, Joel Kvitky, Benjamin S. Lambeth, Jefferson P. Marquis, and Matthew Waxman, *Aerospace Operations in Urban Environments*, Santa Monica, Calif.: RAND Corporation, MR-1187-AF, 2002. As of January 9, 2014:
http://www.rand.org/pubs/monograph_reports/MR1187.html

Warner III, Edward L., and Glenn A. Kent, "A Framework for Planning the Employment of Air Power in Theater War," Santa Monica, Calif.: RAND Corporation, N-2038-AF, 1984. As of January 9, 2014:
http://www.rand.org/pubs/notes/N2038.html

CHAPTER FOUR

Defense Planning After the Cold War

Andrew R. Hoehn

I first met Ted Warner in the late 1980s. Ted was a senior RAND analyst, and I was a junior staff officer in the Office of the Secretary of Defense (OSD). Ted was giving a talk at a government-sponsored event on the future of Soviet strategic nuclear forces. I was attending to learn what I could about latest thinking on likely Soviet decisions and what these might mean for U.S. policy, strategy, and investments. Ted impressed me with his deep knowledge and clear thinking. He did not mince his words but showed remarkable patience in taking my questions, serving in a way as teacher, as well as analyst. Little did I know that Ted would be my boss a few short years later.

As Ted took on his new responsibilities as Assistant Secretary of Defense for Strategy and Requirements, I was assigned to his new organization as member of the staff of the Deputy Assistant Secretary of Defense for Requirements and Plans. I later served in his Strategy office, which I eventually headed. Over the next eight years, I worked closely with Ted on a wide range of defense planning topics. Ted and his small staff had tremendous reach during that period. And while he was known for a flurry of activity, he never lost his touch as a teacher.

༄

Defense strategy is made not only in the broad strokes of official pronouncements and taglines but also in narrow strokes comprising the numerous, almost uncountable actions associated with the day-to-day decisions of governing. The broad strokes of defense strategy make for effective goal setting, the rough alignment of strategic objectives and supporting resources, and communications—to both internal and external audiences—of the major tenets of that strategy. But it is the narrow strokes of implementation—the day-to-day decisions that align institutions, activities, and people behind the bigger ideas—that bring about real change.[1]

---

[1] This chapter attempts to describe the process of making and implementing defense strategy during the eight years of the Clinton administration. This focus is on the role that Ted Warner and his staff played in that process. The activities described here are but a sampling of the many, many activities that were under way during this time. The subsequent chapter in this volume by Dr. Christopher Lamb offers a contrarian view on the difficulties, if not impossibility, of developing and implementing a coherent defense strategy. I accept some of Dr. Lamb's arguments but not all of them. There is no question that the fragmented organizational structure of the current Department of Defense makes it far more difficult to conceive and implement effective strategy. Dr. Lamb and I worked as colleagues for many years inside that structure and can attest to its many idiosyncrasies and inefficiencies. We have witnessed many missed opportunities, as well as a few successes. Dr. Lamb is also correct in

Ted Warner was instrumental in aligning institutions, activities, and people behind the nation's first post–Cold War defense strategy, a strategy initially conceived by the George H. W. Bush administration but one that did not really take form until the Clinton administration took office in 1993 with Warner serving as the Assistant Secretary of Defense for Strategy and Requirements. Warner was given the responsibility of drafting and implementing the nation's defense strategy, a position he held from spring 1993 until fall 2000, in a period that has been called "the post–Cold War era."

A Long Struggle Ends

The story of one era inevitably begins with the final notes of the era that preceded it. The post–Cold War era was no different. The long struggle with the Soviet Union, which many thought might end in nuclear calamity, ended in a whimper. The Soviet empire, including the Soviet Union itself and the "satellite" communist states of Eastern Europe, which Moscow once ruled through fear, collapsed as a result of fatigue and mismanagement. An effort by a desperate or perhaps courageous Soviet leader, Mikhail Gorbachev, to introduce reform within the Soviet Union and in its relations with the vassal states of Eastern Europe provided an opening, an erosion of fear, which led, in turn, to the very rapid and unprecedented collapse of the Soviet empire, all without war. The states in Eastern Europe broke free; a new Soviet leadership group initially stood its ground on the fringes of Red Square; and an old international order that was once defined by the actions and reactions of the two Cold War superpower foes, the Soviet Union and the United States, began to give way to new ambitions— some associated with freedom, others associated with dominance and destruction. The toppling of the Berlin Wall on November 9, 1989, marked the end of the Cold War era and the beginning of the next.

A New Era Takes Shape

A little over two years after the fall of the Berlin Wall, the Soviet Union itself collapsed and was replaced by 15 newly independent states formed from the former republics of

---

observing that the lack of a single organizing principle or focus impedes the ability to frame choices and marshal coherent efforts behind a common set of goals. These matters certainly make the strategy-making process more difficult. But is it impossible? As I hope this chapter will establish, core security challenges can be identified, and the strategy for dealing with them can be crafted and implemented in a reasonably effective fashion, albeit with expected frustrations and setbacks. Moreover, I would argue that the effort to identify core challenges and develop strategy to deal with them, along with the many efforts needed to connect that strategy to a set of specific decisions and actions, albeit imperfect, is better than not attempting at all. But achieving these successes requires the strong and constant leadership of the kind that Ted Warner offered during his tenure. This is one matter on which Dr. Lamb and I are in full agreement.

the Union of Soviet Socialist Republics. It was in the context of this dramatically new situation in Eastern Europe and in the Soviet Union that the Bush administration took a hand in crafting a new U.S. national security policy and defense strategy. It acted on many fronts, often with wisdom and foresight but, in the end, did not have sufficient time to fully work out its new approach.

Perhaps the Bush administration's pinnacle achievement during that period was to initiate the process of bringing a safe and secure end to the threat that Soviet nuclear weapons might fall into the hands of terrorists or irresponsible states. It did so by undertaking a complex set of actions now little remembered, but the result was profoundly important. As the Soviet Union crumbled, many of its strategic nuclear weapons remained on combat alert or stored in supposedly secure nuclear weapon storage sites, spread across various parts of the former Soviet Union. With determination, timely action, and innovative help from the U.S. Congress (in the form of the Cooperative Threat Reduction Program authored by Senators Sam Nunn [D-Georgia] and Richard Lugar [R-Indiana]), the former Soviet nuclear threat was controlled, contained, and ultimately transformed with the help of actions the Bush administration undertook in cooperation with Russia, Ukraine, Kazakhstan, and Belarus, which the Clinton administration substantially expanded. This extensive and sustained effort represents perhaps one of the greatest expressions of cooperation between former adversaries in the modern era. The "loose nukes" that so many feared never really materialized.

At the same time, the "balance of terror" between Washington and Moscow that had occupied so much thought and attention was transformed with the conclusion of the first and second Strategic Arms Reduction Treaties—START I and START II. These treaties involved commitments from each side to substantially reduce its strategic nuclear forces; implementing the treaties involved an unprecedented level of transparency and highly intrusive on-site inspections.

The Bush administration was equally skilled in its handling of Germany. Although some wavered on the question, including key British and French allies, the Bush administration saw an opportunity to unify East and West Germany within the North Atlantic Treaty Organization (NATO). The Bush administration partnered with Chancellor Helmut Kohl; brought along skeptical British and French allies; and even secured the acceptance, however grudging, of the Soviet leadership. As a result of unification, a formerly divided Germany was anchored securely in the West, and a previously divided Europe now had a chance to pursue a very different future.

Despite these accomplishments, the Bush administration may be best remembered for fighting and winning the first Gulf War in the wake of the August 1990 invasion of Kuwait by Saddam Hussein's Iraq. However, this seemingly decisive military response to a looming regional threat ultimately produced a lingering stalemate in the vital Persian Gulf region. That, and other challenges associated with the rest of the opening years of the post–Cold War era, would await the newly elected Clinton administration in January 1993.

In the realm of defense strategy and policy, the first Bush administration will be remembered for a controversial draft planning document—the 1992 Defense Planning Guidance (DPG)—which, among other goals, called for the United States to preclude hostile domination of key regions around the world, an indication of an ambitious and activist foreign and defense policy at a time when some were calling for more prudent restraint. This strategic approach was later refined and released publicly as "the Regional Defense Strategy." This new strategy was accompanied by a set of decisions that significantly reduced the U.S. armed forces in the context of what was labeled "the Base Force," the first dramatic adjustments of the U.S. military in the post–Cold War era.

Defense Strategy for a New Era Forged During the Bottom-Up Review

The Clinton administration entered office with an ambitious domestic agenda, along with a goal to reshape U.S. defense policy. Congressman Les Aspin (D-Wisconsin), who had served for eight years as the Chairman of the House Armed Services Committee, became Secretary of Defense. Aspin had spent the previous few years engaged in a debate with the Bush administration about the shape of the future U.S. defense strategy and how to better connect that strategy to force structure and resourcing decisions. In taking his oath of office, Aspin outlined four new dangers that he believed would dominate the security environment in the era to come: (1) new nuclear dangers associated with the possibility that a handful of nuclear warheads could fall into the hands of terrorists or terrorist states; (2) the danger of regional conflicts, in the form of a hostile Iraq or defiant North Korea; (3) the dangers associated with the failure of reform in the newly independent states that had emerged from the former Soviet Union; and (4) the danger associated with not achieving economic well-being within the United States.

Aspin decided to explore these dangers and the defense strategy and policy needed to address them in what he called "the Bottom-Up Review" (BUR), a major review of U.S. defense policy, strategy, and force structure. Warner and his staff found themselves at the very epicenter of that ambitious defense review, convening key stakeholders, staking out policy positions, narrowing and refining options, and ultimately crafting the new U.S. National Defense Strategy, which provided the guidelines that would set the course for the Clinton administration's defense policy.

Establishing the sizing criteria for U.S. military forces was a core element of the defense strategy and a foundation for the BUR. For decades, U.S. military forces were sized and structured to deter a Soviet nuclear attack on the United States, as well as Soviet conventional and nuclear threats in Europe; Asia; and, later, the Middle East. If deterrence failed, U.S. forces were expected to halt Soviet aggression, relying on the threat of nuclear escalation when necessary. U.S. forces had never been of sufficient size to fight in all areas of the globe simultaneously, so priorities were established among regions, with the expectation that U.S. forces would be prepared to undertake large-scale military operations in response to aggression in more than one region at a time. Some came to call this approach a "two-war strategy."

Following the fall of the Berlin Wall and the collapse of the Soviet Union, there was no clear conceptual guidance on how to size and structure U.S. military forces. The Bush administration signaled a desire to maintain a two-theater or two–major regional conflict (MRC) posture but lacked specific plans to draw out the implications of this commitment in any detail. The BUR took up the challenge by building on U.S. military capabilities employed during the recent Gulf War. It did so by defining what it termed "building blocks" for a future MRC, the elements that would be needed to halt a regional adversary's initial invasion and then mount a major counteroffensive to decisively defeat the aggressor. To the Clinton administration, the Gulf War represented the type of military challenge the United States might expect for the foreseeable future, with Iraq and North Korea identified as the most likely potential foes in the years ahead.

The National Defense Strategy, which was developed during the BUR, posited the anticipated phases of a future regional war:

- Halt the invasion.
- Build up the U.S. combat power in the theater while reducing the enemy's combat power and will to resist.
- Decisively defeat the enemy.
- Provide for postwar stability.

This construct was applied to help ascertain the major force elements needed to execute the new defense strategy. After an extensive, high-stakes internal debate within the Pentagon, the BUR settled on a combination of the following force building blocks as required to prevail in an MRC:

- four to five Army divisions
- four to five Marine expeditionary brigades
- ten Air Force fighter wings
- one hundred Air Force heavy bombers
- four to five Navy carrier battle groups
- special operations forces.

The numbers of transport aircraft and sealift ships, both military and mobilized from the civil sector, that would be needed to move the forces to the theater and sustain them throughout the conflict were subsequently calculated in the follow-on Mobility Requirements Study.

For the purpose of sizing U.S. military forces, the BUR concluded that the United States needed to be capable of fighting and winning in two regions nearly simultaneously, that is, with the second MRC initiated by a different, opportunistic aggressor 30 to 45 days after the beginning of the first MRC. It thus defined U.S. core conventional capabilities around the idea of preparing for two overlapping MRCs while also recognizing that other missions, such as maintaining a forward presence with a range of forward deployed and periodically deployed forces, in particular naval forces, could create special demands for military capabilities and might require certain additional forces or specialized training and preparation. The strategy assumed that lesser regional contingencies, including limited interventions, punitive strikes, peacekeeping operations, and humanitarian assistance and disaster relief operations, might require specialized capabilities but that these contingencies could be conducted within the overall force structure designed to prevail in two MRCs.

The two-MRC construct may appear simple in retrospect—too simple, according to some of the Clinton administration's critics—and for some, the focus on Iraq and North Korea as the canonical planning cases was too narrowly cast. Others questioned the preparation for nearly simultaneous major conventional wars in only two regions when the United States had fundamental interests in at least three—Europe, East Asia, and the Middle East. The Clinton administration countered that it considered it highly unlikely that the United States would confront more than two major regional wars at any given time. Still other observers expressed concerns about the size of the building blocks or parts of them—for example, five Army divisions—being adequate to the demanding tasks. These observers typically felt that more forces, especially more ground forces, were needed, not fewer, to successfully execute the strategy. A smaller group argued that too many forces were being retained.

In a time of dramatically shrinking defense dollars due to the post–Cold War drawdown, all the key stakeholders understood the simple arithmetic associated with the two-MRC construct. More forces from a given service in the designated building blocks meant more dollars for that service. Fewer forces meant fewer dollars.

But the arguments went even deeper and were more passionate. For years, technologists and military planners had anticipated significant changes in modern warfare, expecting particular advantages to accrue from investments in breakthrough areas, such as stealth technology and precision weapons. As David Ochmanek points out in Chapter Three, the Gulf War showed the real promise of these new technologies. For the first time in modern warfare, aircraft armed with conventional weapons demonstrated devastating strategic and battlefield effects. High-value targets throughout the Iraqi rear area were destroyed rapidly with precisely delivered conventional weapons carried by cruise missiles and combat aircraft. On the front lines, Iraqi armored forces deployed in Kuwait were subjected to more than a month of sustained air attacks before American and allied ground forces entered the fray. Many ground-force enthusiasts touted the successes of the so-called 100-hour war, in which allied ground forces outfought, outpaced, and outmaneuvered Iraqi ground forces. But others, including many top decisionmakers, believed that much of this success was made possible by the crushing effect of precision weapons delivered from the air, and that this was just the beginning of a new airpower era.

All this played out in the course of the BUR. Airpower enthusiasts argued in favor of new investments in stealth and precision weaponry. They wanted to exploit the advantages that were demonstrated so vividly in the Gulf War and have those new-found advantages reflected in overall force size and budget shares. They saw this as a shift in warfare and wanted to take advantage of the opportunities that technology—now apparently proven technology—had to offer. They wanted to exploit the potential of what some were now calling the latest revolution in military affairs.

Ground force advocates remained skeptical of these conclusions. They recognized the advantages stealth and precision weapons offered—indeed the U.S. Army was investing in precision weapons for its forces—but they were not ready to concede that this represented a change in the fundamental roles of the U.S. armed forces. The debate was not just between the Army and Air Force, but involved the Navy and Marine Corps as well. Warner and his team were in the thick of the debate and helped mediate it; they were generally perceived as being associated more closely with the views of the airpower enthusiasts, although not with the most extreme of the airpower advocates. Warner and his Deputy Assistant Secretary of Defense for Strategy, David Ochmanek, were, after all, former Air Force officers and had been analysts for the RAND Corporation's Project AIR FORCE before joining the administration.

The BUR yielded a compromise on these matters or, perhaps more appropriately, a truce, which hardly resolved the debate. Investments continued to flow to stealth and precision—investments that would play out importantly later in the decade as new weapons, such as the Joint Direct Attack Munition, a highly accurate Global Positioning System–guided bomb, became so prominent in the U.S. arsenal. The issue would rear its head again a few years later in the controversial Deep Attack Weapons Mix Study.

This was but one of many issues associated with setting a new U.S. post–Cold War defense policy and strategy. Other issues surrounded the future role of Marine Corps amphibious forces, the anticipated contributions of naval aviation, the prospective role of heavy bombers, the future of Army "light" forces, the expected contributions of special operations forces, and the contributions of Navy attack submarines, to name a few.

In the end, the BUR set forth the broad strokes of a new U.S. National Defense Strategy and identified the forces and modernization programs needed to support that strategy—establishing overall outlines and putting defense planning on a new course. Warner played an instrumental role in helping complete the review and, in many ways, drafting the outline for the narrow strokes associated with implementing that strategy that would follow over the coming eight years. This work included the refinement of this defense strategy, force structure, force posture, and force modernization plans for the 1997 Quadrennial Defense Review, a congressionally mandated review that took place at the beginning of President Clinton's second term.

Connecting Planning to Resource Decisions

Throughout the 1990s, the Secretary of Defense issued annual planning guidance to the military departments and defense agencies for the preparation of multiyear budget plans, commonly known to insiders as program objective memoranda. Each year the staff of the Under Secretary of Defense for Policy would work carefully with other organizations in OSD and with the Joint Staff, the military departments, and defense agencies to prepare the annual guidance, known as the DPG.[2]

The DPG is a formal vehicle for communicating recent major policy decisions, such as those coming out of the BUR and Quadrennial Defense Reviews. It also provides the venue for updating resource plans, refining overall guidance, and initiating analyses that are to be used in upcoming planning efforts. In some ways, the DPG can be viewed as the overall tool for guiding the supply of U.S. military forces, just as its companion guidance document, the Contingency Planning Guidance (CPG), was the overall tool for identifying the anticipated demand for military forces and the ways the forces might be employed. The CPG is discussed in a subsequent section.

The military departments look to the DPG to codify force structure and personnel end-strength numbers, maintain emphasis in key readiness areas, support modernization priorities, and articulate key support and infrastructure needs. They welcome guidance to the extent that it supports their preferred positions but were ever anxious that new guidance might depart from their preferred positions, pointing them in directions they were not comfortable following, or put them in the position of not competing well for overall defense resources.

Warner and his Requirements and Plans staff had responsibility for annually drafting and coordinating the DPG. This typically started at the beginning of each calendar year and culminated in a signed guidance document by late spring.

To some, the drafting process appeared as a routine staff exercise—important but not exciting or even very important. To others, it provided an annual opportunity to engage the Secretary of Defense and his top advisors in an exercise to introduce new concepts, codify decisions, refine policy, and sustain the uneasy consensus that surrounds the making of defense policy and strategy. It was a vehicle to set a course or direction and, in some cases, to try to settle arguments before the military services and defense agencies engaged the detailed undertaking of drafting multiyear defense program and budget plans.

---

2   This practice has continued, although the name of the document has changed from time to time.

Because of the many substantial changes in policy and strategy following the end of the Cold War and because of the need to fine-tune resource plans as the new defense policy and strategy adopted following the BUR were being implemented, the mid-1990s were a particularly important time for the DPG. Its drafting provided an opportunity to refine the strategy, reflect on how the strategy was being implemented, and look at issues that had not been appreciated or anticipated in earlier years. It provided a year-to-year check to be sure that strategy, forces, and resources were connected in the ways that were intended. The DPG itself had two major sections: (1) planning guidance and (2) programming guidance. The planning guidance focused on overall policy, planning details (including approved planning scenarios), force sizing criteria (recall the discussion on the two-MRC construct above), and regional and functional priorities. The planning guidance might be thought of as providing the context for how overall resource decisions were to be made.

In contrast, the programming guidance provided specific instructions to the military services and defense agencies on forces, the force mix (active, reserve, and national guard), readiness levels, training requirements, investment priorities (including numbers of systems to be purchased in prominent cases), personnel end-strength numbers (military and civilian), infrastructure requirements (including plans for base closures), and so forth. The guidance typically focused on specific numbers or outcomes but could include a range of numbers or outcomes when greater flexibility was desired or when there was less certainty about a goal or outcome.

The process for preparing the DPG began with an internal staff draft, written by Warner's Requirements and Plans staff.[3] The draft would be reviewed first by Warner and his closest colleagues in OSD and Joint Staff, especially the Director of Program Analysis and Evaluation and the Director of Force Structure, Resources, and Assessment (Joint Staff J8).[4] This review typically involved an informal set of interactions to ensure that the initial draft captured the appropriate scope and content. The back-and-forth associated with producing the first draft usually consumed four to six weeks.

Warner understood well the importance of being heavily engaged at this stage of the drafting process, because decisions about scope and content would have important implications as the process unfolded. For example, the military services typically wanted guidance that was more general rather than more specific, unless, of course, the guidance reinforced one of that military service's preferred positions. In such instances, a military service would welcome detailed guidance both to reinforce positions within its own organization and to ward off opposition elsewhere in the Department of Defense. If detailed guidance was needed or desired, it needed to be reflected in the earliest drafts. Adding detail later in the process, unless it was detail to reinforce

---

[3]   I was the lead author of the DPG from 1993 through 1996.

[4]   The office of Program Analysis and Evaluation is now the office of Cost Analysis and Program Evaluation.

an already accepted position, would raise serious objections, typically prompting an anguished cry of "process foul."

Once the first draft was prepared, it would be circulated to the recipients for comment. The initial comment period typically lasted another four weeks and was accompanied by a series of meetings with the military service three-star planners and programmers to explain the draft. In some years, the meetings with the three-star planners and programmers would begin before the first draft was circulated, as a way of surfacing issues and gauging expectations. The recipients would return their specific comments and requested changes, which typically would number in the tens but occasionally in the hundreds, depending upon how close the product came to meeting recipients' expectations. Warner's staff would collect all the comments, review them, and then engage in a set of deliberations with Warner on the most important suggestions or requested changes.

This would provide the basis for a second and typically final DPG draft. This draft would be sent directly to the three-star community, including the three-star service programmers and directors of the defense agencies, and would be followed by a series of high-level meetings with the key stakeholders, often culminating in meetings with the service chiefs. These interactions would provide the substance for the final draft that would be reviewed and approved by the Secretary of Defense or, in some cases, the Deputy Secretary of Defense. During Warner's tenure as an assistant secretary of defense, this typically involved a set of private interactions with the secretary or deputy secretary, followed by a formal meeting of the department's top military and civilian leaders. The meeting would serve as a final check before the DPG was issued.

Although the deliberations associated with the process were never made public, the internal stakeholders certainly kept score. It was a process that was perceived as producing winners and losers. Warner and his staff worked closely with the full range of stakeholders throughout the process, ensuring that all important perspectives were heard, and therefore ensuring that the Department of Defense's top leaders were provided the best information possible to make effective decisions.

Offering appropriate levels of transparency, including transparency on when and how key decisions would be made, was essential for a smooth process and timely outcome. Not every issue that surfaced was ready for decision, and not every controversial issue was settled with a clear-cut decision. More than a few issues were "kicked down the road." Some were kicked to the second term of the Clinton administration and some to the Clinton team's successors in the second Bush administration. Overall, however, the annual drafting and dissemination of the DPG provided an effective vehicle for connecting and refining the broad strokes of policy and strategy to the detailed day-to-day program and budget decisions of the Department of Defense.

Beyond the guidance, of course, there were opportunities to review the military service and defense agency resource plans on a regular basis. The annual program review, led by an OSD sister office, Program Analysis and Evaluation, looked in depth at the multiyear program plans the military services and defense agencies developed. This provided an opportunity to see how spending plans aligned over time and whether key aspects of the strategy and planning were indeed reflected in the spending plans of the various DoD components. Similarly, that annual budget review, led by the DoD Comptroller, provided an occasion to look at the detailed spending plans for the coming year, to reconcile any anomalies, and to further ensure compliance with overall DoD guidance. Warner and his staff participated actively in these processes, always with an eye toward ensuring the strongest possible connections among strategy, forces, and resources.

Remaking War Plans

An important element of defense planning in the 1990s was the effort to connect strategy to military contingency plans, often referred to as "war plans," in ways that had not been done in the past. The 1986 Goldwater-Nichols legislation called for formal civilian oversight of military war plans by the Secretary of Defense and his staff. The first Bush administration began efforts to do so by assigning this support to the Under Secretary of Defense for Policy, who set up an office for war plan review. Progress, however, in completing this new task was slow, and most of the effort awaited implementation during the Clinton administration.

In the aftermath of the BUR, an intensive effort was needed to align forces and resources to planning, especially regarding the actual plans to implement the requirement of being capable of fighting and winning two, nearly simultaneous MRCs— the two-MRC construct, as discussed above. Warner and the plans component of his Requirements and Plans staff had responsibility for preparing the annual CPG on behalf of the Secretary of Defense. They were also responsible for assisting the Under Secretary of Defense for Policy and the Secretary of Defense in their reviews of the various contingency (war) plans prepared by the combatant commanders in accordance with the direction contained in the CPG. As noted above, the CPG was the vehicle that provided guidance on the preparation of all "deliberate" war plans and established more-general expectations regarding the major demands for military forces. The preparation of the CPG and subsequent review of the war plans the regional and functional combatant commanders developed provided opportunities to plan in detail for how to meet the defense strategy's two-MRC planning requirement. This included the identification of the specific forces to be made available to a particular combatant command for a given plan, their readiness levels (what level of unit preparation field commanders could expect), deployment times, deployment modes (air, sea, rail, and ground movement), arrival times in theater, and support and replenishment needs. Importantly, it also required combatant commanders to submit for review their plans for how they planned to fight a particular conflict under specified conditions.

Just as drafting the DPG involved careful management of competing interests among highly influential stakeholders, so too did the preparation of the CPG. Four-star combatant commanders are expected to be bold in executing war plans and are typically just as aggressive in competing for the forces and resources needed to underwrite their war plans. No combatant commander will agree to less of or different types of forces if he thinks he needs a specific force element or more of a particular type of force. Yet, in implementing any planning construct, there are finite resources and assets to meet competing demands. The CPG set expectations among combatant commanders about what forces they could plan on getting and adjudicated competing demands in the context of the overall defense strategy.

Warner's role in this effort began by working with his Strategy and Requirements and Plans staffs to assess what it would mean to support a two-MRC construct by connecting forces and resources to the actual war plans. In any sequence of two nearly simultaneous or overlapping events, there is always a first event and a second. The theater commander whose war starts first in the sequence will seek the largest number of the most capable and ready forces that are located closest to his area of responsibility (AOR). The commander whose war comes second in the sequence will have to make do with whatever capabilities remain.

When warfighting conditions are very different, the various kinds of military forces can be allocated to where they are most needed. When warfighting conditions are similar, commanders will be competing for the same capabilities. The problem of fighting the second of two wars pertains especially when warfighting conditions are similar. Yet the overall contingency planning process could and had to ensure that the division of forces between the two possible wars was such that the commander whose war came second had a set of MRC building block forces that would provide him with a reasonable chance of success. If the defense strategy's two-MRC construct was to meet its fundamental objective of deterring opportunistic aggression when the United States was embroiled in a major theater war, U.S. war plans had to allocate major force elements and critical enabling capabilities among the potentially overlapping wars to provide effective support to the commander responsible for prosecuting the second war.

As contingency planning evolved in the early to mid-1990s, two main cases dominated the planning debate: a ground invasion of a U.S. ally in the Middle East and a ground invasion of a U.S. ally in East Asia. The challenge to the planning community was the sequencing of forces to meet these two potential military challenges. What forces and assets could theater commanders expect if a war began first in the Middle East, followed by a subsequent war in East Asia? Conversely, what forces and assets could these commanders expect if a war began first in East Asia followed by a subsequent war in the Middle East? The problem would be difficult enough if all forces were at equal readiness levels and deploying from the same locale. But the problem was made much more difficult because not all forces—divisions and tactical fighter wings—provided the same level of capability and were not maintained at equal readiness levels—some were at peak readiness because of recent training and equipment upgrades, while others were well below peak because they had not benefited from recent training, had recently experienced equipment and personnel changeovers, or perhaps had just returned to their home base from another commitment. And, of course, U.S. military forces are deployed across the globe. Those stationed closest to a given conflict can respond rapidly. But not all forces are located close to a conflict. And in some cases, all forces of a given type might be quite distant from a given conflict. For example, in cases involving war on the Korean peninsula, the only U.S. ground forces that were at all close to the area were those already stationed on the Korean peninsula and on Okinawa.

So the task for contingency planning in the early to mid-1990s was to determine what forces were to go where and when while implementing the two-MRC planning construct. This was no small feat. It involved Warner and his Plans staff; the Joint Staff; the combatant commanders and their staffs (including U.S. Transportation Command, which had responsibility for moving all the forces and supplies to the theater of operations); and the military services, which were responsible for day-to-day training of the force elements to supply ready forces when needed.

Combat simulation tools had to be used to help determine what forces and capabilities were best suited to different conditions and sequencing concepts. Planning conferences had to be organized to identify available substitutes and workarounds when commanders could not assume that their preferred forces would be available where and when they believed the forces were needed. Planning conferences also helped inform discussions regarding operational risks. For example, risk of not meeting planned objectives within agreed time lines rather obviously increased when forces could not be available at the time a commander thought they were needed. But was the risk primarily associated with executing a particular plan or with winning or losing a war? All these matters, and many more, had to be debated and settled as policy and strategy were reflected in the details of war plans.

Planning became even more complicated as new variables were introduced. For example, as the 1990s unfolded, it became evident to the war planning community that the forces thought to be available for major wars were being used on a day-to-day basis for a variety of other needs, what came to be known as smaller-scale contingencies. These could range from short-duration punitive airstrikes in Iraq and long-term peacekeeping operations in the Balkans to the sustained enforcement of no-fly zones over Iraq and the conduct of a range of humanitarian assistance and disaster relief operations in response to natural and man-made disasters. The likelihood of continued involvement in these types of contingency operations had to be factored into war planning considerations. Among the questions posed at the time was: Would the forces be available at all—that is, would they be withdrawn from the smaller-scale contingencies and made available for other wartime needs—or did commanders of both the first and second MRCs need to assume they would have to make do without the forces engaged in such operations? These issues had to be resolved in a theoretical sense, since the plans were never tested, but the debate about what forces would be available for which purposes would surface again in a more-specific way during the next decade as the United States found itself involved in two wars that became drawn-out counterinsurgencies in Iraq and Afghanistan yet still had to confront security challenges elsewhere around the globe.

Another challenge had to do with the implications of an aggressor's possible use of chemical and biological weapons on the modern battlefield. As the decade of the 1990s progressed, military planners became more and more convinced that regional adversaries might very well resort to the use of chemical or biological weapons if they concluded that their hold on governing power was threatened. This came at the same time when U.S. objectives became more expansive; in some contingencies, the United States would no longer be content to restore the *status quo ante* if confronted by regional adversaries; it would now seek to forcibly expel the regime that had brought war to their neighbors or even their own people.

The planning community understood that chemical or biological weapons could have important implications for the conduct of contemporary warfare. Ground forces, for example, had the greatest potential for success when they concentrated their efforts at the point of attack and were able to exploit breakthroughs in enemy defenses. But, of course, concentrating forces made them more vulnerable to chemical or biological weapons attack. Chemical and biological defenses—including protective equipment, vaccinations, and battlefield treatment capabilities—could partially offset the effects of these weapons, but the defenses were unproven and typically in very short supply. Dispersing troops across the battlefield could offset the vulnerabilities associated with large force concentrations but would also negate the advantages associated with massing forces at the point of attack. Moreover, because troops would need to deploy to the warfighting areas, they would inevitably be concentrated at the points of arrival—the ports of debarkation and airfields where American forces would be arriving by ship and transport aircraft.

Ships and transport aircraft arriving or departing from areas contaminated by chemical or biological weapon strikes would also pose a different and special problem. Ships and aircraft must move in and out of the theater of operation transporting troops and supplies. A key American warfighting advantage is the ability to deploy rapidly and then resupply deployed forces on a continuing basis. But if the ships and aircraft that moved troops and supplies were to become contaminated, would they be able to move from the contaminated areas to the rear area to collect new troops and supplies? How rapidly could these ships and transport aircraft be fully decontaminated? Would allies and partners, who are crucial for the resupply of American forces, allow contaminated or previously contaminated ships and aircraft into their ports and airfields? Would they be allowed back into American ports and airfields?

The threat of chemical and biological weapon use might be offset by the threat of nuclear escalation, that is, the threat that the United States would retaliate with nuclear weapons in the event of a chemical or biological attack on American or allied forces, but little was known about decisionmaking within the offending regimes. Would regional adversaries be deterred by the threat of American nuclear retaliation, particularly if they judged that the use of chemical and biological weapons might be the only way to preserve their positions of power, lest they be overrun by clearly superior American conventional forces? Less clear still would be the willingness of an American President to resort to nuclear weapons in the face of a chemical or biological attack. It would be one thing to conclude that an American President would retaliate with all means available in the face of mass casualties or widespread use of chemical and biological weapons. What if the chemical or biological weapons were used in limited ways with limited casualties or if there were ambiguity about the use of the weapons—perhaps attributed to a renegade field commander? Would an American President be prepared to retaliate with nuclear weapons? If so, against what targets?

It was in this context that Warner worked with the commanders of U.S. Pacific Command, U.S. Forces Korea, and the U.S. Central Command to establish what came to be known as the Breeze series of planning exercises. Working closely with a former RAND colleague, Bruce Bennett, and the OSD Plans staff, Warner oversaw the development and conduct of a series of step-by-step planning exercises—Coral Breeze and Desert Breeze—to engage the combatant commanders and their staffs on the policy and warfighting considerations associated with fighting effectively to execute the given war plan in the face of the enemy's possible use of chemical or biological weapons on the battlefield.

These exercises, which Warner and members of his Plans staff attended, were designed first to engage combatant command staffs on the many challenges associated with operating in the presence of chemical or biological weapons and ultimately to involve the four-star combatant commanders in simulating the decisionmaking that would be necessary should such circumstances come to pass. The goal was not only to factor the results of the exercises back into the war planning process but also to involve top civilian leaders at the departments of State and Defense to prepare them for the types of decisions they might one day confront and to inform the research and development processes to perhaps identify technologies that would offset the most serious effects of these weapons.

Peacetime Plans to Complement War Plans

As the decade continued, it became clear that a variety of peacetime activities undertaken to shape the international security environment were as demanding in terms of day-to-day commitments of forces as preparing for war. The combatant commanders, along with the military service components assigned to them, were engaged in a wide array of outreach and training activities across the globe. New relationships were being forged, which brought new commitments and demands. Detailed guidance was available to prepare for wartime needs, but the Secretary of Defense issued little or no guidance to establish priorities for the peacetime engagement activities of U.S. military forces or of civilian and military personnel from OSD or the military departments or to sort out the many competing demands for support of peacetime engagement activities that were coming from the combatant commands.

In time, it became clear that some form of peacetime engagement guidance would be needed to establish priorities within and among regions, or combatant command AORs, as they are known. Warner and his Strategy staff led this effort. The new guidance was developed in cooperation with the combatant command staffs, the military service staffs, the Joint Staff, and various parts of OSD. It set out to establish priority countries to be engaged and activities to be undertaken, realizing the need to support well-established relationships—say with the Republic of Korea, Japan, or the original NATO member states—as well as to develop new relationships—say with the new NATO member states, other members of the former Warsaw Pact, and many of the former Soviet republics that were now independent states. Because the new guidance would have implications for broader diplomatic activities, drafts were shared with staff at the Department of State and the National Security Council Staff. The new product, which was known as the "Prioritized Regional Objectives," was ultimately approved by the President.

An important issue of jurisdiction surfaced in the preparation of the guidance that would not be settled until several years later. Combatant commands were traditionally allocated forces through a process led by the Joint Staff. That process yielded what is known as the "Forces For" document or more formally "Forces for the Unified and Specified Commands." By tradition, combatant commanders had authority to make decisions regarding the location and use of those forces within their assigned AORs. Combatant commanders, of course, would need authority from the President and Secretary of Defense to use military force, but they had broad discretion regarding training, positioning, and various outreach activities. Commanders had to request permission to move forces from outside their commands or AORs but not within them.

Some in the combatant commands saw development of new guidance on the use of military forces for peacetime engagement activities as an infringement on the combatant commanders' prerogatives. Those making the arguments were amenable to general guidance setting priorities for the particular countries to be engaged and the major types of activities to be undertaken, but they resisted guidance on specific activities or on how commanders might use forces within their AORs.

Warner and his staff had to manage this source of tension—a classic problem of headquarters and field command relationships—carefully. Most of the major concerns were resolved as various drafts of the guidance were being developed. However, an interesting pattern of caucusing and consensus building developed over time. Combatant command staffs would complain to their Department of State counterparts in the various embassy staffs that headquarters (the Pentagon) wanted to place restrictions or demands on what they were able to do with "their" forces. Most of these issues were resolved through dialogue and negotiation, although at times there was a sense of "Washington versus the field" in some of the deliberations.

Two particular areas of peacetime engagement activity involved Warner and his staff directly: NATO enlargement and outreach to the former Soviet states.

Early in the Clinton administration, a substantial debate unfolded regarding the future of the NATO alliance. Some argued that the alliance had succeeded in its purposes and should move to the background as a new era unfolded. Others were advocating for NATO to take on new responsibilities and new member states. A shorthand message emerged: NATO needed to go "out of area or out of business." In the midst of this debate, many in the administration and Congress asked what it would cost to expand the alliance and how potential new members would contribute to overall alliance capability. In short, what new burdens would current allies be taking on by inviting new members to join the alliance? Analysis was needed to assess the overall military capability of the potential new members.

Warner and his Strategy office conducted that analysis for the Department of Defense, working closely with the Joint Staff and the U.S. European Command. The analysis pointed to various ways that new NATO members could contribute to the alliance. It also highlighted important areas for possible investment. One overall conclusion from the analysis had implications for the larger security assistance debate: It was clear that the new NATO members would not be best served by investing in expensive new aviation capabilities, such as the latest-generation fighter and attack aircraft. The existing 16 NATO members already possessed ample aircraft inventories, and any new investments by the NATO aspirants would be best targeted elsewhere. Since that time, NATO has undergone several rounds of expansion, with subsequent rounds much less contentious within the alliance and the United States than the first. (Russian negative reactions to NATO expansion grew sharper as NATO member states came closer to Russian territory and even included former Soviet republics in the form of the Baltic states.) It is no exaggeration to say that the analysis that Warner and his team undertook in response to congressional direction played an important role in convincing a reluctant Congress to support the Clinton administration's goal of opening the NATO alliance to new members.

Beyond NATO enlargement, there also was a need for the United States to connect with other former Warsaw Pact member states and the newly independent states of the former Soviet Union. This took many forms and involved much of the U.S. government. One particular activity was focused on exchanging defense planning experiences with often newly created defense ministries—first in Eastern Europe, later in the Caucasus, and eventually in Central Asia. Much of the activity was focused on defense-to-defense relationship building in general. Some of the activity was taken in response to specific needs of the new partners. In several cases, this outreach laid important groundwork and established relationships that would be needed in the immediate aftermath of 9/11. Warner and his staff led many of these interactions, with Warner occasionally participating himself. These often week-long interactions typically led to more detailed cooperation that was orchestrated by the combatant commanders and their staffs.

A New Era Soon to Follow

By the time the Clinton administration left office in early 2001, the stage had already been set for the era that was to come. As the United States worked closely with its new allies and partners in Europe, brought peace to the Balkans, forged new relationships throughout the Middle East, worked to align relationships in East Asia, and helped partners confront nagging insurgencies in the Western Hemisphere, new threats were looming and new competitions were arising. Osama bin Laden was successful in targeting U.S. forces and personnel in the Middle East and East Africa and was engaged in planning attacks against the United States from the protection of the mountains of Afghanistan; North Korea and Iran continued their pursuit of nuclear weapons, following a path set by India and Pakistan, both of which had recently joined the nuclear club; and China entered the third decade of its unprecedented economic modernization program and had begun a massive military modernization buildup. The problems of the 1990s would soon fade into memory, but the post–Cold War transformation of the U.S. military was well under way and would continue. Broad strokes and narrow strokes of a new U.S. defense policy and strategy had been combined to create a more effective approach to the pursuit of American national security.

CHAPTER FIVE

Pentagon Strategies

Christopher J. Lamb

When Ted arrived in 1993 as the new Assistant Secretary of Defense for Strategy and Requirements, I was working in the Pentagon office created by Congress to oversee special operations and low-intensity conflict. Soon after Ted's arrival, it was clear his organization would be a significant center of power in the Office of Secretary of Defense. We also quickly learned that he took seriously the proposition that strategy was a holistic enterprise enveloping all the subsidiary functional bodies of expertise in a grand chain of logical reasoning from policy to plans to requirements to operations and associated resource issues. To engage Ted's attention, it helped to argue the strategic merits of any issue with reference to how it fit in this larger framework. Previously, our office had been viewed skeptically in the Pentagon because of its origins and unpopular mission areas, but we discovered that Ted and the team he brought in were ready to accept good thinking from any source. In 1998, Ted invited me to join his Requirements and Plans office, and I had the opportunity to observe and learn more about his approach to organization and strategy.

୧୬

This chapter is about the intersection of strategy and organizational capacity. The common understanding of strategy is that it encompasses what one is trying to achieve, as well as the way it will be achieved and the resources that will be required. The "way" strategy will be achieved must always take into account the strengths and weaknesses of the organizations that implement the strategy. The assertion made here is that organizational impediments of the Department of Defense (DoD) handicap the creation and execution of strategy, so much so that good defense strategy cannot be generated through the formal process. In this chapter, I will argue that strong leadership is required to compensate for such limitations. In particular, leaders like Ted Warner must take responsibility for strategy with an "end-to-end" management approach if they want to overcome the most deleterious organizational limitations that impede strategy. Ted was able to do this, and consequently, it was exciting to work for him. In theory, there are better ways to organize, but in practice, Ted's approach was necessary for reasons I will discuss. Moreover, it was successful because he remained resolutely focused on national rather than parochial interests. This was evident in the way his conception of strategy took precedence over personal and political relationships.

The Formal Strategy-Driven Defense Process

> Just because a government drafts a document which proclaims the existence of a grand strategy … there is no guarantee that the baronies of officialdom will behave cohesively, coherently, and comprehensively. Strategy … is never self-executing.

Colin Gray
Director, Centre for Strategic Studies
University of Reading[1]

To set the stage for arguing that formal DoD strategy documents cannot communicate good strategy, it helps to provide a brief explanation of the defense strategy process and its organizational components. DoD has a massive, well-honed process for formulating and implementing defense strategy. The process evolves, but its basic components are stable. A defense strategy document is developed and used to inform force management decisions, plans for near-term contingencies, and the development of future forces. In this manner, strategy is supposed to propel detailed plans that determine defense programs and associated budgets. How well the process is executed and the actual real-world performance of military forces are then evaluated, and adjustments to the strategy are made on an emergency basis or in the next decision cycle. The process is elaborate. There is only one defense strategy, but there are many subordinate strategies; there is an overarching defense planning and programming guidance document, but there are multiple subordinate planning documents and activities; and there are also multiple ongoing program and budgeting activities designed to support this overall process.

Equally important is the fact that different offices in the Office of the Secretary of Defense lead each part of the process, and the Chairman of the Joint Chiefs of Staff and the military services manage parallel, but ostensibly complementary, processes. Lead offices change over time, but the policy component in the Office of the Secretary of Defense always generates strategy, and another policy office is typically responsible for major supporting planning documents. (See Chapter Four, by Andy Hoehn, for a more-detailed description of the planning process in particular.) In theory, these many organizational components work in close harmony to ensure tight linkages between strategy and supporting plans, programs, and budgets.

During Ted's tenure, the linchpin in his organization was the strategy office, which was widely agreed to house his best talent and receive the most critical tasks. Over time, he recruited and built up the rest of his organization, including the

---

[1]   Colin S. Gray, *The Strategy Bridge. Theory for Practice*, Oxford: Oxford University Press, 2010, p. 28. I am indebted to Frank Hoffman for this quotation (Frank G. Hoffman, "50 Shades of Gray," panel presentation, University of Reading, May 18, 2013).

Resources and Plans office.[2] Resources and Plans used the defense strategy that the strategy office formulated to generate planning guidance that, in turn, would guide defense programs needed to implement the defense strategy. Before Ted left the Pentagon, he was strongly enjoining the leaders of these two suborganizations to work more closely together. Relations were even more problematic between Ted's strategy office and the majority of regional offices located elsewhere in the Policy office that were beyond Ted's organizational control.[3] These offices managed U.S. military relations with other countries and ostensibly pursued regional policies in keeping with the broader U.S. defense strategy. The other elements of DoD that led the program and budgeting portion of the process, in particular, the Office for Program Analysis and Evaluation (now titled the Office for Cost Assessment and Program Evaluation), were even further removed from the policy offices that produced the department's major strategy and planning documents. These elements were prone to ignore the documents and look for program and budgeting efficiencies based on their own conceptions of priorities. Intradepartmental tensions thus complicated strategy development and execution. In fact, it can be argued they precluded it.

Richard Rumelt's book, *Good Strategy, Bad Strategy*,[4] makes a persuasive case that all good strategy requires three essential elements: (1) a penetrating diagnosis that identifies the root cause of the problem or challenge to be overcome; (2) a preferred approach that directs and constrains action to overcome the problem; and (3) supporting actions that are clear and feasible, given scarce resources. Other criteria for good strategy can be added, but these three elements are the core of good strategy according to Rumelt. Theoretically, Rumelt's understanding of what good strategy requires is completely consistent with the DoD process for creating and executing strategy. However, as with most things, it is much easier to articulate the requirements for success than it is to execute them. This is certainly true for defense strategy as it is formulated and executed in DoD.

Defense Strategy Limitations

Rumelt identifies some common problems that compromise the efficacy of the three core elements required for good strategy.[5] They can be used to explain the limitations

---

[2]   At the time, the office included a third component for counterproliferation, a major focus during Ted's tenure.

[3]   The regional office overseeing defense relations with Russia, Ukraine, and most of the other newly independent states that emerged following the dissolution of the Soviet Union in 1991 fell within Ted's expanded Strategy and Threat Reduction organization, formed in November 1997.

[4]   Richard P. Rumelt, *Good Strategy, Bad Strategy: The Difference and Why It Matters*, New York: Crown Business, 2011.

[5]   See the discussion of Rumelt's "common strategy sins" in Andrew F. Krepinevich and Barry D. Watts, *Regaining Strategic Competence*, Washington, D.C.: Center for Strategic and Budgetary Assessments, 2009, p. x.

associated with the formulation and implementation of defense strategy in DoD. These common impediments help explain why it is difficult to diagnose a core problem, choose a guiding way to solve the problem, and focus energies on that course of action. Failure to diagnose a core strategic problem complicates the ability to choose a guiding way to solve the problem. A failure in strategy diagnosis and prescription precludes focusing organizational energy on strategy execution. Strategy impediments thus build on one another and compound their impact. However, for purposes of illustration, each can be considered in turn.

Failure to Face the Problem

The first requirement for good strategy is a diagnosis of the essential problem to be resolved. Strategy presumes competition, and before determining how one might use a competitive advantage to good effect, it is necessary to fully comprehend the nature of the strategy challenge at hand. As Rumelt notes, "unless leadership offers a theory of why things haven't worked in the past, or why the challenge is difficult, it is hard to generate good strategy."[6] For both substantive and political reasons, however, it is quite difficult to narrow the range of defense challenges to one overriding concern. To illustrate this point, Rumelt relates the conclusions from a gathering of prominent defense strategists in Washington, D.C.[7] These defense experts lamented the poor quality of strategic thinking since the fall of the Soviet Union, observing that too many security strategies fail to identify a core problem as the focus of attention. Instead, these experts believed, too many U.S. security strategy documents offer up fluffy prose and laundry lists of diverse, desirable, and unachievable goals that obscure their lack of substance.

The strategy experts were impressed by the substantive problem of providing a good diagnosis, one that "simplifies the often overwhelming complexity of reality by identifying certain aspects of the situation as critical."[8] They drew a contrast between the period "during and after World War II [when] national leadership took national security strategy very seriously" and the post–Cold War and post–9/11 periods when, it is implied, national leaders have not taken strategy seriously. One might think that secret strategic assessments hidden from public view would do a better job of problem diagnosis, but the strategists, all of whom benefited from many years of Pentagon experience, assured Rumelt that the classified strategy documents were no better than the unclassified ones.

By focusing on the substantive challenge involved in diagnosing a core strategic problem, the participants in Rumelt's strategy seminar may have underestimated political impediments. History suggests it is not possible to generate a strategic diagnosis for U.S. security strategy absent a compelling external threat that shocks the Amer-

---

6   Rumelt, 2011, p. 55.

7   Rumelt, 2011, pp. 33ff.

8   Rumelt, 2011, p. 77.

ican public by demonstrating their vulnerability. Arguably, this has happened only three or four times in a manner sufficient to generate a political consensus on a core threat to the American way of life.[9] John Lewis Gaddis argues that the nation's grand strategy for preserving American institutions changed markedly only after three external shocks: the British burning of Washington, the Japanese attack on Pearl Harbor, and al-Qaeda's attacks on September 11, 2001. Some might separate the Pearl Harbor shock from the post–World War II rise of the Soviet Union and its nuclear arsenal. In any case, periods of strategic consensus on an overarching threat to American institutions are scarce and soon give way to acrimonious political debate.

The Cold War period is considered a time of relative strategic unity compared to more recent decades, but the relative bipartisan consensus following World War II evaporated in the late 1950s and 1960s. Similarly, the strategic imperative President George W. Bush emphasized following the terror attacks on 9/11—preventing terrorists from acquiring and using weapons of mass destruction—eroded quickly over the ensuing decade.[10] Without a manifest and existential threat to the American way of life, American public opinion fractures into a wide range of views on what the nation's overriding national security focus ought to be. Whenever blue-ribbon commissions are convened to forge a consensus on the nation's security agenda, the proper scope of national security (and by extension, the focus of security strategy) is sure to be the single most contentious issue.[11] This stands to reason, since all subsequent priorities flow from the diagnosis of the central problem requiring attention. Invariably, large blocks of public opinion will be more concerned about the security implications of global warming than about Iran acquiring nuclear weapons, about the security benefits of eliminating poverty than about the need to lead an emerging transformation in military capabilities, about the benefits of soft power than about hard military power, and so on.

Thus, a singular focus on one core strategic challenge would risk alienating large elements of public opinion interested in other problems. It would open an administration to the charge of simple single-mindedness and willfully ignoring other threats to vital interests. Identifying a central strategic problem also may seem too negative to

---

[9]   Michael Lind has argued that the central problem for American strategy is preserving the American way of life, which means preventing the rise of another power strong enough to require Americans to sacrifice their liberties to preserve their independence. Michael Lind, *The American Way of Strategy*, Oxford: Oxford University Press, 2006.

[10]   Preventing terrorists from acquiring weapons of mass destruction is still a critical objective but one that has lost its place of central importance. In discussing the future security environment and risks, the Chairman of the Joint Chiefs of Staff has noted that the consequences of a terrorist attack "are relatively insignificant in terms of national survival." General Martin Dempsey, "From the Chairman: Risky Business," *Joint Forces Quarterly*, No. 69, 2nd Quarter 2013, p. 3.

[11]   This was true in the Princeton Project on National Security and the Project on National Security Reform, for example.

many who would prefer to stress the positive and embrace opportunities. For example, it would be much safer politically to speak of the need to cooperate with China as one of many security objectives than to focus on containing rising Chinese power. This point was driven home following the end of the Cold War. At that time, strategists concluded American interests required preventing the rise of any regional hegemon that might eventually emerge as a peer competitor to the United States. Their classified document was leaked and the resultant public outcry forced leaders to disavow the document. It was a lesson in the political perils of strategic clarity.[12]

The concern about leaks has grown rather than dissipated over time. During my tenure in the Office for Resources and Plans, there was a concerted effort to block a specific classified defense planning scenario for fear it would be leaked and cause a public uproar. The issue went all the way to the Secretary of Defense for resolution, even though the identity of the country in question could have been easily guessed by anyone interested in international affairs. The White House blocked another planning effort for over a year for similar reasons, even though the situation the planning addressed had been demonstrated by real-world events years earlier.

Absent a national political consensus on one overriding existential threat to the American way of life, there really is no political alternative to having national security strategy documents cover a wide range of potential problem and opportunity areas. Rather than resist political reality, national security strategists have abandoned attempts to capture a central challenge in classified documents and accustomed themselves to working with strategy documents as if they were broad public policy statements. The norm now is for national-level strategy documents to be unclassified, and they are made to serve multiple public policy purposes. They call attention to the *relative* priority of multiple security and defense objectives, with the hope being that downstream defense planning, budgeting, programs, and execution assessments will reflect these priorities. A diverse set of priorities is also helpful for justifying resources from Congress. Finally, diverse strategy objectives communicate the breadth of American security interests and objectives to domestic and foreign audiences in a politically acceptable manner.

None of these public policy purposes benefit from Rumelt's first "good strategy" imperative: clearly diagnosing a single, important, high-stakes challenge. Such a diagnosis devalues the broader range of strategy problems and reduces their utility for securing resources from Congress. In addition, identifying a singular challenge would alarm many countries, even if it reassured some. For these and other reasons, the first prerequisite for good strategy is ignored in defense strategy. DoD has a lot of company in this regard. As Rumelt notes, it is now commonplace among organizations of all types to confuse strategy with goal-setting and "assume strategy is a big-

---

[12] Patrick Tyler, "U.S. Strategy Plan Calls for Insuring No Rivals Develop: A One-Superpower World," *New York Times*, March 8, 1992.

picture overall direction divorced from any specific action."[13] It is substantially easier to articulate "broad goals, ambition, vision, and values" than to actually identify the core, thorny problem that must be solved. For this reason, some critics believe post–Cold War national security leaders suffer from a dearth of strategic "grey matter." However, given the fact that it is politically necessary to embrace a range of security objectives, it is just as easy to argue that Pentagon strategists simply have an accurate appreciation of their political circumstances.

Failure to Identify the Solution

The second requirement for good strategy is choosing a guiding policy or overall approach for solving the strategic problem. Logically it is not possible to identify a good problem-solving path unless the problem first has been clearly identified. But assuming the core strategic challenge is ably diagnosed and stated—for example, containing Soviet power—it is necessary to consider the alternative ways to approach the challenge and then to *choose* one particular approach. Rumelt agrees good strategy is substantively difficult and that strategic miscalculation is possible, but he insists this is not the reason that there is so much bad strategy. Strategists avoid the work strategy demands because choosing is painful and difficult. "When leaders are unwilling or unable to make choices among competing values and parties, bad strategy is the consequence."[14]

Choosing a priority approach is painful for the same reason it is difficult to identify a central strategic problem: It opens up political vulnerabilities. If a particular strategic approach is chosen, the strategist will be attacked by political opponents for taking the wrong approach when untoward developments occur or when quick success is not evident. Choosing a clear priority approach to help align resources for priority tasks is also bureaucratically challenging. Organizations wanting to safeguard their autonomy, capabilities, programs, and budgets will object to emphasis on any approach that does not give priority to their activities.

The current U.S. defense strategy accommodates these political and bureaucratic realities by enumerating ten priority defense missions ranked in a "loose, not strict" order of priority.[15] The list allows all the components of DoD to attach their preferred activities to the defense strategy and thus justify their programs and budgets. The range and ambiguity communicated by lists of strategic objectives trickles down. For example, a subsidiary "force planning construct" has accompanied all post–Cold War defense strategies because the defense strategy priorities articulated are not discriminating enough to make it possible to extrapolate the number and types of missions

---

[13] Rumelt, 2011, p. 6.

[14] Rumelt, 2011, p. 58.

[15] Catherine Dale and Pat Towell, *In Brief: Assessing DoD's New Strategic Guidance*, Washington, D.C.: Congressional Research Service, 2012, p. 3.

military forces must be able to execute at any given moment. Over time, the Pentagon's force planning construct has become less discriminating and more complicated, just like defense strategies. It now stretches to encompass "multiple possible combinations of simultaneous contingencies in addition to steady-state efforts," without clearly stating the risks associated with embracing the wider range of diverse missions.[16]

The same willingness to embrace multiple approaches to meeting a defense challenge is evident in strategic guidance for individual mission areas. Consider counterterrorism. There is an ongoing debate in the defense community about whether it is better to defeat terrorist organizations by directly targeting their key leaders or by building political support for host-nation counterterrorism efforts. Israeli counterterrorism officials refer to their country's periodic efforts to decimate terrorist leader cadres as mowing the lawn and consider it a necessary approach because they do not believe winning political support from Palestinians is a viable alternative. The United States targets terrorist leaders but also tries to build political support in other nations for counterterrorism. Unfortunately, the two approaches conflict, particularly when attempts to hit terrorist leaders inadvertently kill, injure, or humiliate bystanders. While one approach should be given priority over others to generate a coherent approach to solving the terrorism problem, this does not happen.

The same holds true for subordinate military operational concepts for fighting large force-on-force military engagements. Consider forced entry operations, a concept for the introduction of U.S. forces into enemy controlled territory as a precursor to larger, sustained operations. One approach would be to give priority to information superiority, which would enable space and air superiority and thus make it possible to reduce enemy defenses and transport U.S. forces to more lightly defended locations. However, making this clear choice would have the effect of moving resources away from amphibious programs to information and aerospace programs, which would raise strong objections from the Marine Corps and other organizations. For this reason, joint doctrine for forcible entry gives equal weight to the principles of surprise; air, space, and sea control; information and special operations; and destroying enemy forces of all types that might threaten our ability to secure, isolate, and expand the lodgment in enemy territory seized by U.S. forces. No distinction is or can be made regarding the value of any military capabilities for "amphibious assault, amphibious raid, airborne assault, air assault, and any combination thereof."[17]

In short, regardless of the scope of the strategy issue involved, senior DoD leaders cannot choose in advance of actual real-world contingencies a prioritized way to respond. Rumelt argues that two problems arise from avoiding such difficult choices.

---

[16] See the discussion in Dale and Towell, 2012, pp. 4–6. For an argument that the new complexity is a virtue, see Kathleen Hicks and Samuel J. Brannen, "Force Planning in the 2010 QDR," *Joint Forces Quarterly*, No. 59, 4th Quarter, 2010.

[17] Joint Publication 3-18, *Joint Forcible Entry Operations*, Washington, D.C.: Joint Chiefs of Staff, 2012, pp. I-2ff.

First, "if one has a policy of resolving [organizational] conflict by adopting all the options on the table, there will be no incentive for anyone to develop and sharpen their arguments in the first place." Thus, over time, strategic thinking tends to atrophy. In this respect, the participants in the strategy seminar mentioned above may have a point about the decline of strategic thinking in extant defense circles. The second problem arising from a failure to choose involves resource scarcity. Edward Luttwak notes that military strategies can be arranged on a theoretical spectrum ranging from war of attrition at one end, where the objective is simply to grind down the enemy forces, to war by relational maneuver at the other end, where the objective is to avoid enemy strengths and use some element of superiority to exploit a perceived enemy weakness, whether it be physical, psychological, technical, or organizational. Attrition warfare is high cost but low risk for the side with greater resources; relational maneuver that exploits a comparative advantage is lower cost but higher risk.[18] As Rumelt observes, despite

> all the ink spilled on the inner logic of competitive strategy ... the essential difficulty in creating strategy is not logical; it is choice itself. Strategy does not eliminate scarcity and its consequence—the necessity of choice. Strategy is scarcity's child and to have a strategy ... is to choose one path and eschew others.[19]

Historically, the United States has been willing and able to devote the resources necessary to win conflicts by relying on attrition—or as some call it, "winning ugly." The hidden assumption seems to be that, when it comes to war, the American people will pay any price; thus, the "choose all options" approach to solving strategic problems is acceptable. Yet resources are never unlimited, and there are always opportunity costs for using them inefficiently. President Dwight Eisenhower is remembered well for appreciating this fact. He decisively chose one of three paths outlined in his "Project Solarium" strategic planning exercise. He was worried about the costs of pursuing all strategic options for competition with the Soviet Union; instead, he chose what he considered a financially feasible course that involved relying more on nuclear weapons for deterrence.

Eisenhower's strategic clarity had multiple benefits, according to Rumelt. Making a clear choice creates several advantages for a strategist. A clear choice allows a strategist to better anticipate the reactions of others; it reduces the complexity and ambiguity in the situation, exploiting the leverage inherent in concentrating effort on a piv-

---

[18] Edward Luttwak, *Strategy: The Logic of War and Peace*, Cambridge: Harvard University Press, 2001, pp. 113–116, 153. Luttwak's formulation broadens one end of the dichotomy Hans Delbruck raised in his classic work, *Die Strategie des Perikles,* where he argues that "there are mainly two forms of war, one focusing on the slow attrition of the enemy's armed forces and the other on a decisive battle of annihilation." (Quoted in Beatrice Heuser, "Strategy," in *Oxford Bibliographies Online: Military History*, June 7, 2013.) Luttwak's distinction is discussed with respect to special operations in David Tucker and Christopher J. Lamb, *United States Special Operations Forces*, New York: Columbia University Press, 2007.

[19] Rumelt, 2011, p. 61.

otal or decisive aspect of the situation; and, finally, it creates policies and actions that are coherent, rather than working at cross-purposes.[20] Eisenhower's decision had these effects and is rightly lionized as a paragon of good national security strategy decision-making.[21] It is clear, in retrospect, that the decision served the nation well. Even so, in the 1960 presidential election, the decision made Eisenhower's political party vulnerable to the criticism that his administration had allowed the Soviet Union to steal a critical advantage in military capabilities, which helps explain why Eisenhower's clear strategic choice is frequently lauded but seldom emulated.

Failure to Orchestrate Coherent Supporting Actions

The third element required for good strategy is a set of actions designed to carry out guiding policy. It is so common to think of strategy as a set of goals or priorities divorced from action that many leaders make a sharp and false distinction between strategy formulation, which they equate with goal-setting, and strategy execution, which they believe is identifying discrete steps to achieve the goals. To be sure, large, complex organizations will have a hierarchy of objectives that drive "a cascade of problem solving at finer and finer levels of detail" and that evolve over time. Concentrating on a singular approach and making it a priority "necessarily assumes that many other important things will be taken care of."[22] Despite this cascade of supporting and ancillary activities, every good strategy identifies key supporting actions with enough clarity to make the guiding approach comprehensible and focus organizational energy.[23]

It is difficult for DoD's leadership to generate an action agenda directly in support of the nation's defense strategy. The failure to specify a central problem hampers choosing an approach to solving the problem. In turn, the failure to choose a guiding approach cripples the ability to take supporting action. Indeed, the lack of clear strategic choice is "the main impediment to action." "It is the hard craft of strategy," Rumelt says, "to decide which priority shall take precedence. Only then can action be taken."[24] Absent a clear priority for defense resources, decisions on programs and budgets are driven by bureaucratic forces and not strategic imperatives.

The absence of good, overarching defense strategy does not prevent DoD from taking action. The necessity to act in many cases compels leaders to make decisions according to someone's strategic calculus or best-informed perspective. For example, with a limited number of vessels, readiness requirements, and rotation schedules, it is not possible to place an aircraft carrier in every location where combatant commanders

---

[20] Rumelt, 2011, p. 85.

[21] Michèle A. Flournoy and Shawn W. Brimley, "Strategic Planning for National Security: A New Project Solarium," *Joint Forces Quarterly*, No. 41, 2nd Quarter 2006.

[22] Rumelt, 2011, pp. 113, 115.

[23] Rumelt, 2011, p. 87.

[24] Rumelt, 2011, p. 88.

might like to have one. The same holds true for the most sought-after heavy and mobile ground forces and for other limited availability assets, such as special operations forces units. The Pentagon has well-established processes in place for allocating these scarce resources, as it does for raising and training forces.

Similarly, DoD executes campaign plans decisively. In the late 1980s, Congress passed legislative reforms that empowered combatant commanders to plan and run military campaigns in their theaters of operations with singular authority. Recognizing that many military problems needed to be solved with integrated joint force employment, Congress reversed the long-standing tendency to manage military campaigns by committee, with each service controlling its portion of the battle space, often irrespective of a larger campaign strategy. Since these organizational reforms, U.S. military campaigns have been executed with historically unprecedented effectiveness, at least the portions involving the destruction of enemy forces, which is what U.S. forces do best.

Thus, the Pentagon can make important decisions, just not necessarily in support of an overarching defense strategy. When senior leaders intervene to make force management and defense program adjustments, they are often driven by bureaucratic, political, or ephemeral considerations other than the consistent demands of an overarching strategy. The net result is the commonplace observation that the United States employs military force with great tactical and operational skill but often without commensurate strategic effect. It has been argued that "in war, good tactics can often save a flawed strategy, whereas bad tactics can rarely make even an excellent strategy succeed."[25] If this is true, the world-leading tactical prowess of U.S. forces is compensating for poor defense strategy and helping mask its fundamental limitations.

Exacerbating Factors

Two major factors that exacerbate the Pentagon's inability to produce strategy require elaboration, one external and the other internal. The external factor that undermines the utility of defense strategy as it is produced in the Pentagon is the increasingly complex and dynamic security environment. The latest edition of the U.S. defense strategy emphasizes the complex security environment,[26] as does the Chairman of the Joint Chiefs of Staff's recent capstone doctrine. The chairman's military doctrine notes that the strategic security environment is "fluid with continually changing alliances, partnerships, and new national and transnational threats constantly appearing and

---

[25] Wilson, James Q., *Bureaucracy: What Government Agencies Do and Why They Do It*, New York: Basic Books, 1989, p. 18.

[26] The strategy notes that "the global security environment presents an increasingly complex set of challenges." Leon E. Panetta and Barack Obama, *Sustaining U.S. Global Leadership: Priorities for 21st Century Defense*, Washington, D.C.: Department of Defense, 2012.

disappearing" and is "characterized by uncertainty, complexity, rapid change, and persistent conflict."[27] The complex and dynamic security environment complicates defense strategy because it creates conditions that demand better interagency collaboration on strategy and faster formulation and execution of strategy.

A complex security environment means security problems have multidisciplinary aspects, and thus can only be solved by drawing on and integrating diverse bodies of functional expertise resident in numerous departments and agencies. To their credit, recent defense strategies note this fact, but they cannot do much about it because other U.S. government and nongovernmental organizations are not obliged to follow the dictates of DoD's defense strategy. As scholars of public administration agree, the President's ability to unify the efforts of the many federal agencies involved in national security affairs is quite limited. As has been noted elsewhere, a President is effectively a "commander-in-brief" who seldom can sustain his management of any national security matter for long and never comprehensively.[28] In fact, the modern executive branch is so large and unwieldy that one eminent scholar argues that "central management of the bureaucracy, in all its important respects, is not possible."[29] Thus, defense strategy tends to honor interagency collaboration in theory but ignore it in practice. When the need for interagency support cannot be ignored—on the ground during a complex contingency operation—we rely on leaders in the field to work cooperatively. Some famous ambassador–joint task force commander teams have been able to partner well together, but many (arguably most) have not been able to do so, and American aspirations suffer as a result.

The dynamic nature of the environment also means problems are difficult to assess with certainty and mutate quickly. The widely acknowledged consequence is that we need nimble and adaptive organizations that can engage, explore, wrestle with, and ultimately solve problems by coevolving solutions as circumstances change and the problem becomes better understood. Thus, strategy execution must include delegation of authority to those who tackle implementation problems most directly, and they must have the latitude to experiment and solve problems as circumstances demand.

Dynamic security problems might seem to play to American strengths, both the widely acknowledged American spirit of pragmatism and the previously discussed tendencies to avoid narrow strategic premises and rely on excellent military forces to perform well without the benefit of good strategy.[30] A pragmatic approach to complex

---

[27] Joint Publication 1, *Doctrine for the Armed Forces of the United States*, Washington, D.C.: Joint Chiefs of Staff, March 25, 2013, p. I-10.

[28] See Christopher J. Lamb and Edward Marks, *Chief of Mission Authority as a Model for National Security Integration*, Washington, D.C.: National Defense University Press, 2011.

[29] Wilson, 1989.

[30] Henry Steele Commager considered pragmatism the central theme in American life and "almost the official philosophy of America." For this citation and a skeptical interpretation of pragmatism's influence in America, see

and dynamic problems would avoid slavish adherence to a rigid strategy approach and instead embrace a spirit of exploration to determine whatever might prove most useful for solving the problem at hand. With redundant, highly proficient military forces capable of executing a wide range of military tactics, the need to clearly diagnose a strategic problem in advance and formulate a guiding approach for solving it might seem less important.

This conclusion is unwarranted, for several reasons. As we learned in Vietnam and more recent military interventions, it is not possible to resolve problems that are poorly understood, even with abundant resources. Moreover, our new era of fiscal austerity precludes reliance on redundant and overlapping military capabilities to overwhelm poorly understood security threats. Finally, dynamic security problems do not eliminate the requirement for penetrating diagnosis and choice of strategic approach; they require performing these functions more quickly, iteratively, and creatively. As Henry Mintzberg long ago noted, "the real world inevitably involves some thinking ahead of time as well as some adaptation en route," so strategy is never purely deliberative or purely emergent, no matter how stable or dynamic the security environment is.[31] It is a question of balance, and a complex and dynamic environment simply requires more en route adaptation, both in adjusting the strategy and while executing strategy actions. Or as one commentator has put it, in an uncertain environment, less foresight (prediction) and more insight (sense making as strategic situations develop) are required.[32] The overarching defense strategy must keep pace with developments in the security environment, and the execution of the supporting actions must be responsive to the rapidly evolving and complex environment without losing coherence (i.e., their relationship with the problem assessment and guiding policy).

A complex and dynamic security environment thus demands sophisticated and nimble organizations, which brings us to the internal factor complicating defense strategy: the way the Pentagon is organized for strategy, which already has been briefly mentioned. The fact that different offices lead each part of this strategy-plans-programs-budget-execution process complicates strategy formulation and execution. These organizations should work closely to ensure strategy coherence with tight linkages between the strategic diagnosis, approach, and supporting actions. However, each organizational boundary crossed opens up an opportunity for the dilution of strategic logic. Each office leading a component part of the strategy process depends on others upstream or downstream from its own activity to do their parts well and protect the

David A. Hollinger, "The Problem of Pragmatism in American History," *The Journal of American History*, Vol. 67, No. 1, June 1980, pp. 88–107. For an argument about pragmatism's continuing influence in American life, see M. Gail Hamner, *American Pragmatism: A Religious Genealogy*, Oxford: Oxford University Press, 2003.

[31] Henry Mintzberg, *The Rise and Fall of Strategic Planning: Reconceiving Roles for Planning, Plans, Planners*, New York: Free Press, 1994, pp. 24–25.

[32] Yves L. Doz and Mikko Kosonen, *Fast Strategy: How Strategic Agility Will Help You Stay Ahead of the Game*, Harlow, England: Pearson/Longman, 2008, p. 20.

integrity of the strategy. However, because defense strategy is compromised from the beginning with lists of objectives rather than identification of a priority strategy challenge, there is more pressure—and more latitude—for each component of the process to satisfy competing objectives with compromises.

Offices managing the process further down the logic chain use the wide-ranging list of priorities as justification for picking and choosing their own areas to emphasize, which loosens the strategy logic, sometimes beyond recognition. For one example, under Ted's leadership, the defense strategy emphasized counterproliferation, including improving the ability of U.S. military forces to fight through enemy use of chemical and biological weapons. However, leaders in the office directing a major mobility study believed resources would be wasted on such programs and that the United States should rely on nuclear deterrence of adversary use of chemical and biological weapons. They engineered the computer modeling of the study so that it would have no additional impact on chemical and biological defense programs. In short, the need for strategy in a complex and dynamic environment is unavoidable and more rather than less demanding, but the Pentagon is not well organized to provide it. This is a key organizational shortcoming, given the nature of our current security environment.

Mitigating Factors

> Strategy, can be taken to be either theoretical—with war in general in mind or a specific situation—or applied. … Once strategic concepts were generated systematically by governments, they were invariably compromise documents drawn up jointly by a number of actors, which usually deprived them of the coherence found in most of the single-authored theoretical works. Moreover, applied strategic concepts (or strategic concepts drawn up in times of peace for the eventuality of war) are often lacking in explicit articulation of the reasons why certain courses of action are preferred.
>
> Beatrice Heuser
> University of Reading[33]

Trying to impose strategic logic on the vast defense enterprise is akin to steering an aircraft carrier by rigging and adjusting numerous small sails arrayed along the length and breadth of the behemoth. The captain's orders to trim and tack are dutifully acknowledged and generate a lot of activity. In addition to all the human energy consumed by the process, strategy documents can have a trickle-down effect on plans and

---

[33] Heuser, 2013.

programs.[34] However, in terms of strategic direction, the vessel generally continues on its way by gross inertia. Only the most determined and well-orchestrated efforts have any chance of effecting even minor course changes. Most of those who labor in DoD to develop and extend strategic logic to the defense enterprise understand the limitations of defense strategy documents. They know the documents communicate policy positions and areas of emphasis that must be relentlessly tracked and reiterated to produce any changes in direction.

Ironically, Pentagon strategists can do a better job of imposing some strategic discipline on DoD when they understand why good defense strategy codified in a document is not possible given current political and organizational limitations. Among other things, it should incline them to cultivate a vibrant strategic debate in nonofficial forums. Strategy theoreticians in academia and elsewhere are less constrained than Pentagon leaders and, in principle, should be better able to formulate good, coherent strategy alternatives. Even though Pentagon leaders cannot commit to good strategy on paper, they can learn from a vibrant strategic discourse and debate among strategy theoreticians posing alternative diagnoses of strategic challenges and the best ways to meet them.

Thus, good strategy can be formulated in the minds of key leaders, who then attempt to execute it through discrete interventions on specific issues. The issue in applied strategy then becomes whether leaders have the clout and supporting organizational reach and capacity to execute what they formulate. A strong argument can be made that organizational reforms would offer the Secretary of Defense more effective means of applying strategy, particularly the use of cross-functional teams that are capable of pursuing a problem in a coherent, collaborative, and accountable manner.[35] Absent such reforms, however, Secretaries of Defense historically have relied on a key figure on their staffs to oversee strategy implementation, which, as some have argued, underscores the importance of "identifying individuals with the mind-set and talents

---

[34] For example, the emphasis on irregular warfare in DoD's 2005 National Defense Strategy led its Office of Force Transformation to focus on developing new irregular warfare programs, such as Project Sheriff, which was a platform for nonlethal weapons. Many critics have concluded, however, that Pentagon strategy reviews amount to "hollow wish lists and an abdication of the fundamental responsibilities of leadership and management." Anthony H. Cordesman and Paul S. Frederiksen, "America's Uncertain Approach to Strategy and Force Planning," Washington, D.C.: Center for Strategic and International Studies, July 5, 2006. For Project Sheriff, see Jason Dechant, *Catalyzing Change in Complex Organizations: The Department of Defense Office of Force Transformation*, Ph.D. diss., Fairfax, Va.: George Mason University, 2013.

[35] Some combatant commands use horizontal teams that combine J-Staff elements to solve complex problems. Also, the 2006 Quadrennial Defense Review advertised a shift away from stovepiped vertical structures to more-transparent and horizontally integrated structures. It promised improved horizontal integration and creation of future horizontal organizations, but this has not happened in any meaningful way. See John S. Hurley, "Cross-Functional Working Groups: Changing the Way Staffs Are Organized," *Joint Force Quarterly*, No. 39, 2005, and the discussion of cross-functional teams in Project on National Security Reform, *Forging a New Shield*, Arlington, Va.: Center for the Study of the Presidency, 2008.

to craft strategy competently."[36] Such a subordinate leader needs the conceptual clarity required for good strategy and the authority and influence to effectively move specific strategy initiatives through the competing bureaucratic forces in the Pentagon. It takes an uncommon combination of intellect and bureaucratic warrior skills to impose some degree of strategic discipline on the Pentagon.

Ted's Informal Strategy-Driven Approach

My first Pentagon meeting with Ted Warner was in response to his summons. He had heard that some strategy-related work we were doing was interesting, and we were asked to come to his office to brief him on it. He began the meeting by assuring me that his mandate to do defense strategy meant that his responsibilities coincided with our own organization's authorities regarding the formulation of strategy for dealing with low-intensity conflicts, and consequently, we should keep him informed on the subject at hand. Rather than being irritated, we were delighted that such an influential figure was interested in special operations and low-intensity conflict, which, up to that point, had been frowned on by senior defense officials. Other offices that traditionally enjoyed more influence in the Pentagon were less pleased with Ted's catholic interests. Toward the end of Ted's tenure, one flag officer on the Joint Staff famously joked that he had thought about agreeing to a formal truce with Ted: He would not attempt to make policy if Dr. Warner would stop trying to direct military operations. Nevertheless, as Ted's influence grew and as his organization became a key locus of major decisionmaking in the Pentagon, he was increasingly able to impose a rough form of strategic logic on the Pentagon's diverse activities, from strategy to programs and budgets. He did so with a great deal of intellectual rigor.

Other contributions in this volume explain how Ted used an "end-to-end" conceptual framework to assess and improve extant operational military capabilities. This approach ensures mission objectives are tightly linked to associated tasks in discrete operational mission areas, such as air operations conducted to gain air superiority. Ted took the same approach when investigating future military capabilities or what were then called "emerging operational concepts." In the latter part of the 1990s, leap-ahead military capabilities that drew on new information-age technologies were widely believed to be transforming military affairs with combinations of new operational concepts, technologies, and organizations. Ted's team broke emerging operational concepts down into a process with a set of steps: Strategy drove mission priorities that were identified as military campaign–level challenges, which led to mission assessments that determined capability shortfalls, which informed concept development and

---

[36] Andrew F. Krepinevich and Barry D. Watts, *Regaining Strategic Competence*, Washington, D.C.: Center for Strategic and Budgetary Assessments, 2009, pp. xi, 49. The authors also recommend some organizational reforms but argue it is more important to find strategists of sufficiently great talent.

experimentation, which led to new programs and ultimately to transformative military capabilities with integrated doctrine, training, programs, etc.

I believe Ted used an end-to-end conceptual framework for most problem-solving activities under his organizational purview, not just force design. He considered any issue in light of its relationship to broader strategy priorities and looked for a logical sequence of activities or steps that would render the problem manageable. His organization used the U.S. National Security Strategy to inform the defense strategy, which it linked, in turn, to force generation and sustainment planning, force posture planning, force management planning, contingency planning, and force design planning, as well as derivative programs and budgets. Each component in this strategy chain received rigorous scrutiny. For example, under Ted's direction, war plans were examined systemically, first for consistency with strategy documents, then on the basis of their political assumptions, key objectives, proposed courses of action, risks, etc. In one case I recall, Ted doubted that the flow of forces in a particular war plan would provide enough interdiction of enemy armored forces in the early days of a conflict. He insisted on seeing the analysis, which ruffled quite a few feathers, but sure enough, there was a capability gap that subsequently was closed by allocating more antiarmor air attack assets.

This penchant for rigorous end-to-end problem solving is not surprising, given Ted's role in helping RAND develop its highly regarded "strategies-to-tasks" framework for defense analysis and the end-to-end operational concepts needed to carry out the key tasks.[37] It also is entirely consistent with the essential elements of good strategy that Rumelt advocated, with one "end" of the process being problem diagnosis and the other "end" being the coherent set of supporting actions that accomplish required tasks. Within the scope of the issue at hand, Ted was always trying to identify the key problem, alternatives for how best to resolve it, and what capabilities and resources the alternatives would require. He valued clear thinking that cut through the fog of complexity and laid bare the essential elements of any problem. He wanted a clear comparison among competing ways to solve the problem, then follow-though on marshaling the programs and resources required for the chosen problem-solving path.

Conclusion

The title of this essay is an intentional double entendre, referring to both the Pentagon's formal defense strategy documents and to the informal strategies Pentagon leaders must employ to push their agendas forward successfully. I do not mean to suggest that formal strategy documents are irrelevant, which would be sacrilegious, particularly in

---

[37] Glenn A. Kent, with David A. Ochmanek, Michael Spirtas, and Bruce Pirnie, *Thinking About America's Defense: An Analytical Memoir*, Santa Monica, Calif.: RAND, OP-223-AF, 2008, p. 17.

an article honoring Ted Warner, but to call attention to their limitations, which are unlikely to change. My hope is that, by recognizing the limitations of formal strategy documents, we will be more willing to honor strategists like Ted and to consider organizational innovations that would help DoD leaders better formulate and implement strategy to the benefit of the nation and those who serve it.

To return to a subject raised in the introduction to this chapter, prior to departing the Pentagon at the end of the Clinton administration, Ted strongly encouraged me to work more closely with the strategy office. At the time, I was helping direct the office that produced planning documents, such as the Contingency Planning Guidance and Defense Planning Guidance, which were the next step down from strategy in the Pentagon's "strategy-plans-requirements-resource" guidance process. Our office was the most immediate beneficiary of the formal defense strategy document. We had to ensure the defense strategy was translated into plans that would direct resources toward priority defense requirements and programs in order to support near-term contingency plans and future defense scenarios.

At the time, I believed the Strategy Office did great work, particularly in discrete issue areas, such as the development of Presidential Decision Directive 56 (discussed in Chapter Six, by Jim Schear), and in identifying the desired U.S. defense posture, where they used innovative thinking to spark needed changes. However, we also had firsthand experience with the frustrating limitations that arose from the broad lists of objectives and priorities contained in the defense strategy. From my point of view, any disinclination to work more closely with Strategy arose from this awareness of the limited utility of strategy documents as they had to be formulated in our system. Looking back, I believe I focused too much on the limitations of "paper strategy" and was not cognizant enough of what could be accomplished informally by partnering across organizational boundaries.

Fortunately, Ted was not so shortsighted. If I was too much aware of the impossibility of generating good defense strategy through the Pentagon's formal process and documents, Ted understood that defense strategy could best be administered informally through capable leaders—subject, of course, to the slings and arrows of outrageous bureaucratic and political fortunes that befall a single leader trying to exert control over the many disparate parts of a large and complex organization. As Andy Hoehn argues elsewhere in this volume, "it is the narrow strokes of implementation—the day-to-day decisions that align institutions, activities, and people behind the bigger ideas—that bring about real change." Ted knew this, and with his attention to method, intellectual rigor, comprehensive vision, personal leadership, bureaucratic fortitude and moxie, he came as close as is possible in the Pentagon to creating and implementing defense strategy.

"Shape, Respond, and Prepare Now for the Future" was the shorthand version of the defense strategy developed during the first Quadrennial Defense Review in 1997. This bumper sticker was used to encapsulate the defense strategy that guided

U.S. defense efforts during the second half of Ted's tenure as an assistant secretary of defense, and it included just the sort of broad, "cover the gamut" list of strategy goals that Rumelt laments. But as a practical matter, Ted moved the Pentagon forward in all three areas. To cite just a few examples, he embraced a wide range of peacetime engagement activities designed to "shape" the international security environment, including the Cooperative Threat Reduction program, which reduced the risk of nuclear weapons falling into the wrong hands. He also helped move the department away from an exclusive focus on fighting large conventional wars by placing greater emphasis on smaller-scale contingency operations, thus seeking to enhance capabilities to "respond" to a broader set of military challenges. And he helped initiate a disciplined process for creating and exploring emerging operational concepts to begin to "prepare" U.S. forces to better respond to future military challenges.

Because Ted took strategy seriously and understood how to pursue it to the greatest extent possible within the large and unwieldy Pentagon organizational structure, it was a pleasure working for him. This was particularly true because Ted's motives were so transparently selfless. Substantive differences aside, everyone knew he was intent on building a better military for the country and for those who populate its ranks. Because that was true, he was willing to accept good ideas from outside his organization and bring in new talent as well. Another contributor to the volume notes that Ted's willingness to engage "seriously with younger analysts" was one of his hallmarks. I would say his willingness to seriously engage anyone with a substantive contribution—regardless of their political, bureaucratic, rank, gender or age attributes—was a hallmark of his. As someone with different political inclinations from Ted, I was one very fortunate beneficiary of his open-mindedness, and I am pleased to have the opportunity to express my appreciation through this essay.

References

Cordesman, Anthony H., and Paul S. Frederiksen, "America's Uncertain Approach to Strategy and Force Planning," Washington, D.C.: Center for Strategic and International Studies, July 5, 2006. As of January 9, 2014:
http://csis.org/publication/americas-uncertain-approach-strategy-and-force-planning

Dale, Catherine, and Pat Towell, *In Brief: Assessing DoD's New Strategic Guidance*, Washington, D.C.: Congressional Research Service, 2012.

Dechant, Jason, *Catalyzing Change in Complex Organizations: The Department of Defense Office of Force Transformation*, Ph.D. diss., Fairfax, Va.: George Mason University, 2013.

Dempsey, Martin, "From the Chairman: Risky Business," *Joint Forces Quarterly*, No. 69, 2nd Quarter 2013, p. 3.

Doz, Yves L., and Mikko Kosonen, *Fast Strategy: How Strategic Agility Will Help You Stay Ahead of the Game*, Harlow, England: Pearson/Longman, 2008.

Flournoy, Michèle A., and Shawn W. Brimley, "Strategic Planning for National Security: A New Project Solarium," *Joint Forces Quarterly*, No. 41, 2nd Quarter 2006.

Gray, Colin S., *The Strategy Bridge: Theory for Practice*, Oxford: Oxford University Press, 2010.

Hamner, M. Gail, *American Pragmatism: A Religious Genealogy*, Oxford: Oxford University Press, 2003.

Heuser, Beatrice, "Strategy," in *Oxford Bibliographies*, June 7, 2013. As of January 9, 2014: http://www.oxfordbibliographies.com/view/document/obo-9780199791279/obo-9780199791279-0057.xml

Hicks, Kathleen, and Samuel J. Brannen, "Force Planning in the 2010 QDR," *Joint Forces Quarterly*, No. 59, 4th Quarter, 2010.

Hoffman, Frank G., "50 Shades of Gray," panel presentation, University of Reading, May 18, 2013.

Hollinger, David A., "The Problem of Pragmatism in American History," *The Journal of American History*, Vol. 67, No. 1, June 1980, pp. 88–107.

Hurley, John S., "Cross-Functional Working Groups: Changing the Way Staffs Are Organized," *Joint Force Quarterly*, No. 39, 2005.

Joint Publication 1, *Doctrine for the Armed Forces of the United States*, Washington, D.C.: Joint Chiefs of Staff, March 25, 2013.

Joint Publication 3-18, *Joint Forcible Entry Operations*, Washington, D.C.: Joint Chiefs of Staff, 2012.

Kent, Glenn A., with David A. Ochmanek, Michael Spirtas, and Bruce Pirnie, *Thinking About America's Defense: An Analytical Memoir*, Santa Monica, Calif.: RAND, OP-223-AF, 2008. As of January 9, 2014: http://www.rand.org/pubs/occasional_papers/OP223.html

Krepinevich, Andrew F., and Barry D. Watts, *Regaining Strategic Competence*, Washington, D.C.: Center for Strategic and Budgetary Assessments, 2009.

Lamb, Christopher J., and Edward Marks, *Chief of Mission Authority as a Model for National Security Integration*, Washington, D.C.: National Defense University Press, 2011.

Lind, Michael, *The American Way of Strategy*, Oxford: Oxford University Press, 2006.

Luttwak, Edward, *Strategy: The Logic of War and Peace*, Cambridge: Harvard University Press, 2001.

Mintzberg, Henry, *The Rise and Fall of Strategic Planning: Reconceiving Roles for Planning, Plans, Planners*, New York: Free Press, 1994.

Panetta, Leon E., and Barack Obama, *Sustaining U.S. Global Leadership: Priorities for 21st Century Defense*, Washington, D.C.: Department of Defense, 2012.

Project on National Security Reform, *Forging a New Shield*, Arlington, Va.: Center for the Study of the Presidency, 2008. As of March 4, 2014: http://0183896.netsolhost.com/site/wp-content/uploads/2011/12/pnsr_forging_a_new_shield_report.pdf

Rumelt, Richard P., *Good Strategy, Bad Strategy: The Difference and Why It Matters*, New York: Crown Business, 2011.

Tucker, David, and Christopher J. Lamb, *United States Special Operations Forces*, New York: Columbia University Press, 2007.

Tyler, Patrick, "U.S. Strategy Plan Calls for Insuring No Rivals Develop: A One-Superpower World," *New York Times*, March 8, 1992.

Wilson, James Q., *Bureaucracy: What Government Agencies Do and Why They Do It*, New York: Basic Books, 1989.

CHAPTER SIX

Orchestrating Complex Contingency Operations: A Forever Bumpy Ride

James A. Schear[1]

I have known Ted Warner since the mid-1980s. Our paths crossed in a world quite different from the one we live in today. Back then, it was the Cold War's Heyday. The Berlin Wall looked impenetrable. Ted was leading the charge for RAND on anything Soviet. I was an eager student of Soviet-American arms control. As a predoctoral fellow at Harvard, I staffed the Aspen Strategy Group, then directed by Joe Nye, another great mentor. As Joe and I brainstormed upcoming group discussions, questions inevitably arose: How can we best frame discussions regarding, say, nuclear deterrence, missile defense, space policy, chemical weapons, or strategic stability, and who can we ask to clearly explicate Moscow's views and behavior? Ted's name, inevitably, came up. He brought expertise and analytic rigor, as well as humor and humility, to the table. Prior service in Moscow as an air attaché enhanced his street credibility, and Ted could easily navigate the wonkish and political dimensions of these Aspen conversations. He also was an utterly dependable, parsimonious author—a pleasure to edit. Once the Berlin Wall fell, I pivoted away from things Soviet toward regionally focused stabilization efforts, initially in Southeast Asia and the Balkans. As fate would have it, Ted ended up working these issues, too, as an assistant secretary of defense in the mid-1990s, and our paths would soon cross again—this time, on the topic framed by this essay.

Introduction

By any measure, the early 1990s was a time of great turbulence. Although ebbing Cold War tides had helped to calm parts of Southeast Asia, Central America, and Southern Africa, conflicts were escalating elsewhere, either on the wings of aggressive (Saddam Hussein) or collapsing (Siad Barre) dictators or amidst an upsurge of ethnic and often sectarian violence. Instability gripped regions as diverse as the Balkans, the Caucasus, Southwest Asia, Central Africa, and Oceania. At the same time, al-Qaeda and its affili-

---

[1] I am most grateful for suggestions and critiques offered by friends and colleagues, including Michèle Flournoy, Leonard Hawley, Christopher Lamb, Eric Schwartz, and Matthew Vaccaro. That said, the views expressed herein are purely mine. I hereby absolve those cited above, as well as our honoree, Ted Warner, of any guilt by association with possibly contentious opinions contained in this essay.

ates were expanding their reach, albeit without much public visibility until the 1998 embassy bombings in Nairobi and Dar es Salaam.

For the United States, international engagement during this era definitely had a contingency flavor. The incoming Clinton administration inherited the messy after-math of Operation Desert Storm in Iraq, as well as responsibilities for enabling, supporting, or leading major United Nations (UN) (or UN mandated) multilateral deployments into Somalia, the former Yugoslavia, and northern Iraq, ostensibly on humanitarian missions.[2]

It was a bumpy ride, to put it mildly. By late 1993, the Somalia operation was not going well. By securing relief supply lines, UNITAF had saved countless lives, but the hunt for Somali warlord Mohamed Farrah Aidid had culminated in the Battle of Mogadishu, the loss of 18 U.S. service members, and a presidential decision to with-draw. Soon thereafter, then Secretary of Defense Les Aspin directed a thorough review of the Somalia operation, to be led by Ted's staff within the office of the Under Secre-tary for Policy.

Somalia was by no means the only looming challenge. By early 1994, Rwanda's civil war was metastasizing into genocidal violence, overwhelming demoralized and unreinforced UN peacekeepers whose mission quickly unraveled. Closer to home, the United States, with strong UN backing, was ratcheting up pressure on Haitian dicta-tor Raoul Cédras to cede power to Jean Bertrand Aristide, his democratically elected opponent. However, lingering memories of the poorly scripted U.S. stabilization opera-tion (Promote Liberty) that followed Panamanian dictator Manuel Noriega's removal in 1989 motivated those at the White House to proceed cautiously. When President Bill Clinton reviewed the proposed plan for intervention in Haiti, he reportedly asked: "How long will it take for us to do the job?" The military briefer answered, "We will secure Haiti in about one week." Then the President asked, "Well, what happens in the second week and thereafter?" No one at the meeting had any answers.[3]

The intersection of a dispirited withdrawal from Somalia and the prospect of a major deployment into Haiti (Operation Uphold Democracy, launched in September 1994) produced a moment of genuine soul-searching for the United States. U.S. lead-ers had begun to sense how unprepared they were to navigate a volatile post–Cold War landscape populated much more by rebel fighters, tribal tensions, ethnosectar-ian violence, and illicit transnational actors (e.g., terrorists or smugglers) than by state adversaries capable of waging large-scale conventional campaigns or mass destruction warfare. To be sure, high-end threats had not disappeared, especially on the Korean

---

[2] Prime examples are Operation Provide Comfort II in Turkey and Kurdish areas in northern Iraq and the United Nations Task Force (UNITAF), which deployed into Somalia in December 1992. The United States pro-vided 25,000 of UNITAF's total of 37,000 personnel.

[3] This story was relayed to me by Len Hawley, who heard it from a senior National Security Council (NSC) staff colleague at the time.

peninsula. For planning and force development purposes, this mission category was henceforth labeled as "major theater wars." But the administration was also fleshing out a more-diverse mission set—so-called smaller-scale contingencies—that would fall short of major theater war but cover a wide array of contingencies (e.g., crisis-driven humanitarian relief operations, no-fly zones, coercive air campaigns, conducting or enabling multinational peace enforcement missions) that U.S. forces should be prepared to conduct or support.[4] The still unanswered question was: Where was the rest of our government?

Why PDD-56?

These small-scale contingencies brought interagency planning and execution requirements to the fore during the Clinton years. At the field level, then Lt. Gen. Anthony Zinni, one of UNITAF's top officers, returned to the United States from Mogadishu flagging the need for more-effective civil-military coordination.[5] But the same was also true in Washington. On the planning side, a widely supported humanitarian relief operation for Somalia had quickly morphed into a more ambitious hunt for warlords and initial efforts at nation-building. However, interagency stakeholders had not rigorously addressed "mission creep" hazards prior to the operation's commencement. Surprisingly, there was no widely agreed playbook for coming to decisions on whether or how to launch these missions, what their presumptive goals should be, how best to prepare for and execute key tasks (i.e., which agency does what task), or what means might be used to distill applicable lessons to help inform after-action learning and training opportunities for the interagency community. The United States was venturing into a new era in which these complex missions were suddenly within our geopolitical reach but, oddly enough, beyond our conceptual grasp.

Ted Warner and two of his interagency partners at the time—Dick Clarke (then on the staff of the NSC) and Ted McNamara (then at the Department of State's Bureau of Political-Military Affairs)—pondered these quandaries while participating in an interagency training session in Carlisle, Pennsylvania, home of the U.S. Army War College. Their initial brainstorming and the work that followed produced one of the

---

[4] The smaller-scale contingency mission category was first introduced in the Clinton administration's 1997 Quadrennial Defense Review, although it was the focus of much experiential learning in the years immediately preceding its issuance. As the shared modifier "small" suggests, there are also some interesting historic parallels with the "small wars" paradigm, authoritatively explicated by Max Boot, *The Savage Wars of Peace: Small Wars and the Rise of American Power*, New York: Basic Books, 2002. That said, the operational tempo of our present-day interagency system cannot fairly be accused of fostering deep reflection on the legacies of America's 19th- and early 20th-century engagements in such places as the Barbary Coast and the Caribbean, not to mention latter-day Vietnam.

[5] Cited by Len Hawley in a presentation to an expert working group crafting a Center for Strategic and International Studies report *Beyond Goldwater-Nichols: Defense Reform for a New Strategic Era*, May 8, 2003.

Clinton administration's most well-known directives: Presidential Decision Directive (PDD) 56, "Managing Complex Contingency Operations."[6] The overriding rationale for this new directive was that it would be a critical gap-filler. The military planning world at the time did not have a roadmap for interagency planning and execution, and none was apparent among non-DoD stakeholders.[7]

Knowing the benefits that accrue from holding the pen, Ted volunteered for drafting duties and immediately drew in his highly talented strategy team, led by Michèle Flournoy, which had undertaken the Somalia lessons-learned study. Crafting an agreed interagency document is always challenging, and several real-world events—most notably, Operation Deliberate Force, the Dayton Accords on Bosnia-Herzegovina, and the Erdut Agreement on Eastern Slavonia—distracted senior leaders' attention but also provided some "learning by doing" opportunities. President Clinton signed PDD-56 in May 1997; two months later, as a freshly minted deputy assistant secretary, I was honored to receive Ted and Michèle's bequest.

How well did the U.S. government implement PDD-56? Let me offer a personal parallel: a few years earlier, while boarding a UN-contracted Ilyushin IL-76 in Zagreb for a flight into Sarajevo, I asked one of the flight crew members how sturdy this aircraft really was. "Oh, it's very, very solid," he exclaimed in broken English. Then, with a grin, he added: "OK, those engines? They're only so-so." Well, after a bumpy ride, this jittery passenger still managed to get into Sarajevo safely. So it was with PDD-56, which endured many bumps but also yielded some positive outcomes. This chapter offers a personal reflection on that experience.

The PDD's Key Features

PDD-56's overarching goals were absolutely Herculean: to develop and institutionalize an integrated, interagency approach to the planning and execution of complex contingencies—in effect, synchronizing the political, military, humanitarian, economic, and other dimensions of these multifaceted operations while also ensuring that all U.S. government entities with statutory authority to participate would be ready and able to support such operations. Within the directive's ambit were peace operations (such as peace accord implementation operations, like the Dayton Accords), humanitarian interventions (such as Operation Provide Comfort), and large-scale foreign disaster

---

[6]   This reference to PDD-56 and those that follow are to the unclassified summary of the classified version of the directive, Presidential Decision Directive 56 (PDD-56), "The Clinton Administration's Policy on Managing Complex Contingency Operations," May 1997.

[7]   After the promulgation of PDD-56, the Chairman of the Joint Chiefs of Staff introduced so-called Annex V (on interagency coordination) into deliberate war plans in 1999, arguably a positive effect of the PDD's issuance. Henry H. Shelton, USA, Chairman of the Joint Chiefs of Staff, posture statement before the Committee on Armed Services, U.S. Senate, February 8, 2000.

relief operations (such as Operation Unified Response, the response to the 2010 earthquake in Haiti, and Operation Sea Angel, the response to the 1991 cyclone that devastated Bangladesh).[8] The PDD set forth five key steps toward these ends:

- *Establishing an Executive Committee (ExComm).* The committee membership was to be appropriate for supervising the day-to-day management of U.S. participation in contingency operations. The ExComm would work on clarifying agency responsibilities, strengthening agency accountability, ensuring interagency coordination, and developing policy options for consideration or adjudication by senior policymakers.
- *Drafting a Political-Military (Pol-Mil) Implementation Plan.* The plan was to include a comprehensive situation assessment, mission statement, agency objectives, desired end states, and performance milestones. It would outline an integrated concept of operations covering major functional tasks (e.g., political mediation and reconciliation, military support, humanitarian aid, police reform, basic public services, economic recovery, and public information).
- *Rehearsing the Plan.* A rehearsal should cover the plan's main elements, with appropriate ExComm officials presenting the elements for which they are responsible. Such an event would help to identify and help resolve differences over mission objectives, agency responsibilities, timing, synchronization, and resource allocation prior to the commencement of the operation.
- *Completing an After-Action Review.* After the conclusion of each operation in which this planning process was employed, such a review would focus on interagency planning and coordination (both in Washington and in the field), legal and budgetary difficulties encountered, problems in agency execution, and proposed solutions to capture and disseminate lessons learned.
- *Developing a Training Repertoire.* The idea here was to create a cadre of professionals familiar with this integrated planning process to improve the U.S. government's ability to manage future operations. Appropriate government educational institutions were to explore appropriate ways to incorporate the pol-mil planning process into their curricula.

Reviewing PDD-56 more than 15 years later, it is worth underscoring the prescience of several passages. "While not relinquishing unilateral capacity," the directive noted, the United States should "conduct future operations in coalitions whenever possible." Coalition operations in Libya in 2011 and Mali in 2013 reflect that guidance. In addition, PDD-56 noted that "we must also be prepared" to manage crises where "chemical, biological, and/or radiological hazards may be present," which could

---

8   Protection of the homeland, domestic disaster relief, counterterrorism, hostage-rescue operations, and international armed conflict were explicitly outside PDD-56's scope, "unless otherwise directed."

"significantly increase" the complexity of a U.S. response. This concern became critical in the response to the tsunami that struck Japan in 2011 and the ensuing challenges at the Fukushima-Daiichi nuclear power plant. Perhaps most poignantly, the PDD stressed that "many aspects" of these operations "may not be best addressed through military measures"; U.S. forces "should not be deployed in an operation indefinitely"; and "integrated planning and effective management" early on can avoid delays and "reduce pressure on the military to expand its involvement in unplanned ways." If only U.S. government agencies had applied such foresight when signing up for LTG (ret) Jay Garner's well-intentioned and adroitly orchestrated but far too narrowly scoped planning exercise—his so-called "rock drill"—in the days leading up to Operation Iraqi Freedom.

Balancing Aspirations and Realities

In the years immediately after PDD-56's issuance, the pol-mil planning "infection" spread throughout our complex interagency system as the tempo of planning drills increased. Major multinational peace operations were being prepared for deployment into Sierra Leone, the Democratic Republic of the Congo, Eritrea-Ethiopia, Kosovo, and East Timor (none of which, except for Kosovo, featured substantial U.S. boots on the ground). We started to think more in "pol-mil" than in purely operational terms when confronting looming contingencies or negotiations among warring factions that could quickly generate requirements to mobilize peacekeeping troop contributors. There were also a number of major sudden-onset disasters—in Central America (a hurricane and flooding), Venezuela (coastal mudslides and hazardous material contamination), Turkey (Izmit earthquake), and Mozambique (cyclones and torrential rains)—that triggered substantial disaster relief efforts, as well as concerns over complex recoveries. While these events offered opportunities to learn by doing, this kind of pol-mil planning occasionally triggered bureaucratic resistance, especially among regional policy stakeholders who feared they were ceding equities to the NSC staff and/or that public knowledge of an ongoing contingency planning drill might actually accelerate the crisis they were trying to prevent through diplomatic means. On balance, though, the results were positive: We hewed to the spirit (if not the letter) of PDD-56 while our bureaucratic "immune systems" also become more resilient and adaptable.[9]

---

[9] For analyses of core issues related to PDD-56 and its legacy, see Len Hawley and Dennis Skocz, "Advance Political-Military Planning: Laying the Foundation for Achieving a Viable Peace," in Jock Covey, Michael Dziedzic, and Leonard Hawley, eds., *The Quest for Viable Peace: International Intervention and Strategies for Conflict Transformation*, Washington D.C.: United States Institute for Peace, 2005, pp. 37–76. See also Clark A. Murdock, Michèle A. Flournoy, Christopher A. Williams, and Kurt M. Campbell, *Beyond Goldwater-Nichols: Defense Reform for a New Strategic Era, Phase 1 Report*, Washington D.C.: Center for Strategic and International Studies, 2004, pp. 6–67.

What specifically did we learn? One lesson was that contextual and public-messaging issues can pose significant challenges—in this case, specifically, how the PDD-56 "brand" might be seen. For example, Hurricane Mitch, one of the largest storms of the 20th century, struck in late 1998; killed more than 10,000 people; left more than two million homeless; and devastated roads and bridges throughout Honduras, El Salvador, Nicaragua and Guatemala. The commander of U.S. Southern Command, General Charlie Wilhelm, established a response task force that eventually launched under the code name Operation *Fuerte Appoyo* [Strong Support]. He also proposed that Washington "hit the PDD-56 button," given the challenges the U.S. Agency for International Development encountered in generating initial needs assessments (many of their personnel were already Kosovo-bound), as well as concerns about the potential complexities of recovery.

The message back from Washington was negative. Anxious over funding shortfalls, White House budgeters wanted more control than they thought the PDD-56 process would give them. In addition, it was argued, we were already into execution mode, given the sudden-onset quality of the event. And notwithstanding Southern Command's visible presence in the response, U.S. policymakers also preferred a purely humanitarian brand over a pol-mil label in Central America.[10]

Another lesson revolved around the issue of ownership. Despite encouragement from some quarters, a formalized ExComm structure was seldom established. In practice, the senior U.S. decisionmakers who constituted the membership of the NSC's Deputies Committee (colloquially referred to simply as "deputies") were not inclined to delegate day-to-day management of a complex contingency.[11] The one notable exception was Kosovo, where senior decisionmakers became so immersed in coalition management and the bombing campaign (Operation Allied Force) that they delegated ExComm-like functions to a small group of senior humanitarian officials. Led by then U.S. Agency for International Development administrator Brian Atwood and the late Julia Taft, Assistant Secretary of State for Population, Refugees, and Migration, this

---

[10] I appreciate Eric Schwartz's and Len Hawley's recollections on this case. Interestingly, there was less sensitivity to showing more muscle elsewhere. When southern Mozambique was hit with terrible flooding and cyclonic wind damage in early 2000, the Vice Director of Operations on the Joint Staff, LTG Russ Honoré, took the Joint Staff's initial concept plan to the staff of the NSC for review. The plan's code name was Silent Promise. Members of the NSC staff, however, wanted a stronger title, so it was adroitly relabeled Atlas Response.

[11] That said, they were definitely inclined to be humorous. Prior to a disputatious deputies' meeting on an unnamed topic, Under Secretary of Defense for Policy Walt Slocombe remarked to Ambassador Dick Holbrooke (who frequently terrorized deputies' committee meetings and even interagency policy committees, although he was a principal at the time): "Dick, I have only ten hours before our next DC to come up with every conceivable objection to your proposal, and in the end we'll probably roll as we usually do!" The next morning, when representatives of the Office of the Secretary of Defense (of which Slocombe's office was a part) arrived in the West Wing, they found that Holbrooke's team (per their boss's direction) had already plastered the White House Situation Room with large-font copies of Walt's statement.

group examined "day-after" scenarios, especially for a massive refugee return that they feared could occur prior to the onset of winter.

Whether deputies should have invested the enormous amounts of time they did on many smaller-scale contingencies (e.g., Congo, East Timor, Sierra Leone) is a fair question. But in the late 1990s, they also lived in the pre-9/11 world. Moreover, and very fortunately, the interagency policy committee–like entity at the time (the Peace-keeping Core Group), led by then NSC Senior Director Eric Schwartz, had morphed into a regional-functional group that could develop policy options for various contingencies. It became the administration's de facto ExComm. Also, and very significantly, senior decisionmakers at the departments of State and Defense found ways to introduce rehearsal-like efficiencies into their deliberations.[12]

In retrospect, it became clear that the pol-mil planning template and process would have to adapt to suit the needs of these senior policymakers. At the staff level, substantial planning work was accomplished at NSC and the Department of State's Office for Contingency Planning and Peacekeeping within the Political-Military Affairs Bureau. Notable successes included pol-mil plans for Croatia's Serb-held regions (prior to PDD-56's issuance), as well as Kosovo, where their efforts produced the foundational design for the UN's mission there following the completion of Operation Allied Force. That said, although deputy-level consumers became accustomed to rigorous interagency analysis generated by pol-mil planning teams, they usually set aside deliberate-style pol-mil plans, preferring to scan shorter summaries of these documents. They also did not want planning to generate requirements for decisions that might box them in too early. The result, as one colleague recalls, was an improvisational "jam band" approach—playing informally, albeit with an established rule set, but adapting and iterating the product along the way.[13]

Amplifying this tendency was what could be termed the "inclusive-exclusive" conundrum. To be truly comprehensive, pol-mil planning needs to be inclusive: Any office with authority and funding to perform a given mission should be at the table. However, the diplomatic and security dynamics generating the need for advanced planning may also propel policymakers toward greater exclusivity. If, for example, U.S. leaders find themselves mediating a fragile peace process—as they did during the 1998–2000 Eritrea-Ethiopia war—or orchestrating complex coalition-building relationships—as they did prior to the deployment of a UN-mandated, Australian-led coalition into East Timor (now Timor-Leste) in 1999—policymakers and especially their regionally focused advisors will want to limit access to their deliberations. Bal-

---

[12] For instance, then Under Secretary of State Tom Pickering would often turn his deputies' committee preparation sessions into de facto rehearsals by inviting representatives from the Office of the Secretary of Defense and the Joint Staff to preview issues for discussion and decision. Watching various groups line up outside his office, I once asked him how he prioritized his meetings. "Wherever the fires are burning," he replied.

[13] Thanks to Matt Vaccaro for this very apt metaphor.

ancing between these competing imperatives proved to be genuinely hard, as it still is today.

Finally, there is the challenge of "competing narratives." From the supply-side standpoint, comprehensive pol-mil planning is easier in a "first-person" narrative (i.e., here is what *we* will do). However, if national interests dictate that the United States should be only supporting, not leading, a looming contingency operation, a second- or third-person narrative may be more appropriate (i.e., here is what *you* or *they* can do). The dilemma, however, is that the institution that plans intensively will often be expected to lead the overall operation.

In short, the PDD-56 "plane" was well designed and solidly built; it achieved takeoff velocity, but the strength and durability of its propulsion systems were greatly stressed by stronger than expected headwinds. That said, it also catalyzed a great deal of creative thinking and helped those charged with implementing the directive to become better navigators in piloting through the mountainous terrain of complex contingencies. Eisenhower's oft-cited admonition that "plans are nothing, but planning is everything" is very apt here. Dynamic and adaptive approaches to planning are always called for.

Future Priorities?

What prescriptive steps might advance PDD-56's goals in the future? While the directive's track record in the years immediately following its issuance is instructive, so too are the experiences of the post–9/11 era. Driven by two large-scale U.S.-led forced-entry and regime-change campaigns, pressures to expand America's stabilization and reconstruction activities skyrocketed, vastly exceeding the capabilities of civilian agencies and posing significant "mission creep" problems for the Department of Defense (DoD). While a newly elected Bush administration in 2001 had effectively rescinded PDD-56—recalling Condoleezza Rice's oft-cited quip that U.S. soldiers in Bosnia shouldn't be "escorting kids to kindergarten"—the Bush team reluctantly came to embrace the inevitability of "nation-building under fire" as the Iraq and Afghanistan campaigns morphed into protracted counterinsurgencies.[14]

Could the adroit utilization of the PDD-56 template possibly have altered or even precluded Operations Enduring Freedom and Iraqi Freedom? Counterfactual histories

---

[14] A successor directive to PDD-56 was scripted but never signed in the Bush administration's first year (so-called NSPD-XX). For Rice's Bosnia quote, see Michael R. Gordon, "The 2000 Campaign: The Military; Bush Would Stop U.S. Peacekeeping in Balkan Fights," *New York Times*, October 21, 2000. Regarding nation-building, Secretary Robert Gates observed: "The United States is unlikely to repeat a mission on the scale of those in Afghanistan or Iraq anytime soon—that is, forced regime change followed by nation building under fire. But ... the United States is still likely to face scenarios requiring a familiar tool kit of capabilities, albeit on a smaller scale." Robert M. Gates, "Helping Others Defend Themselves: The Future of U.S. Security Assistance," *Foreign Affairs*, May/June 2010.

are inherently contentious, and I cannot claim insights based on personal involvement in the policymaking dimensions of these operations. Conceivably, PDD-56's rigorous application might have encouraged senior decisionmakers to examine critically the always tenuous—and ultimately untenable—assumption that Iraqi government ministries and police would survive Saddam's removal intact.[15] Such an examination did not happen. A PDD-centric assessment might have also triggered concerns over the likelihood of rising sectarian violence in post-Saddam Iraq, as well as the risks of orchestrating Afghan stabilization and reconstruction operations without the appropriate or necessary resources following the Iraqi invasion. On the other hand, it is hard to imagine that a PDD-56–driven review would have ultimately changed the intelligence community's assessments of Iraqi weapons of mass destruction capability or would have resolved tensions between the departments of State and Defense over chain of command issues at the operational level (since the PDD never addressed these issues). And, of course, it would not have changed the mix of personalities in President George W. Bush's inner circle.

History's real path, as it turned out, revealed just how problematic a "liberate and leave" strategy turned out to be once these operations got under way. As the Bush administration began to recognize this reality, it launched its own review of presidential policy. The result was National Security Presidential Directive (NSPD) 44, issued in December 2005. This new directive formally superseded PDD-56 and shifted the locus of interagency coordination for complex contingencies from the NSC to the Department of State. It specified that the newly established Office of the Coordinator for Reconstruction and Stabilization (S/CRS) would assist the Secretary of State in strengthening interagency efforts aimed at "stabilizing and reconstructing countries or regions, especially those at risk of, in, or in transition from conflict or civil strife."[16]

Those in S/CRS faced many challenges as well. On the positive side, they spearheaded efforts to improve the rigor of conflict assessments, develop critical expertise on planning and field activities, and orchestrate the provision of stabilization assistance to at-risk countries under the so-called Sec. 1207 program, with funds from DoD.[17] That

---

[15] See interview with then National Security Advisor Condoleezza Rice, cited in Michael Gordon and Bernard Trainor, *Cobra II: The Inside Story of the Invasion and Occupation of Iraq*, New York: Pantheon Books, 2006, p. 142.

[16] National Security Presidential Directive 44 (NSPD-44), "Management of Interagency Efforts Concerning Reconstruction and Stabilization," December 7, 2005. For a useful comparison of PDD-56 and NSPD-44, see Christopher Lamb, "Redesigning White House and Interagency Structures," in Hans Binnendijk and Patrick M. Cronin, eds., *Civilian Surge: Key to Complex Operations*, Washington, D.C.: National Defense University Press, 2009, pp. 39–43.

[17] Section 1207 of the National Defense Authorization Act for Fiscal Year 2006 authorizes the Secretary of Defense to provide services and transfer defense articles and funds to the Secretary of State for the purposes of facilitating the secretary's provision of reconstruction, security, or stabilization assistance to a foreign country. The aggregate value of all services, defense articles, and funds provided or transferred to the Secretary of State under this section in any fiscal year may not exceed $100,000,000.

said, its construct for interagency coordination—the so-called Interagency Management System—never achieved much traction, and effective coordination with NSC-centric policy processes proved difficult. Ironically, the size and controversial nature of the very campaigns that had so dramatically spiked demand for civilian capability in 2005 also inhibited subsequent efforts to conduct preventive planning for "at risk" countries.[18] That inhibition has not prevented S/CRS's successor, the Bureau of Conflict and Stabilization Operations (CSO), from providing value in such diverse venues as Burma/Myanmar, Kenya, or Syria, but the Department of State's ability to sustain a civilian response corps on the scale anticipated several years ago has shrunk dramatically in the face of budget austerity.

Given this track record and in light of looming real-world challenges, I would underscore four priorities for the future. The first is to strengthen *intraagency* collaboration. Effective two-way communication across portfolios within agencies is an essential component of achieving whole-of-government coherence. Traditionally, the largest challenge has been coordination between regional and functional offices, that is, ensuring that regional offices understand the tools, funding, and equities functional offices offer. Now, with the growing nexus between the "counter-tops" (e.g., counterterrorism, countertrafficking, counter–weapons of mass destruction) and the "bleeding hearts" (e.g., peacekeeping, humanitarian, and stabilization missions), internal cross-functional (and regional) synchronization is even more important, from the Sahel in Africa to Central America's northern quadrant. In this regard, DoD's Office of the Secretary of Defense has made some positive strides.

A second priority is to improve the balance between contingency planning's "horizontal" and "vertical" dimensions. Much of PDD-56–related pol-mil implementation planning in the late 1990s was generated at staff levels across federal agencies, with supervision typically no higher than by a director or deputy assistant secretary. Today, as U.S. combatant commands have increasingly become their own interagency hubs—a positive development, on balance—there is logic in having them increasingly be a locus for planning, working closely with our country teams and mil-groups teams in a prospective host nation and/or in coalition partners. The challenge here is vertical review. Combatant commands are understandably reluctant to have their products circulating in Washington (and prone to rapid escalation to deputies) without the review of their senior four-star commanders, but the time associated with such reviews often leads to frustrating delays. Rough-order-of-magnitude planning constructs, a Joint Staff innovation, have helped to expedite this process somewhat, but high-level reviews of the basic commencement, scope, substance, and delivery dates of pol-mil planning are required to keep the process moving. We need, in particular, to avoid conflating

---

[18] For a more in-depth discussion of this issue, see James A. Schear and Leslie B. Curtin, "Complex Operations: Recalibrating the State Department's Role," in Hans Binnendijk and Patrick M. Cronin, eds., *Civilian Surge: Key to Complex Operations*, Washington, D.C.: National Defense University Press, 2009, pp. 93–114.

the policy and operational levels of interagency planning. Each has distinct challenges: Offices in Washington need to focus on their responsibilities, while operational leaders need the support of the departments and agencies in Washington going forward.

Third, we need a better roadmap for navigating through the increasingly complex security assistance and capacity-building terrain as part of today's crisis action contingencies. As we have seen in recent cases, an incredibly broad swath of assistance is highly relevant—indeed, critical—to achieving positive outcomes. The United States or others can provide humanitarian relief (e.g., "human security assistance") to severely affected civilian populations (and allocated by international organizations and nongovernmental organization implementers purely on the basis of need), as well as progressively more partisan-leaning stabilization assistance, which helps civic groups provide basic services while countering the influence of insurgent actors or predatory autocrats. In addition, the international community can offer security force assistance (both nonlethal and lethal), which aims at building the operational capacity of coalition partners, host-nation security forces, or even freedom fighters to act responsibly in defense of their people's legitimate aspirations. Moving adroitly, however, is no easy matter: Legal authorities and funding complexities, agency-centric programming, and partners' absorptive capacity all weigh heavily on planners; advisors; and, ultimately, the deciders. There are two keys to reform: establishing a process for vetting assistance requirements that is widely agreed early on and ensuring that those responsible for funding allocations discipline choices on how to meet validated needs.

Finally, we must concentrate more time, attention, and resources on the human capital dimensions of this enterprise. PDD-56's most compelling components—that is, building a knowledge base via rehearsals, after-action reports, and curricula for practitioner education—have received the least visible attention. Even so, our professional military education community made some useful strides in this area. The establishment of academic centers for research and analysis provided a wellspring of expertise that was not apparent over a decade ago.[19] Today's interagency system is more open to—indeed, very keen on—the idea of tabletop exercises that can simulate key decision points and alternative courses of action in complex contingencies. The Department of State's CSO Bureau has become a good reservoir for planning expertise. And interagency after-action reports are now becoming a more familiar part of the landscape.[20]

---

[19] The Peacekeeping and Stability Operations Institute at the Army War College was an output of the early move toward PDD-56, and the Center for Complex Operations at the National Defense University came into being as a congruence of PDD-56 imperatives and Bush-era stabilization directives.

[20] Two comparatively recent after-action reviews were completed in the aftermath of Operation Unified Response in Haiti, and Operation *Tomodachi* [Friendship] in response to the radiological hazards triggered by the Fukushima Daiichi dimensions of the March 2011 earthquake and tsunami in Japan.

Closing Observations

The priorities cited above align well with the Obama administration's preferences regarding conflict stabilization. Boiled down to its essentials, today's White House's narrative could fairly be characterized as follows: We are responsibly transitioning out of the Operation Enduring Freedom era, but isolationism is not the destination. New security challenges are looming, and regional conflicts that feed terrorism and extremist violence, risk mass atrocities, or pose spillover hazards will affect U.S. security and humanitarian interests. However, just as inaction may impose costs, we also need to weigh the full range of impacts, including unintended ones, associated with alternative courses of action. Finally, given fiscal realities and public fatigue with large, protracted U.S. counterinsurgency campaigns, the U.S. approach must emphasize greater reliance on partner-focused capacity-building. Of critical value are the forms of assistance (e.g., advisory support and persistent reconnaissance) that can help achieve successful partner-led operations while also catalyzing a host nation's economic recovery and its ability to develop accountable governance over the longer term. Working with, by, and through partners is completely consistent with PDD-56 precepts.

Our colleague Ted Warner might disclaim any clairvoyance when he helped launch this country into the PDD-56 era nearly two decades ago. But he certainly knew there would be an overwhelming need to better understand and act more coherently and collaboratively in an increasingly complex global environment. All that has happened since bears out that supposition: from the wave of popular uprisings throughout the Middle East and North Africa to the continued rise of transnational actors, the stunning growth of social media, the mobilization of increasingly complex multilateral contingency operations, and continuing dramas surrounding fragile states and their struggle for legitimacy and the loyalty of their citizens. Thank you, Ted, for helping us to navigate much more adroitly through this complex terrain.

References

Boot, Max, *The Savage Wars of Peace: Small Wars and the Rise of American Power*, New York: Basic Books, 2002.

Gates, Robert M., "Helping Others Defend Themselves: The Future of U.S. Security Assistance," *Foreign Affairs*, May/June 2010.

Gordon, Michael R., "The 2000 Campaign: The Military; Bush Would Stop U.S. Peacekeeping in Balkan Fights," *New York Times*, October 21, 2000.

Gordon, Michael, and Bernard Trainor, *Cobra II: The Inside Story of the Invasion and Occupation of Iraq*, New York: Pantheon Books, 2006.

Hawley, Len, presentation to an expert working group crafting a Center for Strategic and International Studies report, *Beyond Goldwater-Nichols: Defense Reform for a New Strategic Era*, May 8, 2003.

Hawley, Len, and Dennis Skocz, "Advance Political-Military Planning: Laying the Foundation for Achieving a Viable Peace," in Jock Covey, Michael Dziedzic, and Leonard Hawley, eds., *The Quest for Viable Peace: International Intervention and Strategies for Conflict Transformation*, Washington D.C.: United States Institute for Peace, 2005, pp. 37–76.

Lamb, Christopher, "Redesigning White House and Interagency Structures," in Hans Binnendijk and Patrick M. Cronin, eds., *Civilian Surge: Key to Complex Operations*, Washington, D.C.: National Defense University Press, 2009, pp. 39–43.

Murdock, Clark A., Michèle A. Flournoy, Christopher A. Williams, and Kurt M. Campbell, *Beyond Goldwater-Nichols: Defense Reform for a New Strategic Era*, Phase 1 Report, Washington D.C.: Center for Strategic and International Studies, 2004.

National Defense Authorization Act for Fiscal Year 2006.

National Security Presidential Directive 44 (NSPD-44), "Management of Interagency Efforts Concerning Reconstruction and Stabilization," December 7, 2005. As of January 10, 2014: http://www.fas.org/irp/offdocs/nspd/nspd-44.html

Presidential Decision Directive 56 (PDD-56), "The Clinton Administration's Policy on Managing Complex Contingency Operations," May 1997. As of January 10, 2014: https://www.fas.org/irp/offdocs/pdd56.htm

Quadrennial Defense Review, 1997.

Schear, James A., and Leslie B. Curtin, "Complex Operations: Recalibrating the State Department's Role," in Hans Binnendijk and Patrick M. Cronin, eds., *Civilian Surge: Key to Complex Operations*, Washington, D.C.: National Defense University Press, 2009, pp. 93–114.

Shelton, Henry H., General, USA, Chairman of the Joint Chiefs of Staff, posture statement before the Committee on Armed Services, U.S. Senate, February 8, 2000.

CHAPTER SEVEN

Dealing with Russia After the Cold War and After

Eugene Rumer

My first recollection of Ted Warner dates back to 1984. A graduate student at the Massachusetts Institute of Technology's Defense and Arms Control Studies program, I went to the American Academy of Arts and Sciences to hear a lecture by two visiting RAND analysts—retired Lt Gen Glenn Kent and Dr. Edward L. Warner III. Their subject was first-strike stability between the United States and the Soviet Union and the impact on it of President Ronald Reagan's recently launched ambitious Strategic Defense Initiative ("Star Wars") missile defense program. Thirty years later, I don't recall much about the lecture—sophisticated charts and the conclusion that the impact on first-strike stability would be decidedly negative, that's about it.

What impressed me more than anything else, though, was the cool, methodical, almost detached manner in which General Kent and Ted Warner presented their arguments on an issue that was at the center of a heated; highly politicized; and, for many at the time, very emotional national debate. Their lecture was very RAND-like. It was also unlike many other lectures I attended in and outside the classroom because the two presenters were dispassionate about nuclear weapons and strategic stability, about the Soviet Union, and about policy analysis—in other words, they were RAND-like. If that was RAND-like, RAND was where I wanted to be.

A few years later, I joined RAND and worked with Ted on several different projects—war games simulating crises in Eastern Europe and the Union of Soviet Socialist Republics (USSR) as Gorbachev's changes were gathering speed, interviewing Soviet officials and leaders of early prodemocracy movements in Moscow as the Soviet Union was coming apart, and thinking through the consequences of it all—from independence for the Baltic States to the fate of former Soviet nuclear weapons deployed in Kazakhstan, Ukraine, and Belarus. It was like getting another graduate education with Ted as a leading voice in RAND's own internal debate and in our briefings to policy customers.

Working with Ted was always an education. It has continued to be the case since our time together at RAND, through his service as an assistant secretary of defense in the Clinton administration and, most recently, in the Obama administration as Ted continued to lead our policy and intellectual efforts on arms control, strategic—no longer first-strike—stability, and relations with Russia.

❧

During the past quarter century, the United States has sped past two major historical milestones on its strategic landscape. The end of the Cold War in the early 1990s opened a period of unbridled optimism and a sense of absolute invulnerability at the end of a long and dangerous chapter in U.S. history. In contrast, the September 11, 2001, terrorist attacks triggered an entirely different sentiment in the U.S. approach to the world—a sense of profound vulnerability and an expectation of an open-ended, generational conflict with an unpredictable and ill-defined enemy. However, with the post–Cold War era well behind us and with the second of the two wars of the post–9/11 era winding down, it should be possible for the United States to look beyond the challenges it had confronted nearly a generation ago. But many of these challenges still remain at the top of U.S. foreign policy agenda. None has presented a more difficult and contentious problem for policymakers and analysts than the relationship with Russia.[1]

At Cold War's End

Looking back at the past quarter century, one cannot help but be struck by the highly uneven, almost cyclical quality of U.S.-Russian relations. The presidency of George H. W. Bush began on a highly promising note, as President Mikhail Gorbachev's domestic and foreign policies triggered the fall of the Berlin Wall in November 1989 and as, shortly afterward, the Soviet military began withdrawing its conventional and nuclear forces from Eastern Europe. The former adversary proved to be a partner, willing to take bold, unprecedented steps to reduce the dangers of nuclear war and a conventional military confrontation in Europe, and even went along with the U.S. military campaign against Saddam Hussein.[2]

However, no sooner did the Soviet Union emerge as a new U.S. partner, holding out the possibility of a cooperative and mutually rewarding relationship with the United States, than changes triggered by Gorbachev's campaigns of *glasnost* and *perestroika* inside the Soviet Union put that promising future in jeopardy. Ironically, the challenge to the cooperative and mutually rewarding relationship between the United States and Russia resulted from the very changes in Soviet domestic politics and economy that the United States had actively encouraged during the many decades of the Cold War and that had finally become possible during Gorbachev's presidency.

Despite (and in some instances because of) his remarkably successful foreign policy and widespread international recognition as an architect of a new world order, Gorbachev grew increasingly unpopular at home. The *glasnost* campaign, initially intended to boost the credibility of the Communist Party and mobilize the population

---

[1]   For an illustration see the ongoing debate about the role of morality in U.S. policy toward Russia on the pages of *The American Interest* magazine (David Kramer, "The Debate Is On," *The American Interest*, April 4, 2013).

[2]   Arriving in Moscow in February 1991, Ted Warner and I called on a leading Soviet expert on arms control and the United States. He looked away from a CNN broadcast from the Persian Gulf as we walked into his office, and greeted us: "Congratulations, gentlemen, you have just won the war!" We were stunned.

in support of Gorbachev's reforms, rapidly exceeded all the limits on public discussion the regime had previously imposed. The result was a complete delegitimization of the Communist Party and the Soviet state.

The veneer of success was stripped from virtually every major accomplishment of the Soviet regime—from the space program to the victory in World War II and Stalin's forced industrialization and, finally, to the very founding of the Soviet state by Lenin. The leaders of the Soviet Union's constituent republics challenged Gorbachev's federal government under the banner of rediscovered nationalism, fueled by popular sentiments of anger and frustration with the regime that had hidden the true historical record for several generations. The people's rediscovery of that record—from Moscow and Leningrad to the most distant corners of the Soviet Union—left them thinking that the Soviet Union had been a raw deal for everyone and that every part of the country would be better off if it took control of its own economic and political life. This powerful domestic political challenge to the Soviet government and Gorbachev personally gained so much momentum so rapidly that it effectively eclipsed his international agenda and any ambitions he might have had to pursue it.

Gorbachev fared no better in pursuing economic reforms. Major government investment programs of the early Gorbachev era intended to spark industrial production and economic growth were targeted at heavy industry and proved to have little impact on the Soviet economy and a public starved for consumer goods. Attempts at defense industrial conversion produced no tangible results. A partial liberalization of the economy that allowed some private business activity proved to be too little and too late and, paradoxically, probably made matters even worse by siphoning off resources into the "black" and "grey" markets.

Facing political unraveling and economic decline, Gorbachev came under fire from both the right and the left. On the right, the conservatives wanted him to stop his reforms and return the country to the condition he had inherited from his geriatric predecessors in 1985. Conservatives denounced him as a traitor who had surrendered the Soviet empire in Eastern Europe to the West and thus betrayed the legacy of the Soviet Union's victory in World War II. On the left, the liberals were frustrated by what they saw as slow, indecisive, and inconclusive reforms; compromises with the conservatives; and occasional retreats from the course of reform. Caught between these two camps, Gorbachev struggled to retain his job and keep the country together.

As the country was slipping away from him, foreign policy became Gorbachev's respite, the place where he could get much-needed support and recognition, but these accomplishments were secondary to the main—domestic—arena where his fate and the fate of the country itself would be decided. Partnership with the United States in pursuit of a new shared agenda and a new world order, where the two former superpower adversaries would come together on behalf of the world, was becoming an increasingly distant prospect. Instead of a partnership dedicated to a global agenda, it became a vehicle for seeking political support and economic assistance to boost Gorbachev's chances at home.[3]

The failed August 1991 coup to unseat Gorbachev that reactionaries determined to put an end to Gorbachev's reforms had launched was the clearest manifestation of the turmoil in Soviet domestic politics. The coup was swiftly defeated. While reformers rescued Gorbachev from his brief detention at his Black Sea dacha, he lost his ability to balance between the two camps and, within a few months, was swept aside by the reformers' momentum and the outpouring of popular support for them.

Having liberalized Soviet politics and given the people of the USSR the freedom to vote and decide their own fate, Gorbachev was left without a country. He was the best partner the United States had ever had in the Soviet Union, but the Soviet Union was no more, and the partnership became hollow almost as rapidly as it emerged. It fell prey to the rebirth of Soviet domestic politics and changes that had long been urged on the Soviet leaders by successive American Presidents.[4] In one form or another, Soviet and after 1991, Russian domestic politics would remain the biggest obstacle to the partnership between Washington and Moscow for the next twenty-plus years.

Dealing with a New Russia

The rapid fall of the Soviet Union and the reemergence of Russia in its place was a strategic surprise for the United States, but one that held out the promise of an even better relationship between Moscow and Washington. Although weakened by years of domestic turmoil and economic decline, the new Russia appeared to embrace many, probably even most, of the ideas that had previously constituted the intellectual core of Gorbachev's reforms—democratic governance and market economy at home and a close partnership with the West and the United States, in particular, in the international arena. One of the key differences between Mikhail Gorbachev and Boris Yeltsin was the speed and scope of the transformation they had pledged to pursue in

---

[3]   This portion of the chapter draws on Robert M. Gates, *From the Shadows: The Ultimate Insider's Story of Five Presidents and How They Won the Cold War*, New York: Simon and Shuster, 1996; David Remnick, *Lenin's Tomb*, New York: Vintage, 1994; Jack Matlock, *Autopsy of an Empire: The American Ambassador's Account of the Collapse of the Soviet Union*, New York: Random House, 1995; and Michael Beschloss and Strobe Talbott, *At the Highest Levels: The Inside Story of the End of the Cold War*, New York: Little, Brown and Company, 1994.

[4]   The paradoxical nature of this development was best illustrated when President George H. W. Bush came under criticism after delivering a speech in Kiev, Ukraine, in which he warned Ukrainians about the dangers of radical, "suicidal" nationalism. The speech was delivered on August 1, 1991, as Gorbachev was making a desperate attempt to hold the Soviet Union together. The speech was widely interpreted at the time as an attempt to buck up Gorbachev politically and to prop up the Soviet Union against the tide of popular sentiments favoring greater or complete independence for the Soviet republics—an idea that successive U.S. Presidents had favored for over a generation, since the Eisenhower presidency, when the Captive Nations Week came into being. Less than a month after President Bush's speech, Ukraine declared its independence from the Soviet Union.

the country's domestic affairs and foreign policy. Yeltsin pledged to move with greater speed and across a wider range of issues than Gorbachev, who had been held back by the reactionaries in the Communist Party and the Soviet government.

Even Russia's serious economic difficulties did not seem to pose a fundamental obstacle to pursuing a new relationship with the West and the United States. Certainly, Russia's attention and energies would be devoted for a considerable period to domestic reconstruction, and it would have only meager resources available to engage in select foreign policy pursuits, let alone play the role of a strategic partner to the United States. But that would not have to be a major impediment to a better relationship with the United States.

Building on U.S. efforts undertaken by the George H. W. Bush administration, during the immediate post-Soviet period, in early 1993, the new U.S. administration of President Bill Clinton embraced support for Russian reforms as one of its most important strategic foreign policy initiatives. It was designed on a sound strategic rationale: Deep, comprehensive U.S. engagement with Russia from the early stages of its fundamental internal transformation not only would be a gesture of good will on behalf of the American people but would also ensure that the United States could provide the intellectual capital and guidance for Russian reform and thus lay the foundations for an enduring strategic partnership between the two countries—a partnership that would more than pay off in the long run. It reflected a combination of good will and pragmatism, entirely consistent with the late Gorbachev era vision of the new world order.[5]

However, once again, the promise of U.S. partnership with Russia proved far more distant and elusive than originally hoped for. There were many reasons, but, as in the Gorbachev era, chief among them was the dynamics of Russia's domestic politics.

Despite the Russian public's frustration with Gorbachev's *perestroika* and early enthusiastic embrace of Boris Yeltsin, his early reforms were deeply unpopular and generated a powerful domestic political backlash. One of the first steps of the new Yeltsin government was aimed at liberalizing prices and economic deregulation—a form of "shock therapy" advocated by Western advisors and liberal Russian economists—and was implemented at a time when the Russian government's coffers were nearly empty. This proved to be too much of a shock for a population whose savings and patience had been depleted by the hardships of previous failed reform attempts. With the economy in a free-fall and no sources of revenue to pay the pensioners, government workers, the military, and the workers of vast state industrial and agricultural enterprises, the Russian government was left to choose between pursuing inflationary policies and borrow-

---

[5]   This section draws on Strobe Talbott, *The Russia Hand: A Memoir of Presidential Diplomacy,* New York: Random House, 2002, and James M. Goldgeier and Michael McFaul, *Power and Purpose: U.S. Policy Toward Russia After the Cold War*, Brookings, 2003.

ing from Western creditors, who refused to lend money to Russia unless it curbed its inflationary policies and implemented even more painful economic reforms.

Russia chose both. The results were a deeply unpopular set of economic policies whose promised rewards were too few and too slow to justify them in the eyes of the public and growing disenchantment with the United States, the West in general, and the policies they had urged the Russian government to pursue. Further feeding that trend was an ambitious campaign of privatization undertaken with the support and involvement of U.S. economic advisors. Its expectations were overly optimistic, while its immediate results fell far short of the mark, thus compounding the negative impression of U.S. involvement in Russian domestic affairs.

The lack of results that the Yeltsin government could demonstrate to the public opened it to a broad attack from the Communists and the ultranationalists, who were able to capitalize on the endless crises thwarting any initiative of the executive branch. The divided government and the economic free-fall in the wake of the dissolution of the Soviet Union created an atmosphere of chaos, both political and economic, and discredited the country's experiment with market and democracy in the eyes of many Russians. Because of its endorsement of the Russian government's policies at that time and involvement in their design and implementation, the United States' reputation suffered as well.

The October 1993 violent clash between the Yeltsin government and the Communist- and nationalist-dominated legislature was another important turning point, not only in Russian domestic politics but also in the bilateral U.S.-Russian relationship. In the United States, the Yeltsin government's attempt to disband and eventual use of force against the Duma was perceived as a clash between the reform-minded executive branch and the reactionary parliament standing in the way of progress. Many Russians, however, saw the conflict in terms of a constitutional crisis between the executive branch pursuing unpopular U.S.-prescribed reforms and the parliament elected in one of the freest elections Russia had had in the 20th century.

U.S. pursuit of an activist international agenda during that same period also contributed to an anti-American backlash in Russian domestic politics. The fall of the Soviet Union opened unprecedented opportunities for the expansion of the West. Responding to the desires of the newly independent states of Eastern Europe and even the Soviet Union, the United States embraced the inclusionary course aimed at bringing them into key Western institutions—the North Atlantic Treaty Organization (NATO) and, subsequently, the European Union.

Neither of the policies was intended to be *against* Russia. To the contrary, some elements of the new policies were very clearly designed to bring stability and prosperity to the borders of new Russia where otherwise conflict and economic stagnation were very real possibilities.

However, that was not how the policies of Western, U.S.-led NATO and European Union expansions were perceived in Russia. Amid disenchantment with democratic and economic reforms, the expansion of NATO into Eastern Europe was perceived in Russia as a geopolitical land grab that was made possible by Russian weakness that had been, in turn, precipitated by U.S. advice and encouragement of the ill-fated economic reforms. The redeployment to Russia of Russian troops from Eastern Europe, the Baltic states, and other former Soviet republics without adequate housing and provisions was another blow to Russian prestige and contributed to the perception of forced retreat under pressure from the United States.

U.S. engagement with the newly independent states of the former Soviet Union generated an equally neuralgic response, fueled by the Communist and nationalist opposition charges that the United States was implementing a deliberate policy of geopolitical encirclement and international marginalization of Russia taking advantage of its weakness. The low point was reached when Russia suffered a devastating financial crisis in August 1998 and when the United States launched the military campaign in Kosovo shortly thereafter, despite the strong objections of the Russian government.

By the end of the 1990s, the vision of partnership between Russia and the United States was a far more distant prospect that it had been at the outset of the decade. Russia was weak and withdrawn, to the point that students of Russia were debating the idea of a world without Russia as an effective actor in the international arena, incapable of acting because of its domestic turmoil.[6] One of the most important accomplishments of early post–Cold War era—the Strategic Arms Reduction Treaty (START) II signed between the United States and the Soviet Union in the last days of the George H. W. Bush administration—languished unratified in both countries. The United States remained committed to NATO enlargement despite Russian objections as groups of Eastern European states were admitted into the Atlantic Alliance. Russia's relevance to the United States appeared greatly diminished, and U.S. relevance to Russia appeared greatly diminished too. The exception, ironically, was in the international arena, where Moscow remained opposed to many U.S. initiatives and sought to oppose them wherever possible as an assertion of its residual relevance, and Washington grew irritated at Russia, which came to be viewed as an obstructionist actor whose ambitions greatly exceeded its capabilities. The vision of productive U.S.-Russian partnership was more aptly described as a ghost.

The Post–9/11 Era

The tragedy of 9/11 appeared to breathe new energy into that vision of partnership. In Russia, the terrorist attacks elicited a strong response from the general public and the leadership; both had grown wary of terrorism and Islamist militants in the course of

---

[6] Thomas E. Graham, Jr., "World Without Russia?" speech at the Jamestown Foundation Conference, Washington, D.C., June 9, 1999.

Russia's own protracted wars in Afghanistan and Chechnya. The image of the United States as no longer invulnerable and acting unilaterally, but seeking to enlist the support of the international community, also probably had a powerful effect on Russian attitudes toward the United States. Russia's geographic position astride the Eurasian landmass, which provided control of some key lines of communications to Afghanistan, made it relevant, even essential, to the United States in a way it had not been since the breakup of the USSR. Russian support for the United States' military campaign in Afghanistan and for its global war on terror created new opportunities for the partnership between Moscow and Washington.

However, these renewed hopes also proved short lived. Ironically, at this stage, one of the key factors behind new frictions between the United States and Russia was not the latter's weakness but its growing strength.

At the outset of the new millennium, Russia found itself on the path of dual—economic and political—recovery. The former was brought about largely by the steady growth in the price of oil and other commodities, fueling growth that cascaded throughout the Russian economy. The latter, also a by-product of economic growth, was the result of President Vladimir Putin's consolidation of political power. After the 1990s, with their seemingly interminable economic decline and political chaos, the majority of the Russian public welcomed the new era of stability and increasing prosperity.[7]

The contrast between the 1990s and the 2000s was reinforced by the emphasis the Putin government made on pursuing its own course in economic and political affairs. Whereas in the 1990s the Russian government limped along from one disbursement of funds from the International Monetary Fund to the next and grew dependent on foreign donors, the Putin government emphasized reliance on Russia's own resources and know-how and paid off its outstanding loans to international lenders.

After the disillusionment with Western aid and advice, this course proved popular with the Russian public. Besides the welcome benefits of strong economic growth, the Russian public showed few signs of disapproval of Putin's pursuit of "sovereign democracy"—a political model that insisted on following a uniquely Russian path to democracy that would ensure greater domestic stability, insulate Russia from Western-inspired upheavals of the 1990s, and—most important—protect its sovereignty from external intrusions and alien influences. As the country's economy grew by 6 to 7 percent a year, few Russians were willing to challenge the Kremlin.

However, what Putin's voters saw as the country's return to stability and prosperity, his critics, mainly in the West, criticized as an authoritarian revival fueled by petrodollars. The most important fault line between the United States and Russia emerged on the issue of democracy promotion. The United States firmly embraced it as a major element of its foreign policy. Russia grew ever more firmly opposed to it as a vehi-

---

[7]   For Russian public opinion data, see the Levada-Center's website.

cle for direct external interference in its internal affairs, a violation of its sovereignty, and a form of geopolitical encirclement intended to undermine Russia's own domestic stability when U.S. democracy promotion efforts appeared to reach the periphery of Russia, as was the case during the so-called "color" revolutions—democratic uprisings in Georgia (the "Rose Revolution") and Ukraine (the "Orange Revolution")—which pitted the United States against Russia. The United States grew more and more critical of Russia as both an increasingly authoritarian state and a neoimperialist one.[8]

The sharpest response from Russia came in 2007, at the Munich Security Forum, where Putin delivered a speech that revealed the depth of Russian frustrations with the West.[9] The West, he charged, had grown accustomed to not taking Russia seriously as a major force in the international arena and criticizing Russia for its lack of democracy at home. NATO expansion, he warned, "represents a serious provocation."[10]

U.S.-Russian tensions reached their highest point, and U.S.-Russian relations reached their nadir, in August 2008 with the outbreak of the Russian-Georgian War. It was the lowest point in relations between the United States and Russia since the Cold War, possibly even since the early 1980s, and in this instance, U.S. and Russia's sharply differing perspectives on democracy and foreign policy once again played a critical role. For the United States, Georgia had emerged as the leader of democratic change in the newly independent states of the former Soviet Union. For Russia, Georgia under President Mikheil Saakashvili was a geopolitical irritant, an agent of U.S.-inspired change, and a promoter of democratic ideals whose spread it, together with the United States, advocated both around and in Russia. It was therefore even more than a rebel satellite state on Russia's turbulent border in the Caucasus. It was a source of challenge to Russia's domestic arrangements and sovereignty.

After Georgia—A Familiar Cycle

Despite the severity of the 2008 crisis in relations between Russia and the United States, the damage was repaired quickly. Moreover, following the U.S. presidential election of 2008, the two sides once again embraced the language of partnership. The new Russian President, Dmitry Medvedev, and his agenda of economic modernization and hints at political liberalization appeared as a far more agreeable partner than Vladimir Putin with his ideas of "sovereign democracy" at home and "energy super-power" foreign policy.

---

[8]   Ilan Greenberg and Andrew E. Kramer, "Cheney Urges Energy Export Routes That Bypass Russia," *New York Times*, May 5, 2006.

[9]   Vladimir Putin, "Prepared Remarks of Russian President Vladimir Putin at the 43rd Munich Conference on Security Policy," February 12, 2007.

[10] Putin, 2007.

Medvedev's stated commitment to a more open political system than during the tenure of his predecessor and his embrace of economic modernization of Russia, intended to wean it from its dependence on the sale of oil and gas and orient it toward high-tech manufacturing, had a dual effect. They triggered an active discussion in Russia about political liberalization and alternative modes of political development, as well as expectations among Russian intelligentsia of impending political changes. This in turn led to expectations that newly liberalized political debates would result in substantial changes in the way Russia was governed.

The change in external perceptions of Russia and of its domestic developments, as well as expectations of impending changes, facilitated renewed Western engagement with Medvedev's government. The saliency of democratization as an issue on the bilateral U.S.-Russian agenda was reduced, thus enabling the two sides to concentrate on other problems—Iran's nuclear program, Afghanistan, and strategic arms control. As a result, the Washington-Moscow relationship had not only recovered but produced important results, such as the 2010 Russian cancellation of the sale of the S-300 air defense system to Iran and conclusion of the New START arms reduction treaty.

However, shortly after the entry into force of New START in February 2011, that relationship came under renewed stress. The cause, once again, was Russian domestic politics. The new Russian awakening was triggered by widespread popular discontent about the conduct of the December 2011 Duma election and charges of fraud, as well as by the prospect of Vladimir Putin's return to the presidency, which frustrated the hopes of the liberal intelligentsia for a new Medvedev-inspired era in Russian politics.[11] The outpouring of popular discontent not seen in Russia since the final days of the Soviet Union generated hopes for a democratic revival in Russia in the West and had profoundly unsettling effects on Russian leaders, including concerns that the United States was behind the revival of Russian prodemocracy movement.

The Kremlin's backlash against the opposition has returned the issue of democracy to the fore of the bilateral U.S.-Russian agenda. In keeping with the long-standing theme of the Putin presidency, the Kremlin has made it clear that it would tolerate neither U.S. criticism of Russia's domestic political arrangements nor perceived U.S. intervention in Russian domestic politics. That is where the relationship remains at present—in limbo—having stumbled once again on the issue of Russian domestic politics and the role of the United States in promoting democratic change in Russia.

Where does the Russian-American relationship go from here? Both sides stand to gain from averting backsliding. For the United States, Russia remains a key player on Afghanistan, on Syria, on Iran, on arms control, and on a host of other less prominent but nonetheless important issues. For Russia, the relationship with the United States reaffirms its special place in the international system as a nuclear superpower. Despite

---

[11] Dmitri Trenin, Alexei Arbatov, Maria Lipman, Alexey Malashenko, Nikolay Petrov, Andrei Ryabov, and Lilia Shevtsova, "The Russian Awakening," Washington, D.C.: Carnegie Moscow Center, November 2012.

Russia's efforts, the United States is a key geopolitical actor around its periphery in Europe and in Asia. It is also potentially a much-needed counterweight to China in the event that Beijing becomes increasingly assertive at Russia's expense.

However, despite the realization on both sides of the potential for mutual benefit, in the view of this author, the relationship is bound to keep running into the same familiar obstacle—Russian domestic politics, U.S. criticism of those politics, and Russian refusal to tolerate such criticism. As long as this tension persists between U.S. foreign policy and Russian domestic politics, a true partnership between the United States and Russia is bound to remain elusive.

Coda

Since this chapter was written in spring 2013, the relationship between the United States and Russia has deteriorated dramatically. In March 2014, the crisis in Ukraine has the United States and Russia at the brink of a new Cold War. At the heart of the current crisis is the same fundamental disagreement that has plagued U.S.-Russian relations for a generation: Washington's values-based foreign policy and support for democratic change versus Russia's hard, realist foreign policy with its emphasis on balancing power, interests, and geographic spheres of influence. With NATO debating how to best reassure the frontline states that share borders with Ukraine and Russia, with Russian troops in Crimea and Moscow asserting its right to send troops into eastern Ukraine to defend compatriots there, with U.S. missile defense components being prepared for deployment in Poland and Romania, and with the Russian Ministry of Defense hinting that it may halt arms control inspections in response to Western sanctions, the problem of first-strike, or strategic, stability does not seem as archaic as one would like it to be.

References

Beschloss, Michael, and Strobe Talbott, *At the Highest Levels: The Inside Story of the End of the Cold War*, New York: Little, Brown and Company, 1994.

Gates, Robert M., *From the Shadows: The Ultimate Insider's Story of Five Presidents and How They Won the Cold War*, New York: Simon and Shuster, 1996.

Goldgeier, James M., and Michael McFaul, *Power and Purpose: U.S. Policy Toward Russia After the Cold War*, Washington, D.C.: Brookings, 2003.

Graham, Thomas E., Jr., "World Without Russia?" speech at the Jamestown Foundation Conference, Washington, D.C., June 9, 1999. As of January 10, 2014: http://carnegieendowment.org/1999/06/09/world-without-russia/eup

Greenberg, Ilan, and Andrew E. Kramer, "Cheney Urges Energy Export Routes That Bypass Russia," *New York Times*, May 5, 2006.

Kramer, David, "The Debate Is On," *The American Interest*, April 4, 2013. As of January 10, 2014: http://www.the-american-interest.com/articles/2013/4/4/the-debate-is-on/

The Levada-Center, website, undated. As of March 10, 2014: http://www.levada.ru

Matlock, Jack, *Autopsy of an Empire: The American Ambassador's Account of the Collapse of the Soviet Union*, New York: Random House, 1995.

Putin, Vladimir, "Prepared Remarks of Russian President Vladimir Putin at the 43rd Munich Conference on Security Policy," February 12, 2007.

Remnick, David, *Lenin's Tomb*, New York: Vintage, 1994.

Talbott, Strobe, *The Russia Hand: A Memoir of Presidential Diplomacy,* New York: Random House, 2002.

Trenin, Dmitri, Alexei Arbatov, Maria Lipman, Alexey Malashenko, Nikolay Petrov, Andrei Ryabov, and Lilia Shevtsova, "The Russian Awakening," Washington, D.C.: Carnegie Moscow Center, November 2012. As of January 10, 2014: http://carnegieendowment.org/files/russian_awakening.pdf

On *Not* Throwing the Nuclear Strategy Baby Out with the Cold War Bath Water: The Enduring Relevance of the Cold War

James M. Acton

I believe I have known Ted Warner for less time than any of the other contributors to this volume, which made it a particular privilege to be asked to contribute. I first met Ted in 2010, at a workshop on the practicalities of implementing the recently completed U.S. Nuclear Posture Review. I had known him by reputation, of course. But, given that he had spent the past year negotiating the New Strategic Arms Reduction Treaty (New START) and that I was—and, for that matter, still am—a young(ish) think tank analyst, it was hardly surprising our paths had never crossed. At the meeting, there was much fairly abstract discussion of the need to "reconceptualize" strategic stability for the "second nuclear age." I was waiting to speak and make the argument that, actually, the basic Cold War conception of strategic stability still had considerable utility when, in a perfect "first strike," Ted preempted me and made the identical point. So, when I was asked to contribute a chapter to this volume, it seemed only appropriate to expand on this theme.

A few months later, Ted invited me to his office for a chat and lunch. To my surprise, delight, and trepidation, I found that Ted had not only printed out my recent book, Deterrence During Disarmament,[1] *and read it cover to cover but had also covered it in sticky notes and annotations in preparation for his cross examination of me (I only found out later that such willingness to engage seriously with younger analysts was a hallmark of his). I can only assume that I passed this second thesis defense because, since then, Ted has been a huge supporter of and contributor to a number of Track II dialogues I have organized with defense experts from Russia and China—for which I am most grateful.*

❧

The epithet "Cold War," as applied to nuclear strategy, is almost never meant kindly. Officials and analysts from both the left and right—for quite different reasons— regularly urge the United States to purge itself of a Cold War mentality. President Obama himself, in a 2009 speech in Prague that recommitted the United States to the goal of a world without nuclear weapons, promised to "put an end to Cold War

---

[1] James M. Acton, *Deterrence During Disarmament: Deep Nuclear Reductions and International Security*, Abingdon, U.K.: Routledge, 2011.

thinking."[2] Ironically, opponents of his nuclear policy also argue for the same goal, albeit on the grounds that received wisdom inhibits the United States from crafting a more-effective nuclear force (which is usually argued to require low-yield, high-accuracy nuclear weapons capable of greater discrimination than the "Cold War" legacy systems in today's U.S. stockpile).[3]

No part of the intellectual inheritance from the Cold War is more frequently maligned than the concept of strategic stability. A detailed definition is presented below. Here, it suffices to say that its advocates generally argue against attempting to undermine the survivability of other states' nuclear forces—at least in the cases of Russia and, more recently, China—out of concern that doing so might lead to arms racing and, even more seriously, preemptive attacks in a crisis. Critics who believe in the utility of nuclear superiority argue that, when applied to today's security environment, "[s]tability metrics from the Cold War can lead to dangerous and sometimes absurd conclusions."[4]

Criticism of strategic stability—at least the Cold War conception of the term—also comes from the other side in the nuclear strategy debate. While very few advocates of disarmament renounce it outright, many propose policies, such as "dealerting," that run contrary to Cold War prescriptions for achieving stability.[5] For example, five senior retired American officials, including Senator Chuck Hagel (who was subsequently appointed Secretary of Defense) and General James Cartwright (a former Vice Chairman of the Joint Chiefs of Staff and commander of U.S. Strategic Command), recently wrote that "[w]e should close the books on the Cold War and immediately put the nuclear arsenals into strategic reserve status on 'modified alert.'"[6]

Simultaneously, most contemporary nuclear strategists generally ignore the understanding of both Soviet and American nuclear decisionmaking processes that was built up during the Cold War and has since been augmented with newly available evidence.[7]

---

[2]   Barack Obama, "Remarks by President Barack Obama," Prague, April 5, 2009.

[3]   See, for example, Keith B. Payne, *The Fallacies of Cold War Deterrence and a New Direction*, Lexington, Ky.: University Press of Kentucky, 2001.

[4]   Thomas Scheber, "Strategic Stability: Time for a Reality Check," *International Journal*, Vol. 63, No. 4, Autumn 2008, p. 894. For other examples of similar criticism, see James M. Acton, "Reclaiming Strategic Stability," in Elbridge A. Colby and Michael S. Gerson, eds., *Strategic Stability: Contending Interpretations*, Carlisle, Pa.: Strategic Studies Institute and U.S. Army War College Press, 2013a, Chapter 4, notes 1 and 2.

[5]   Dealerting involves taking nuclear weapons off alert by, for example, separating warheads from missiles.

[6]   James Cartwright, Richard Burt, Chuck Hagel, Thomas Pickering, Jack Sheehan, and Bruce Blair, "Modernizing U.S. Nuclear Strategy, Force Structure and Posture," Global Zero, May 2012.

[7]   Shortly after the end of the Cold War, oral history became practical, resulting in such important studies as John G. Hines, Ellis M. Mishulovich, and John F. Shull, *Soviet Intentions 1965–1985*, Vol. I: *An Analytical Comparison of U.S.-Soviet Assessments During the Cold War*, McLean, Va.: BDM Federal, 1995, and Richard Ned Lebow and Janice Gross Stein, *We All Lost the Cold War*, Princeton, N.J.: Princeton University Press, 1994. In addition, the declassification of archival documents in the United States, Russia, and elsewhere has provided a

Presumably, they view such understanding as nothing more than a historical curiosity, irrelevant to contemporary deterrence challenges.

No serious analyst can argue that the profound changes that have taken place since the end of the Cold War do not have important implications for nuclear strategy. But, equally, it is important not to throw the baby out with the bathwater. The Cold War experience has many lessons relevant to today. Some of these lessons are negative—mistakes it is important not to repeat; other lessons are more positive—principles and practices that should be preserved.

This chapter addresses the continuing relevance of two lessons from the Cold War, which Ted Warner helped the United States to learn the first time around: the enduring importance of strategic stability and the importance of understanding that an adversary may not be a unitary actor. As described further below, both lessons provide insights useful for preventing and managing crises and for correctly interpreting the behavior of potential adversaries during peacetime.

The Enduring Importance of Strategic Stability

The Obama administration has made "strategic stability" the centerpiece of its approach to nuclear relations with Russia and China.[8] Yet it has been somewhat reticent to present—in public at least—a clear definition of the term. This failure has played into the hands of critics who argue, simultaneously and contradictorily, that the term is so ill defined as to be virtually meaningless and also that is an example of outdated Cold War thinking.[9]

As good a starting point as any for defining strategic stability for today's world is the definition Warner and two coauthors, Glenn A. Kent and Randall J. DeValk, used in a 1985 RAND study examining options for the then ongoing U.S.-Soviet strategic arms reduction talks. In their view, strategic stability (which was identified as one of three goals for arms control, along with credible deterrence and essential equivalence in strategic offensive capabilities) required a set of conditions that it is worth quoting at length:

> Neither side is likely to be sufficiently tempted or fearful to resort to the initiation of nuclear operations, even (*especially*) in a time of severe political crisis.

---

steady stream of new information that has informed numerous studies (even if few aimed to draw lessons for contemporary nuclear strategy). The Woodrow Wilson Center's Cold War International History Project and George Washington University's National Security Archive are notable for making archival documents easily available.

[8]   U.S. Department of Defense, *Nuclear Posture Review Report*, April 2010, pp. 28–29.

[9]   For the flavor of the current debate about this term, see Elbridge A. Colby and Michael S. Gerson, eds., *Strategic Stability: Contending Interpretations*, Carlisle, Pa.: Strategic Studies Institute and U.S. Army War College Press, 2013.

Neither country could escape devastating urban-industrial retaliation even if it executed a massive, surprise, would-be disarming first strike.

Neither can greatly alter this retaliatory stalemate by means of a "breakout" in attack or defense capability. …

Both superpowers are sensitive to the risks of nuclear war and have been willing to establish procedures and capabilities to facilitate communications in crises and actually use these arrangements as a means of reducing the chances of direct super-power military conflict.[10]

With the exception of the references to "superpowers" and "superpower conflict" in the final paragraph, this description of what a desirable relationship between nuclear-armed near-peer potential adversaries should look like has aged remarkably well (especially the part about crisis management, which is discussed further below). Unlike other Cold War approaches (particularly quantitative ones based on counterforce exchange ratios and the like), this definition stresses goals that are still important, even if the practical challenges of attaining them have evolved. In 1985, for example, concerns about Soviet missile throw-weight (a term that has virtually disappeared from the arms control lexicon) were in vogue. Warner et al. worried that "pattern bombing" with "*only* a few million kg of ballistic missile throw-weight" could undermine the survivability of the U.S. bomber force.[11] While such concerns (thankfully) receded with the end of the Cold War, technological developments have raised new fears—particularly outside the United States—about nuclear force survivability.

During the Obama administration, Warner has been at the forefront of official U.S. efforts with Russia and has been deeply involved in unofficial efforts with China to develop a shared understanding of how to define and ensure strategic stability in today's world. The implications of developments in *non*nuclear technologies are central to this debate. While such technologies were not entirely ignored during the Cold War, they have significantly increased in importance over the last two decades.[12] In this regard, four new, or rapidly advancing, technologies could have implications for

---

[10] Edward L. Warner III, Glenn A. Kent, and Randall J. DeValk, "Key Issues for the Strategic Offensive Force Reduction Portion of the Nuclear and Space Talks in Geneva," Santa Monica, Calif.: RAND Corporation, N-2348-1-AF, December 1985, pp. 1–2. Italics in original.

[11] Warner et al., 1985, p. 5. My italics. A few million kilograms of ballistic missile throw-weight are equivalent to a few thousand megatons in yield.

[12] For an interesting Cold War discussion of what might be termed nonnuclear strategic weapons, see Carl H. Builder, *Strategic Conflict Without Nuclear Weapons*, Santa Monica, Calif.: RAND Corporation, R-2980/FF-RC, 1983. For a recent overview of thinking on this subject during the Cold War, see James M. Acton, *Silver Bullet? Asking the Right Questions About Conventional Prompt Global Strike*, Washington, D.C.: Carnegie Endowment for International Peace, 2013b, pp. 10–13.

strategic stability in future: ballistic missile defense, long-range conventional precision strike, antisatellite weapons, and cyber weapons.

Russian and Chinese concerns that ballistic missile defense and conventional prompt global strike (a program to develop long-range hypersonic conventional weapons) might ultimately be able to undermine their nuclear forces have been discussed extensively elsewhere and do not need to be rehearsed here.[13] It is, however, worth stressing three points. First, Russian and Chinese experts have articulated particular concern that, in combination, ballistic missile defense and high-precision conventional weapons could enable the United States to execute a disarming first strike without crossing the nuclear threshold.[14] Second, Chinese and Russian experts generally do not, in fact, disaggregate prompt and nonprompt conventional munitions (such as cruise missiles or gravity bombs), arguing that the latter also pose a potential threat to their nuclear forces.[15] Third, however paranoid these concerns seem to U.S. audiences, they could have implications for strategic stability, which (like deterrence more generally) depends on the perception of a threat rather than its reality. The very real challenge of managing these concerns is a central part of ensuring strategic stability with Russia and China.

By coincidence (or perhaps not), the three states with the most sophisticated antisatellite capabilities are also China, Russia, and the United States. Both the United States and Russia use satellites to detect missile launches. Attacks on such satellites could be extremely destabilizing (since the victim could well interpret them as the prelude to a first strike). Fortunately, the probability of deep U.S.-Russian crisis is low and, even if one were to occur, Washington and Moscow would probably have some shared understanding of how destabilizing attacks on early warning satellites could prove to be.

There are reasons to be less sanguine about the implications of antisatellite weapons for strategic stability in the U.S.-China context (not the least of which is the greater likelihood of a U.S.-China crisis or conflict). China does not have early warning satellites, but it does have an active antisatellite weapon program. While it may lack the capability to launch kinetic attacks on U.S. early warning satellites at the moment,

---

[13] For a summary, see Acton, 2013b, pp. 120–126.

[14] See, for example, the quotation from Anatoly Antonov, Russian New START negotiator and now Deputy Defense Minister, in Eugene Miasnikov, "On the Relationship Between Nuclear and Conventional Strategic Arms in the New START Treaty," Center for Arms Control, Energy and Environmental Studies at Moscow Institute of Physics and Technology, September 10, 2010, p. 3, and M. Taylor Fravel and Evan S. Medeiros, "China's Search for Assured Retaliation: The Evolution of Chinese Nuclear Strategy and Force Structure," *International Security*, Vol. 23, No. 2, Fall 2010, p. 83.

[15] See, for example, Alexei Arbatov, *Gambit or Endgame? The New State of Arms Control*, Washington, D.C.: Carnegie Endowment for International Peace, 2011, pp. 19–22, and Yao Yunzhu, "China Will Not Change Its Nuclear Policy," China-U.S. Focus, website, April 22, 2013. Note that Yao simply refers to "conventional strategic strike capabilities."

it may be able to "dazzle" them (thus rendering their infrared sensors inoperable for some period or burning out their optics altogether), and it could acquire the capability for kinetic destruction in future.[16] There could be at least two reasons for Beijing to use such capabilities in a conflict. First, U.S. early warning satellites provide cueing information for many (if not all) U.S. missile defense systems.[17] Second, early warning satellites could, in theory, help the United States locate—and hence destroy—the transporter erector launchers for conventional missiles after they had launched their missiles.[18] In practice, locating, tracking, and destroying dispersed mobile missiles would probably present insurmountable challenges to the United States.[19] Nonetheless, given well-documented Chinese concerns about the survivability of its land-based nuclear forces, which mostly consist of mobile missiles, it seems eminently possible that Beijing would worry, in a conflict, that very similar conventional missiles were vulnerable. This concern, coupled with fears about the impact of U.S. ballistic missile defenses, could create a plausible incentive for China to attack U.S. early warning satellites in a serious conventional conflict in which Beijing was using, or planning to use, its large and growing arsenal of conventionally armed regional ballistic missiles.

Attacking U.S. early warning satellites would obviously be very provocative—but just how provocative is hard to say. Because China could not hope to execute a disarming first strike on U.S. central strategic forces, it is possible that Washington would not interpret attacks on its early warning satellites as signaling the possibility that Beijing might be planning to employ nuclear weapons. But, in practice, much would inevitably depend on how the conflict was unfolding and what other indications of Chinese intent Washington was receiving.

The implications of cyber weapons for strategic stability are also murky. U.S. early warning systems are one possible target for cyberattacks. For exactly the same reasons that Beijing might try to attack U.S. early warning satellites in a conflict, it could attempt to interfere with the systems that are used to transmit and process data from these satellites. If such interference succeeded either in denying the United States timely access to early warning information or in replacing this information with false and misleading data, it could have effects very similar to those of direct attacks on the early warning satellites themselves. Of course, how vulnerable early warning systems

---

[16] Instability could also arise if the United States uses communication satellites in low earth orbit for nuclear command and control because such satellites are vulnerable to kinetic attacks.

[17] National Research Council, *Making Sense of Ballistic Missile Defense: An Assessment of Concepts and Systems for U.S. Boost-Phase Missile Defense in Comparison to Other Alternatives*, Washington, D.C.: National Academies Press, 2012, p. 116.

[18] Forrest E. Morgan, *Deterrence and First-Strike Stability in Space: A Preliminary Assessment*, Santa Monica, Calif.: RAND Corporation, MG-916-AF, 2010, p. 20.

[19] See, for example, Alan J. Vick, Richard M. Moore, Bruce R. Pirnie, and John Stillion, *Aerospace Operations Against Elusive Ground Targets*, Santa Monica, Calif.: RAND Corporation, MR-1398-AF, 2001, especially pp. 57–81. On whether current U.S. technological efforts can solve this problem, see Acton, 2013b, pp. 82–84.

are to this kind of cyberintrusion is impossible to assess with unclassified information. It is also hard to predict how escalatory cyberinterference would be. For at least two reasons, however, such interference might prove somewhat less escalatory than direct attacks—especially kinetic attacks—on early warning satellites. First, cyberinterference would presumably be easier to reverse than direct attacks. Second, it might take a significant length of time for the United States to establish that cyberinterference had occurred. In fact, by the time it did so, it would hopefully have become clear that such attacks were not the prelude to a nuclear strike. That said, the assertion that cyberattacks on early warning systems would be less escalatory than direct attacks on satellites sets a rather low bar; either type of attack could be highly escalatory.

Another possibility is that vulnerabilities in cyberspace could be exploited to enable the unauthorized use of a nuclear weapon. Interestingly, U.S. lawmakers recently requested a National Intelligence Estimate about the vulnerabilities of foreign nuclear weapons to such assaults.[20] Whether such vulnerabilities exist and could plausibly be exploited depends on a number of factors. Are command and control systems "hooked up" to the Internet, or are they effectively isolated? What safeguards exist to enable those in charge of nuclear weapons to confirm the authenticity of a launch order? It is possible to bypass such safeguards by transmitting orders directly to nuclear weapons? For understandable and obvious reasons, nuclear-armed states refrain from providing sufficient information to even attempt to answer these questions. Indeed, when asked whether Russia and China "have the ability to stop some cyber attack from launching one of their nuclear intercontinental ballistic missiles," Gen Robert C. Kehler, then Commander, U.S. Strategic Command, replied "I don't know."[21]

A quite distinct concern is that cyberweapons could be used to disable a nuclear command and control system and hence *deny* a state the use of its nuclear forces, potentially generating preemptive pressures similar to those kinetic forces can create (not least because of the possibility that kinetic and nonkinetic forces could be used simultaneously). Once again, it is impossible, at least on the basis of publicly available information, to know whether cyberweapons could actually be used in this way. However, there is some evidence that China worries that they could. Michael Pillsbury, a former U.S. defense official, has argued that

> [t]he fears of the Second Artillery Corps, China's strategic missile force, are revealed in reports published by China's *Rocket Force News* that training exercises have emphasized strategies to counter air attacks, attacks by special forces, electro-magnetic jamming, live-troop reconnaissance, and network attacks using hackers

---

[20] Aliya Sternstein, "Officials Worry About Vulnerability of Global Nuclear Stockpile to Cyber Attack," Nextgov, website, March 13, 2013.

[21] Sternstein, 2013.

and computer viruses. Electronic warfare and cyber attacks on China's missile forces are also a growing concern.[22]

A separate but extremely important aspect of strategic stability—also emphasized in Warner et al.'s 1985 definition—is crisis management. In this regard, the question of command and control in a crisis is intensely relevant to contemporary deterrence challenges. These issues came to the fore in the Soviet context at the very end of the Cold War. Testifying before Congress in 1991, Warner put the problem this way:

> Even ... when the [command and control] system remains intact, some vulner-abilities could emerge in a deep international crisis. The weakest link in the system under these conditions would appear to be at the point when the Soviet politi-cal leadership had neutralized several of its safeguards by directing the mating of nuclear weapons with delivery systems, by bringing nuclear forces to states of heightened combat readiness, but had not yet ordered the initial use of nuclear weapons.[23]

Just under five months later, the Soviet Union was dissolved, dramatically reduc-ing the likelihood of a deep crisis with Russia. Unfortunately, a deep crisis with China, while still rather unlikely, is now significantly more likely than it was during the second half of the Cold War. The primary strategy that China has adopted to enhance the sur-vivability of its nuclear forces—mobility both on land and at sea—could also exacer-bate command and control challenges with potentially catastrophic results in a crisis.

If Beijing believed (rightly or wrongly) that the United States might attempt to eliminate its nuclear forces, it could disperse them. Not only might this have the (pos-sibly unintended) effect of escalating the crisis, but it could also increase the possibility of an unauthorized launch for precisely the reasons Warner outlined in 1991 in regard to the Soviet Union.[24] To make matters worse, although the United States and China do have a crisis hotline, Beijing has refused to use it in past crises.[25] This underscores Warner et al.'s prescience in arguing in 1985 that crisis management tools are worthless if they are not accompanied by a willingness to use them.

---

[22] Michael Pillsbury, "The Sixteen Fears: China's Strategic Psychology," *Survival*, Vol. 54, No. 5, October–November 2012, p. 157.

[23] Hearings Before the Defense Policy Panel of the Committee on Armed Services of the U.S. House of Repre-sentatives on "The Grand Bargain—Should the West Bankroll Soviet Transformation to a Free Market Econ-omy?" HASC No. 102-26, Washington, D.C., July 31, 1991, p. 242.

[24] See also Michael S. Gerson, "No First Use: The Next Step for U.S. Nuclear Policy," *International Security*, Vol. 35, No. 2, Fall 2010, pp. 37–39.

[25] For detailed case studies, see Michael D. Swaine and Zhang Tuosheng, eds., with Danielle F. S. Cohen, *Man-aging Sino-American Crises: Case Studies and Analysis*, Washington, D.C.: Carnegie Endowment for International Peace, 2006, especially Chapters 9 and 10.

Similar escalatory dynamics could occur in a crisis with the Democratic People's Republic of Korea, as underlined by recent U.S. concerns about its progress toward a road-mobile intercontinental ballistic missile (not to mention its large arsenal of shorter-range mobile weapons). These dynamics could be even more acute than in a crisis with China, for any number of reasons. North Korea's nuclear forces are presumably much less survivable than China's. There is even less reason to hope that Pyongyang would use crisis communication mechanisms.[26] And, however poorly Washington and Beijing would understand one another's behavior in a crisis, it is a fair bet that the potential for misunderstanding would be much higher in a U.S.–North Korea crisis. Moreover, whereas the United States is prepared to seek strategic stability with China and has expressed some willingness to reassure Beijing about the survivability of its nuclear forces, it is not prepared to accept a similar relationship with North Korea (and neither should it be).

Balancing the legitimate objective of damage limitation in a nuclear conflict with North Korea against the possibility that trying to achieve that objective might actually make a nuclear attack more likely presents a profound challenge for U.S. policymakers. In trying to find the least bad solution to this problem, one potentially productive starting point could be the analysis of Cold War crises. The most relevant crisis in this regard is probably the 1969 Sino-Soviet border conflict, in which China became wrongly but intensely worried that a Soviet first strike on its nascent nuclear arsenal was imminent.[27] While there would, unquestionably, be many and important differences between this crisis (or any other Cold War crisis) and a future U.S.–North Korea crisis, the fact remains that the Cold War is the only source of actual evidence for a how a nuclear crisis, in which one side fears for the survivability of its nuclear forces, might unfold.[28]

---

[26] As this essay was being written, North Korea cut off all hotlines with South Korea. Even if these are ultimately reinstated, there seems to be a significant probability that they would be severed or ignored in a future crisis. Choe Sang-Hun, "North Korea Cuts Off the Remaining Military Hot Lines with South Korea," *New York Times*, March 27, 2013.

[27] Michael S. Gerson, *The Sino-Soviet Border Conflict: Deterrence, Escalation, and the Threat of Nuclear War in 1969*, Alexandria, Va.: Center for Naval Analyses, 2010.

[28] Of course, there have been nuclear crises since the end of the Cold War, most obviously the 1999 crisis between India and Pakistan. However, there is no evidence that, in this case, either side feared for the survivability of its nuclear weapons. It is interesting to wonder whether Pyongyang feared for the survivability of its nuclear forces in March 2013 when, following North Korea's third nuclear test and a series of exceptionally belligerent statements, the United States flew B-52 and B-2 bombers to South Korea to participate in ongoing military exercises. There is, however, little evidence on which to base a firm conclusion.

Nuclear Strategy and the Nonunitary State

Strategic stability is an important concept because it provides policymakers with insight into preventing and managing crises. Although not discussed above, it also alerts policymakers to the circumstances that may encourage a state to build up its nuclear forces. Warner et al.'s definition, for example, highlights the importance of neither state in a deterrence dyad being able to "greatly alter [the] retaliatory stalemate by means of a 'breakout' in attack or defense capability."[29] However, other authors stress the possibility that a state worried for the survivability of its own nuclear forces might augment them.

Although confidence in force survivability is a necessary condition for deterring either the use of nuclear weapons or a nuclear buildup by an adversary, it is not sufficient. One of the key lessons from the Cold War is that, where nuclear decisionmaking is concerned, states are not necessarily unitary actors. Indeed, group politics—and other manifestations of nonunitary behavior—help explain certain aspects of Soviet and U.S. procurement policy and crisis behavior, providing today's policymakers with useful insights.

Throughout the Cold War, there was a strong tendency within the United States, particularly among nuclear strategists, to view the Soviet Union as a unitary actor. Country specialists—the Kremlinologists—were more inclined to recognize the existence of group politics within the Soviet Union but had a relatively limited impact on nuclear strategy debates. As a nuclear strategist and a Soviet watcher, who wrote his doctoral dissertation on Soviet bureaucratic politics, Ted Warner was one of the few to straddle both camps.[30]

Nowhere was the impact of internal Soviet politics more significant than on weapon procurement. At the time, few Western analysts had any conception of the extent to which pressures from the design bureaus shaped Soviet policy. Warner was, in fact, one of the few who argued it might be a significant factor. In 1975, for example, he noted that "weapons designers have a great deal at stake that prompts them to generate new weapons systems proposals" and argued that "entrepreneurial self-promotion" probably influenced procurement decisions.[31]

We now know that even Warner underestimated the extent to which bureaucratic politics must be invoked to explain Soviet procurement, which, it turns out, was largely *supply* driven. In particular, the extraordinary proliferation of different strategic weapon systems was largely the result of the powerful defense-industrial sector foisting

---

[29] Warner et al., 1985.

[30] Edward L. Warner III, *The Military in Contemporary Soviet Politics: An Institutional Analysis*, New York: Praeger, 1977.

[31] Edward L. Warner III, "The Bureaucratic Politics of Weapons Procurement," in Michael MccGwire, Ken Booth, and John McDonnell, eds., *Soviet Naval Policy: Objectives and Constraints*, New York: Praeger, 1975, p. 76.

whatever it wanted to build onto the military. Shortly after the end of Cold War, Vital-lii L. Katayev, a senior advisor to the chairman of the Defense Industrial Department of the Communist Party Central Committee from 1967 to 1985, explained Soviet procurement this way to U.S. interviewers:

> In order to avoid slighting design bureaus, Katayev explained, missiles of the same class that were developed by different design bureaus were put into series production simultaneously. The [Strategic Rocket Forces] at one time had 10 different missiles serving the same mission. Katayev characterized this process as a kind of *internal arms race* carried out inside the defense sector.[32]

The Soviet General Staff officer and noted military strategist Colonel-General Andrian A. Danilevich concluded that "strategic objectives were often subordinated to, and built around, weapon systems."[33]

The influence of intragovernment dynamics on Soviet procurement "policy" could help inform contemporary debates. There is, for example, a vigorous ongoing debate within the United States about the purpose of China's ongoing strategic modernization and its gradual nuclear buildup. Generally, U.S. analysts and officials fall into one of two camps: Either they argue that this process is offensively oriented and part of a long-term strategy to give Beijing the option of achieving its political objectives by force or the threat of force, or they argue that this process is defensively motivated and intended to preserve the survivability of China's nuclear forces in the face of a perceived growing threat from the United States. Cold War history should, however, alert us to a third possibility: that China's modernization and buildup is not primarily strategically motivated but is the result of defense-industrial considerations and/or other forms of internal politics.

The nonunitary nature of governments also has implications for the avoidance and management of crises.[34] Indeed, the seminal study on bureaucratic politics, Graham T. Allison's *Essence of Decision*, was based on the Cuban Missile Crisis (even if newly emerged evidence has forced a rethink of some of its original conclusions).[35] The theory of bureaucratic politics has been used extensively since then to study U.S. national security policy (although its application to weapon procurement has attracted much less attention since the end of the Cold War). However, the ways in which intragovernmental competition shaped Soviet national security policy has, for understandable reasons, attracted less attention. Yet there are clear indications that its influence was signif-

---

[32] Hines, Mishulovich, and Shull, 1995, p. 63. Italics in the original.

[33] Hines, Mishulovich, and Shull, 1995, p. 61.

[34] See Chapter Two, by Michael Sulmeyer and Michael Albertson, for a discussion of the theory of bureaucratic politics.

[35] Graham T. Allison, *Essence of Decision: Explaining the Cuban Missile Crisis*, Boston: Little, Brown and Company, 1971.

icant. For example, historians Richard Ned Lebow and Janice Gross Stein have argued that, in addition to other motivations, Soviet Premier Nikita Khrushchev may have perceived his decision to place missiles in Cuba as a way to placate "militants" after a series of failed domestic reforms.[36] In addition, his need for a face-saving solution to the crisis—in particular, the secret deal to remove Jupiter missiles from Turkey—suggests that his freedom of action was circumscribed by elements of the Soviet system that he could not simply ignore, resulting in an internal bargaining process.

Experts on Sino-U.S. relations have argued that the nonunitary nature of both governments—but the Chinese government, in particular—has had a significant impact on past crises. For example, the American scholar Michael D. Swaine has stated that one reason the Chinese leadership refused to answer phone calls from the White House after the 1999 bombing of the Chinese embassy in Belgrade was a desire to reach an internal consensus before dealing with the United States.[37] He has also argued that this problem could become more acute in future crises because in "China, in particular, an increasingly complex and fragmented decisionmaking process and a stovepiped intelligence structure have apparently slowed reaction time and distorted both the assessment of information and clear signaling in a crisis."[38] Of course, China and the Soviet Union are quite different, and it would be wrong to assume that the former suffers from exactly the same bureaucratic pathologies that afflicted the latter. For this reason, one of the most significant lessons the United States can learn from the Cold War is simply its own tendency to underestimate how splintered the other protagonist in a crisis might be.

Nowhere could nonunitary behavior be more portentous than in a future India-Pakistan crisis. Although the United States would not be a direct participant, it could well be involved as a mediator (as it has in past crises). India has threatened to retaliate with decisive conventional force against a terrorist attack sponsored by the Pakistani state. In practice, however, it could be very difficult to determine whether Pakistani terrorists were actually acting on behalf of Pakistan's intelligence agency (Inter-Services Intelligence, or ISI) and, if they were, whether that agency was following orders from elected national leaders. The implications of this uncertainty for stability are potentially significant. For example, U.S. analyst George Perkovich has observed that, if Islamabad did not authorize a terrorist attack, but India nonetheless retaliated,

> Pakistani leaders, feeling that they had not authorized aggression against India, would feel that India was initiating war. It is widely recognized that victims of

---

[36] Lebow and Stein, 1994, p. 59.

[37] Michael D. Swaine, "Sino-American Crisis Management and the U.S.-Japan Alliance," in Akikazu Hashimoto, Mike Mochizuki, and Kurayoshi Takara, eds., *The Japan-U.S. Alliance and China-Taiwan Relations: Implications for Okinawa*, Sigur Center for Asian Studies, 2008, p. 86.

[38] Swaine, 2008, p. 87.

aggression—defenders—are more highly motivated to retaliate because they have suffered an injustice. Knowing this, Pakistani defenders would feel that their threats to escalate in response to an Indian attack would be more credible than if they had been the initiators of the conflict.[39]

However, Indian leaders—believing that Islamabad had initiated the attack—would feel equally strongly that they were the defenders and, hence, that Islamabad would ultimately back down. The resulting escalatory dynamics—in which each side felt it enjoyed the moral advantage—could be particularly difficult to manage.

Conclusion

In looking back at the Cold War experience of nuclear deterrence, now more than 20 years distant, two fundamental mistakes can be made: assuming that everything has changed and assuming that nothing has changed. Right now, students of nuclear strategy in the United States seem in much greater danger of making the former mistake than the latter. In the first decade after the end of the Cold War, there was considerable optimism that the problems associated with nuclear weapons would simply melt away in the geopolitical thaw. Ted warned against this view, and he has, unfortunately, been proved right.[40] As U.S. policymakers seek to navigate this new array of challenges, they should take account of the Cold War experience.

Out of the many lessons that could be culled from the Cold War, the enduring importance of strategic stability and the realization that a potential adversary (or, for that matter, the U.S. government) may not be a unitary actor have important implications for preventing and managing future crises, as well as for interpreting and shaping the peacetime behavior, especially the procurement policies, of potential adversaries. The most important lessons relate to crisis management. Serious crises in which the use of nuclear weapons would be conceivable remain possible (even if crises in which the United States would be a protagonist have become less likely). The same threats to stability, including vulnerable nuclear forces, that could have precipitated nuclear use during the Cold War could still do so in a future crisis. In fact, given the increasing ability of nonnuclear weapons to interact with nuclear assets and ballistic missile early warning systems, technological developments could compound these "Cold War" problems. To make matters worse, North Korea and China, the two states currently most likely to enter into a nuclear crisis with the United States, appear more disinclined than the Soviet Union was to use crisis communication mechanisms. Likewise,

---

[39] George Perkovich, "The Non-Unitary Model and Deterrence Stability in South Asia," Washington, D.C.: Stimson and Carnegie Endowment for International Peace, November 13, 2012, p. 13.

[40] Edward L. Warner III, "Nuclear Deterrence Force Still Essential," prepared statement for the Senate Armed Services Committee, March 31, 1998.

the complications to crisis management that nonunitary governments create did not end with the Cold War. In fact, Pakistan, arguably the state most likely to employ its nuclear arsenal, is plagued by a pathologically fragmented government with potentially catastrophic implications for any future Pakistani-Indian crisis.

To ignore the Cold War is to ignore virtually the only source of empirical evidence available for the practice of nuclear deterrence. And, for that reason, I believe Ted's considerable contribution to academic literature and discourse, much of it from Cold War, will be of enduring value.

References

Acton, James M., *Deterrence During Disarmament: Deep Nuclear Reductions and International Security*, Abingdon, U.K.: Routledge, 2011.

———, "Reclaiming Strategic Stability," in Elbridge A. Colby and Michael S. Gerson, eds., *Strategic Stability: Contending Interpretations*, Carlisle, Pa.: Strategic Studies Institute and U.S. Army War College Press, 2013a. As of January 10, 2014:
http://www.strategicstudiesinstitute.army.mil/pdffiles/PUB1144.pdf

———, *Silver Bullet? Asking the Right Questions About Conventional Prompt Global Strike*, Washington, D.C.: Carnegie Endowment for International Peace, 2013b. As of January 10, 2014:
http://carnegieendowment.org/files/cpgs.pdf

Allison, Graham T., *Essence of Decision: Explaining the Cuban Missile Crisis*, Boston: Little, Brown and Company, 1971.

Arbatov, Alexei, *Gambit or Endgame? The New State of Arms Control*, Washington, D.C.: Carnegie Endowment for International Peace, 2011. As of January 10, 2014:
http://carnegieendowment.org/files/gambit_endgame.pdf

Builder, Carl H., *Strategic Conflict Without Nuclear Weapons,* Santa Monica, Calif.: RAND Corporation, R-2980/FF-RC, 1983. As of January 10, 2014:
http://www.rand.org/pubs/reports/R2980.html

Cartwright, James, Richard Burt, Chuck Hagel, Thomas Pickering, Jack Sheehan, and Bruce Blair, "Modernizing U.S. Nuclear Strategy, Force Structure and Posture," Global Zero, May 2012. As of January 10, 2014:
http://www.globalzero.org/files/gz_us_nuclear_policy_commission_report.pdf

Choe Sang-Hun, "North Korea Cuts Off the Remaining Military Hot Lines with South Korea," *New York Times*, March 27, 2013. As of January 10, 2014:
http://www.nytimes.com/2013/03/28/world/asia/north-korea-shuts-last-remaining-hotline-to-south.html?_r=0

Colby, Elbridge A., and Michael S. Gerson, eds., *Strategic Stability: Contending Interpretations*, Carlisle, Pa.: Strategic Studies Institute and U.S. Army War College Press, 2013. As of January 10, 2014:
http://www.strategicstudiesinstitute.army.mil/pdffiles/PUB1144.pdf

Fravel, M. Taylor, and Evan S. Medeiros, "China's Search for Assured Retaliation: The Evolution of Chinese Nuclear Strategy and Force Structure," *International Security*, Vol. 23, No. 2, Fall 2010.

Gerson, Michael S., *The Sino-Soviet Border Conflict: Deterrence, Escalation, and the Threat of Nuclear War in 1969*, Alexandria, Va.: Center for Naval Analyses, 2010.

———, "No First Use: The Next Step for U.S. Nuclear Policy," *International Security*, Vol. 35, No. 2, Fall 2010.

Hearings before the Defense Policy Panel of the Committee on Armed Services of the U.S. House of Representatives on "The Grand Bargain—Should the West Bankroll Soviet Transformation to a Free Market Economy?," HASC No. 102-26, Washington, D.C., July 31, 1991.

Hines, John G., Ellis M. Mishulovich, and John F. Shull, *Soviet Intentions 1965–1985*, Vol. I: *An Analytical Comparison of U.S.-Soviet Assessments During the Cold War*, McLean, Va.: BDM Federal, 1995.

Lebow, Richard Ned, and Janice Gross Stein, *We All Lost the Cold War*, Princeton, N.J.: Princeton University Press, 1994.

Miasnikov, Eugene, "On the Relationship Between Nuclear and Conventional Strategic Arms in the New START Treaty," Center for Arms Control, Energy and Environmental Studies at Moscow Institute of Physics and Technology, September 10, 2010. As of January 10, 2014: http://www.armscontrol.ru/pubs/en/em091010.pdf

Morgan, Forrest E., *Deterrence and First-Strike Stability in Space: A Preliminary Assessment*, Santa Monica, Calif.: RAND Corporation, MG-916-AF, 2010. As of January 10, 2014: http://www.rand.org/pubs/monographs/MG916.html

National Research Council, *Making Sense of Ballistic Missile Defense: An Assessment of Concepts and Systems for U.S. Boost-Phase Missile Defense in Comparison to Other Alternatives*, Washington, D.C.: National Academies Press, 2012. As of January 10, 2014: http://www.nap.edu/catalog.php?record_id=13189

Obama, Barack, "Remarks by President Barack Obama," Prague, April 5, 2009. As of January 10, 2014: http://www.whitehouse.gov/the_press_office/Remarks-By-President-Barack-Obama-In-Prague-As-Delivered

Payne, Keith B., *The Fallacies of Cold War Deterrence and a New Direction*, Lexington, Ky.: University Press of Kentucky, 2001.

Perkovich, George, "The Non-Unitary Model and Deterrence Stability in South Asia," Washington, D.C.: Stimson and Carnegie Endowment for International Peace, November 13, 2012. As of January 10, 2014: http://carnegieendowment.org/files/George_Perkovich_-_The_Non_Unitary_Model_and_Deterrence_Stability_in_South_Asia.pdf

Pillsbury, Michael, "The Sixteen Fears: China's Strategic Psychology," *Survival*, Vol. 54, No. 5, October–November 2012.

Scheber, Thomas, "Strategic Stability: Time for a Reality Check," *International Journal*, Vol. 63, No. 4, Autumn 2008.

Sternstein, Aliya, "Officials Worry About Vulnerability of Global Nuclear Stockpile to Cyber Attack," Nextgov, website, March 13, 2013. As of January 10, 2014: http://www.nextgov.com/defense/2013/03/officials-worry-about-vulnerability-global-nuclear-stockpile-cyber-attack/61855/

Swaine, Michael D., "Sino-American Crisis Management and the U.S.-Japan Alliance," in Akikazu Hashimoto, Mike Mochizuki, and Kurayoshi Takara, eds., *The Japan-U.S. Alliance and China-Taiwan Relations: Implications for Okinawa*, Sigur Center for Asian Studies, 2008. As of February 6, 2014:
http://carnegieendowment.org/files/Swaine_Chapter.pdf

Swaine, Michael D., and Zhang Tuosheng, eds., with Danielle F. S. Cohen, *Managing Sino-American Crises: Case Studies and Analysis*, Washington, D.C.: Carnegie Endowment for International Peace, 2006.

U.S. Department of Defense, *Nuclear Posture Review Report*, April 2010. As of January 10, 2014:
http://www.defense.gov/npr/docs/2010%20nuclear%20posture%20review%20report.pdf

Vick, Alan J., Richard M. Moore, Bruce R. Pirnie, and John Stillion, *Aerospace Operations Against Elusive Ground Targets*, Santa Monica, Calif.: RAND Corporation, MR-1398-AF, 2001. As of January 10, 2014:
http://www.rand.org/pubs/monograph_reports/MR1398.html

Warner III, Edward L., "The Bureaucratic Politics of Weapons Procurement," in Michael MccGwire, Ken Booth, and John McDonnell, eds., *Soviet Naval Policy: Objectives and Constraints*, New York: Praeger, 1975.

———, *The Military in Contemporary Soviet Politics: An Institutional Analysis*, New York: Praeger, 1977.

———, "Nuclear Deterrence Force Still Essential," prepared statement for the Senate Armed Services Committee, March 31, 1998. As of January 10, 2014:
http://www.defense.gov/Speeches/Speech.aspx?SpeechID=683

Warner III, Edward L., Glenn A. Kent, and Randall J. DeValk, "Key Issues for the Strategic Offensive Force Reduction Portion of the Nuclear and Space Talks in Geneva," Santa Monica, Calif.: RAND Corporation, N-2348-1-AF, December 1985. As of January 10, 2014:
http://www.rand.org/pubs/notes/N2348-1.html

Yao Yunzhu, "China Will Not Change Its Nuclear Policy," China-U.S. Focus, website, April 22, 2013. As of January 10, 2014:
http://www.chinausfocus.com/peace-security/china-will-not-change-its-no-first-use-policy/

CHAPTER NINE

Strategic Stability Between the United States and Russia

Dean A. Wilkening

It was a warm sunny spring morning in Santa Monica, like every other day, when I glided into the parking lot at the RAND Corporation on my motorcycle. As I walked toward the main entrance, there stood Ted Warner, looking rather frantic, pacing up and down the sidewalk and looking into the distance in search of something. I had heard a lot about Ted and had seen him in action on more than one occasion holding forth on arms control with the former Soviet Union, but we didn't know each other well. "Where is that cab, he was supposed to be here half an hour ago! I just flew in from Seoul, came to RAND to pick up some briefing materials, and need to head back to the airport to catch a flight to Frankfurt in an hour!" Ted announced with more than a bit of irritation. A look of frustration darkened his face. Then he turned to me and asked if I had a car. "No," I replied "I just have my motorcycle." Ted grew dark again as he continued to contemplate his fate. "But I can give you a ride to the airport if you wish," I added. Ted looked up, his face brightening slightly. A faint look of mischief crossed his face. "But I have this luggage and briefing materials," he said. Ted had a large garment bag and a briefcase overflowing with papers. "That's OK," I said, "You can put the garment bag between us, hold your briefcase with one hand and the motorcycle with the other." Ted seemed to be studying the option for a moment, then realized he had no other choice. So, off we went, with me straddling the gas tank, the garment bag sandwiched between us, and Ted on the back with his briefcase resting on one leg while holding onto me with his free hand. We "white lined" the entire way, which is motorcycle talk for splitting lanes. Ted's knees came within a foot of cars to either side of us as I raced through traffic. I think the near misses distracted him from his concern about making his flight, at least for a few moments. Who knows, he may even have been enjoying himself back there. At any rate, we arrived at the Los Angeles Airport International Terminal in record time. Ted jumped off the bike, thanked me with a big grin on his face, and disappeared into the terminal. I later heard that he caught his flight, those being the days before Transportation Security Agency security checks. That was the first of what would become many beneficial and enjoyable collaborations with Ted since that memorable spring day.

While working at RAND in the 1980s and early 1990s, Ted Warner worked with David Ochmanek, Glenn Kent, and others on a range of issues involving strategic planning, arms control, and strategic stability—the situation in which both the United States and the Soviet Union maintained an assured nuclear retaliation capability against the other, this being the central goal of strategic arms control with the

Soviet Union at that time. Ted was committed to finding paths by which the United States and the Soviet Union, now Russia, could reduce tensions and improve security on both sides by engaging in strategic dialogue and formal arms control. This belief has animated Ted's work as long as I have known him. But his was not simply a belief in the virtues of arms control diplomacy. Ted had a keen sense of what was required on a military level to provide security for the United States, as well as a cautious optimism about the results that could be achieved through negotiations with Moscow.[1] So it was that Ted and I worked on nuclear targeting in the early 1990s at a time when Gen Lee Butler headed U.S. Strategic Command, examining the extent to which U.S. nuclear war plans would have to change if the overall numbers of nuclear weapons on both sides came down significantly—a question that remains relevant today as further cuts in U.S. and Russian nuclear arsenals are being contemplated. We also worked together on a "road map" for U.S. Air Force strategic nuclear force modernization in the early 1990s, with questions of the stability of the balance of offensive nuclear force postures always in the back of our minds.

Although Ted Warner worked mostly on offensive nuclear forces and their possible reduction for much of his career, he was no stranger to the argument that strategic ballistic missile defense also could have a significant impact on strategic stability—the central premise of the Anti-Ballistic Missile (ABM) Treaty signed between the United States and the Soviet Union in 1972.

Today, the issue of strategic stability between the United States and Russia has the same two facets: first, how to maintain a stable balance of offensive nuclear forces that guarantees mutual retaliatory deterrence as the number of nuclear weapons deployed by both sides is reduced and, second, the extent to which a limited U.S. homeland missile defense might upset this balance as force levels are reduced (Russia has yet to deploy a limited nationwide missile defense system, although it maintains a long-standing regional missile defense around Moscow). Put another way, under what circumstances could the U.S.-Russian nuclear balance of terror, often described as "mutual assured destruction," become delicate if strategic nuclear force levels are reduced and limited ballistic missile defenses are deployed?

Ted and I have examined this issue several times over the past three decades using drawdown curves—a graphical depiction of the nuclear balance popularized by Lt Gen (ret) Glenn Kent and used extensively by Ted Warner, myself, and others at RAND. It is this analytic technique, along with the conclusions regarding strategic stability under New Strategic Arms Reduction Treaty (New START) force levels, that I wish to present in this chapter.

---

[1]   See, for example, Glenn A. Kent, Randall J. DeValk, and Edward L. Warner III, *A New Approach to Arms Control*, Santa Monica, Calif.: RAND Corporation, R-3140-FF/RC, 1984, and Edward L. Warner, Glenn A. Kent, and Randall J. DeValk, "Key Issues for the Strategic Offensive Force Reduction Portion of the Nuclear and Space Talks in Geneva," Santa Monica, Calif.: RAND Corporation, N-2348-1-AF, 1985.

During the closing days of the Cold War, the United States had approximately 12,000 deployed strategic nuclear weapons in its arsenal, in addition to a large number of tactical or theater nuclear weapons. The Soviet Union had a comparable number of deployed strategic nuclear weapons. Today, this number has been reduced dramatically through a series of arms control treaties—START I, the Strategic Offensive Reductions Treaty (the Moscow Treaty), and New START. Under New START, signed in 2010, the number of U.S. and Russian deployed strategic nuclear warheads will be reduced by February 2018 to 1,550 accountable weapons mounted on no more than 700 strategic nuclear delivery systems. Originally, it was hoped that negotiations between Washington and Moscow on further reductions would get under way in the second term of the Obama administration, with the President stating in Berlin in June 2013 that reductions to a level of approximately 1,000 operational strategic warheads would be consistent with U.S. security interests—another step toward the President's goal of "the peace and security of a world without nuclear weapons." Whether Russia is prepared to agree to further nuclear force reductions is an open question because Moscow currently relies more heavily on the possible limited use of nuclear weapons to compensate for its relatively weak conventional military forces. Moreover, Russia has tied further progress on offensive force reductions to constraints, preferably legally binding, on U.S. missile defense deployments—a concern that Russia highlighted in the preamble to New START by noting the critical importance of "the interrelationship between strategic offensive arms and strategic defensive arms" and that "this interrelationship will become more important as strategic nuclear arms are reduced." In any event, with Russia's forcible annexation of Crimea in March 2014, the possibility of further nuclear arms control between the United States and Russia looks bleak indeed.

Nuclear deterrence, and hence strategic stability in the classic sense, rests on the mutual ability of opposing states to deliver a crushing nuclear retaliatory blow against an adversary even after absorbing a massive nuclear attack. As was pointed out by Albert Wohlstetter over 50 years ago in "The Delicate Balance of Terror,"[2] deterrence rests not on the mere existence of nuclear weapons in one's arsenal but rather on the ability to deliver nuclear weapons against the opponent's homeland after being attacked first. Therefore, deterrence and, hence, strategic stability require opposing sides each to maintain strategic offensive forces that can survive an opponent's counterforce first strike, operate reliably in the postattack environment, and penetrate any strategic air and missile defenses in sufficient quantity to threaten devastating consequences that outweigh any conceivable benefit of attacking first. If either side begins to doubt that it possesses such a "secure second strike" capability, the disadvantaged side may feel pressured to launch its vulnerable forces first during an intense crisis, especially if by attacking first it can gain a meaningful advantage in the ensuing conflict. But before such

---

2   Albert Wohlstetter, "The Delicate Balance of Terror," Santa Monica, Calif.: RAND Corporation, P-1472, November 6, 1958.

first-strike incentives develop, the disadvantaged side will be pressured to modernize its forces to reduce their vulnerability and thereby regain a secure second-strike capability, thus leading to the kinds of arms races witnessed between the United States and the former Soviet Union throughout much of the Cold War. Therefore, the question of maintaining strategic stability between Washington and Moscow can be reduced to whether or not the United States and Russia can maintain secure second-strike capabilities in the face of the other's offensive and defensive strategic force postures.

It may seem to some observers that concerns about the stability of the U.S.-Russian strategic nuclear balance are a relic of the Cold War and that such concerns today should be consigned to history books. However, smoldering Russian resentment over North Atlantic Treaty Organization (NATO) expansion and the dissolution of the Russian empire makes the possibility of conflict between NATO and Russia real in the eyes of some Russian officials and military planners, quite apart from the desire that this not occur. Thus, the United States and Russia could find themselves embroiled in a future crisis—not unlike the conflict that arose in 2008 between Russia and Georgia or that between Russia and Ukraine in 2014—in which the underlying nuclear balance between Russia and the United States might become relevant to the outcome of the crisis. Recognizing that nuclear weapons are less important today than they were during the Cold War does not mean they are irrelevant or that U.S. leaders should be indifferent to the stability of the U.S.-Russian nuclear balance if only because Russian leaders appear to be quite concerned about the continuing viability of their strategic nuclear deterrent in the face of highly capable U.S. strategic nuclear forces, long-range conventional precision strike capabilities, and expanding homeland missile defenses.

Quantifying Deterrence

The extent to which a country's retaliatory potential is secure can be quantified by determining the fraction of its strategic nuclear forces that would survive a counterforce attack, operate reliably, and penetrate any defenses that may oppose their delivery to the attacker's homeland. Arriving, as opposed to inventory, weapons deter.

This section examines the stability of the U.S.-Russian offensive nuclear balance, absent ballistic missile defenses, assuming these strategic arsenals are constrained by New START. Table 9.1 illustrates one possible New START force structure, equal to approximately 1,550 accountable weapons for each side. The U.S. force structure is assumed to consist of 420 single-warhead Minuteman III intercontinental ballistic missiles (ICBMs) deployed in silos; 12 Trident submarines deployed with 20 D-5 submarine-launched ballistic missiles (SLBMs), downloaded from eight to a mix load of four or five warheads each; and a bomber force with 60 nuclear-capable B-52H and B-2A heavy bombers carrying light loads, for a total of approximately 320 bomber

Table 9.1
Illustrative New START Forces

	Delivery Vehicles	Countable Warheads	Actual Warheads
U.S. forces			
Minuteman III ICBM	420	420	420
D-5 SLBM	12 x 20	1,040[a]	1,040
B-52 H	42	42	252
B-2A	18	18	72
Total U.S.	720	1,550	1,814
Russian forces			
SS-18 follow-on	10	100	100
SS-27 silo	90	270	270
SS-27 mobile	135	405	405
SS-N-23 (Delta IV)	3 x 16	192	192
R-30 Bulava (Dolgorukiy)	8 x 16	512	512
Bear H heavy bomber	50	50	300
Total Russian	461	1,529	1,779

[a] In this analysis, each D-5 SLBM is assumed to be loaded alternately with four or five warheads to maximize the operational force level under New START.

weapons (each bomber counts as only one accountable strategic warhead against the New START 1,550-warhead ceiling).

Greater uncertainty surrounds possible future Russian strategic force structures. For this analysis, we assume Russia deploys approximately 235 ICBMs, including a few new heavy ICBMs (i.e., an SS-18 follow-on) carrying ten warheads, and a three-warhead variant of the SS-27 deployed in fixed silo and mobile basing modes, for a total of 775 ICBM warheads. The Russian SLBM force is assumed to consist of 11 new Dolgorukiy and older Delta IV missile-carrying submarines deployed with 176 SLBMs carrying a total of 704 warheads, assuming four warheads per missile. The Russian bomber force is assumed to consist of 50 Bear H long-range bombers carrying light loads, for a total of approximately 300 bomber weapons.

Of the weapons in these inventories, only those not undergoing maintenance are available for retaliation (this analysis assumes that 10 percent of the strategic nuclear delivery systems are undergoing maintenance at any given time). Of the available forces, only those that survive the opponent's counterforce first strike, operate reliably, and penetrate the opponent's defenses contribute to deterrence.

Table 9.2 provides notional planning factors that capture these effects for U.S. and Russian strategic forces at different states of readiness. The fraction that survives

Table 9.2
Illustrative Planning Factors

System	Availability	Day-to-Day Alert Survival	Generated Alert Survival	Reliability	Penetration Probability
U.S. forces					
MMIII ICBM	0.90	0.2/1.0[a]	0.2/1.0	0.95	1.00
D-5 SLBM	0.90	0.67[b]	1.0	0.95	1.00
B-52H	0.90	0.0	1.0	0.95	0.80
B-2A	0.90	0.0	1.0	0.95	0.95
Russian forces					
SS-18 silo	0.90	0.2/1.0[a]	0.2/1.0	0.90	1.00
SS-27 silo	0.90	0.2/1.0[a]	0.2/1.0	0.90	1.00
SS-27 mobile	0.85	0.27/1.0[c]	1.0	0.90	1.00
SS-N-23	0.85	0.18/0.73[d]	1.0	0.90	1.00
SS-N-32	0.85	0.18/0.73[d]	1.0	0.90	1.00
Bear H	0.85	0.0	1.0	0.90	0.80

[a] Based on the assumption that one accurate U.S. or Russian warhead attacks each ICBM silo. For LUA scenarios, the survival probability is assumed to be 1.0 for systems that launch reliably.

[b] Based on the assumption that eight out of 12 U.S. missile-carrying submarines are at sea during peacetime.

[c] On day-to-day alert, four Russian mobile ICBM regiments are assumed to survive in the field yielding a day-to-day alert rate of 4/15 (0.27). If Russian mobile ICBMs remain in garrison, their survival probability is very low, unless they launch out from under the attack in which case their survival rate is assumed to be 1.0.

[d] On day-to-day alert, two Russian missile submarines are assumed to be at sea, for a survival rate of 2/11 (0.18). Six additional submarines are assumed to be on pier-side alert, yielding a day-to-day survival probability of 0.73 if these SLBMs launch out from under the attack.

an opponent's counterforce first strike is a function of the alert posture.[3] On day-to-day alert, all U.S. silo-based ICBMs are assumed to ride out the attack; eight out of 12 U.S. missile-carrying submarines (SSBNs) are assumed to be at sea; and none of the U.S. bomber force is assumed to be on strip alert, that is, with bombers fueled, loaded with nuclear weapons, and prepared to take off quickly to get out from under a missile attack in less than 15 minutes. On the Russian side, silo-based ICBMs are assumed to either ride out the attack or launch out from under it, depending on the scenario; four

---

[3]   This analysis assumes that a single nuclear weapon arriving on a bomber base, submarine base, or mobile ICBM garrison will destroy any delivery systems at that base. Once dispersed, these systems should survive because bombers can escape the blast zone around their base if they take off quickly on warning; submarines at sea are difficult to find and, hence, to destroy; and mobile ICBMs are difficult to locate and attack once deployed out of garrison. Only ICBMs in silos remain fixed, although they are hardened. For this analysis, we assumed silo-based ICBMs on both sides survive attack with a probability of 0.2 unless they are launched before the incoming attack arrives.

mobile ICBM regiments with nine mobile ICBMs each are assumed to be out of garrison; two SSBNs are assumed to be at sea; and none of the bombers are assumed to be on alert. ICBMs in silos are vulnerable unless they launch before the attack arrives. Table 9.2 lists notional penetration probabilities for airborne systems. The penetration probability for ballistic missile reentry vehicles (RVs) is calculated separately in the analysis below. The reliability for all U.S. strategic delivery systems (0.95) is assumed to be somewhat higher than for Russian systems (0.90) because, historically, this has been the case. Finally, both U.S. and Russian strategic command and control systems are assumed to survive well enough to make retaliation highly likely, an assumption that could be changed if one is interested in truly worst-case scenarios.

A common tactic to ensure that vulnerable strategic missiles (i.e., ICBMs in silos, mobile ICBMs in garrison, and SLBMs on submarines in port) survive is to launch these forces prior to the arrival of the incoming attack, based on tactical warning. Launch under attack (LUA), as this tactic is known, improves the survival of vulnerable forces but introduces the worrisome prospect of an accidental or unauthorized missile launch because these systems are on hair-trigger alert. On generated alert, LUA options are more plausible because the ballistic missile warning system and nuclear command and control system are on a heightened state of alert, thus making LUA decisions by the National Command Authorities increasingly plausible. Table 9.2 provides alternate survival rates if one assumes LUA tactics are employed.

Multiplying these factors together for each delivery system and summing over the entire force structure gives the expected number of arriving or "effective" weapons for a given alert posture. The number of targets that can be destroyed for a given number of effective weapons depends on how the attack is allocated. This analysis does not examine targeting issues, i.e., the extent to which a given target set can be destroyed. Rather, it stops at calculating the number of effective weapons that are successfully delivered against the adversary's homeland, thus providing a more straightforward characterization of each side's secure second-strike capability.

Mutual Deterrence Without Ballistic Missile Defense

The extent to which the United States and Russia can maintain a secure second-strike capability for deterrence can be viewed pictorially by means of a drawdown curve. This graphic is used here to illustrate the stability of the U.S.-Russian nuclear balance with strategic offensive forces constrained by New START. Drawdown curves are simply plots of the number of weapons remaining on both sides after one side initiates a counterforce first strike against the opponent's strategic nuclear forces. Besides providing a convenient pictorial representation of the U.S.-Russian strategic nuclear balance before and following counterforce attacks, they also can be used to illustrate many of the strategic arguments that influenced nuclear debates during the Cold War.

Drawdown curves are also useful for analyzing many contemporary issues, as will be illustrated when we examine the impact of limited homeland missile defenses on deterrence. Again, the important point to note is the extent to which the defender's retaliatory strike is "secure," that is, survivable in the face of an adversary's attack. Drawdown curves capture the quantifiable dimensions of deterrence, leaving the reader to judge for himself whether deterrence remains robust or whether the balance of terror is delicate in a given scenario.

To introduce the concept of a drawdown curve, Figure 9.1 illustrates the number of surviving and effective (i.e., deliverable) U.S. strategic nuclear weapons after a hypothetical Russian counterforce first strike, assuming New START–constrained forces under day-to-day alert conditions. The initial point on the drawdown curve, in the upper right-hand corner, represents the total U.S. and Russian arsenals, measured in terms of the number of effective weapons (weapons that would actually detonate on the opponent's homeland), before the attack begins. The slope of the curve at any point determines the counterforce exchange ratio, i.e., the ratio of U.S. effective warheads destroyed to Russian effective warheads consumed at this point in the attack. Hence, the slope indicates the relative attractiveness of this particular portion of the counterforce attack. The curve is plotted so that the most lucrative counterforce targets—heavy bombers off alert and SSBNs in port—are attacked first, with the least attractive

Figure 9.1
Russian Counterforce First Strike on U.S. Strategic Forces (day-to-day posture)

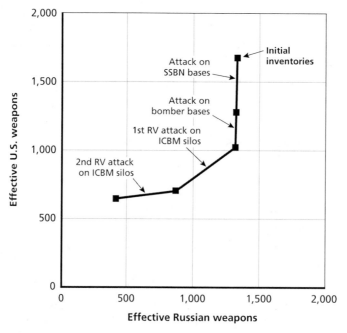

targets, silo-based ICBMs, last. SSBNs at sea and mobile ICBMs deployed in the field are assumed, in this analysis, to be invulnerable.

Initially, the drawdown curve is nearly vertical because a Russian attack against U.S. SSBN bases (two are assumed in this analysis) and bomber bases (three are assumed under day-to-day conditions) destroys a large number of U.S. weapons off alert (i.e., U.S. SSBNs in port and nonalert bombers on the ground) with the expenditure of very few Russian weapons (two weapons are allocated to each base for confident destruction). Hence, by attacking a total of five targets with approximately ten weapons, Russia can destroy a large fraction of the U.S. strategic nuclear arsenal under day-to-day alert conditions. After this, U.S. single-warhead ICBM silos would be attacked, where the drawdown curve is broken into two segments, the first portion illustrating the effectiveness of a single Russian weapon targeted at each silo and the next segment where a second warhead is allocated to each silo. If one assumes the objective in launching this hypothetical attack is to limit damage to the Russian homeland from the presumed U.S. retaliation, Russia might allocate two weapons to each U.S. Minuteman III silo, even though the exchange ratio is not very favorable for Russia. Notwithstanding the traditional argument that single-warhead ICBMs in silos are stabilizing, this does not mean that they will not be attacked in a nuclear exchange. The benefits in terms of reducing the size of the expected retaliation are illustrated here. After an attack on U.S. Minuteman silos, no attractive counterforce targets remain. The stopping point illustrates the size of the surviving U.S. and remaining Russian arsenals, measured in terms of effective weapons.

Whether or not Russia can limit damage to a significant degree by striking first in this scenario is determined easily by noting how close the drawdown curve comes to the x-axis in Figure 9.1. Approximately 650 U.S. effective weapons survive a maximal Russian counterforce attack under day-to-day alert conditions. Therefore, Russia cannot limit damage to its homeland in any meaningful sense even after taking into account weapon system reliability and bomber weapon penetration probabilities through air defenses (assuming the notional values used in this analysis are representative). In fact, by attacking Minuteman silos with a second warhead each, Russia ends up with fewer remaining effective weapons than the United States does, which suggests that this portion of the Russian counterforce attack might not occur, although attacking each single-warhead U.S. ICBM with a single Russian warhead seems likely.[4]

Figure 9.2 repeats the Russian drawdown curve for day-to-day alert and adds a drawdown curve for generated alert, as well as one if the United States chooses to launch its vulnerable ICBMs out from under the attack on generated alert. On generated alert, approximately 1,200 effective weapons would survive. Hence, the U.S.

---

[4]   During the Cold War, some analysts argued that the ratio of surviving forces at any given point along the drawdown curve was important because this was an indication of the coercive potential of the remaining arsenals at that point. Thus, it was argued, counterforce attacks might proceed so long as the resulting point on the drawdown curve was below (or above) a 45-degree line drawn from the origin.

Figure 9.2
Russian Counterforce First-Strike Scenarios Against Varying U.S. Strategic Force Postures

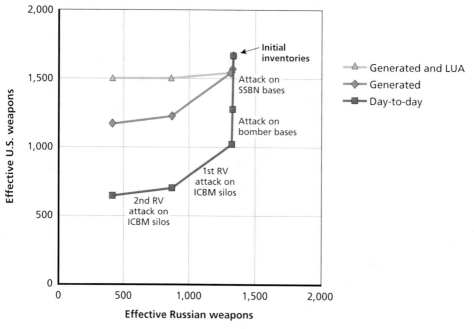

retaliatory potential is very robust, even without having to launch vulnerable ICBMs out from under the attack. LUA options would increase the U.S. retaliatory potential by about 300 effective weapons, to a total of approximately 1,500 effective weapons. Hence, the U.S. deterrent appears to be very robust under all three scenarios.

The Russian Strategic Nuclear Deterrent

Turning to the effectiveness of the Russian strategic deterrent, particularly as it might appear to Russian political and military leaders, Figure 9.3 illustrates U.S. counterforce attack options against Russian New START–constrained forces. Again, the inventory point in the upper right-hand corner represents the total U.S. and Russian arsenals prior to any attack (measured in effective weapons). The most lucrative U.S. attacks are directed against Russian SSBN bases (two are assumed here) and Russian bomber bases (two are assumed under day-to-day alert conditions and four when Russian strategic forces are on generated alert). The next most attractive options are attacks on mobile ICBM garrisons, 15 of which are assumed in this analysis, followed by single-warhead attacks against Russian ICBM silos, the most attractive of which are occupied by the presumed new heavy multiple independently targeted reentry vehicle (MIRV)–

Figure 9.3
U.S. Counterforce First Strike Against Varying Russian Strategic Force Postures

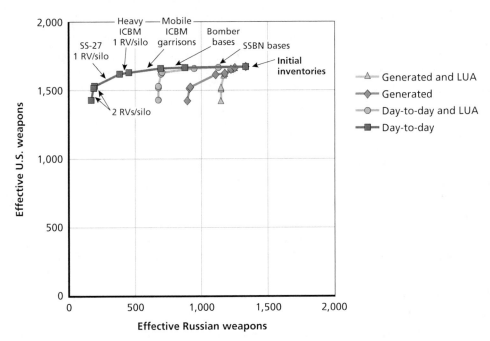

RAND *CP765-9.3*

equipped ICBM that Russian leaders have said they may deploy in the future, followed by attacks using one U.S. warhead against each of the silo-based MIRVed SS-27s. The United States might allocate a second warhead to each Russian ICBM silo, as illustrated in Figure 9.3. After this, no attractive counterforce options remain. Hence, the likely stopping point for a U.S. counterforce first strike would be after one or two missile warheads had been allocated against each Russian ICBM silo.

Several interesting points emerge from Figure 9.3. First, a U.S. counterforce first strike against the most attractive Russian counterforce targets requires only about 240 weapons, fewer than for a Russian counterforce attack against the United States because Russia is assumed to deploy MIRVed ICBMs in a relatively small number of silos. Second, under day-to-day alert conditions, without assuming a LUA scenario, only approximately 170 Russian effective weapons would survive and arrive on the U.S. homeland in the absence of a U.S. homeland ballistic missile defense. This is far smaller than the Russian surviving arsenal during the Cold War and is less than the U.S. day-to-day alert retaliatory potential under New START limits illustrated in Figure 9.2 because of Russia's presumed low day-to-day alert rate, i.e., the relatively small number of SSBNs at sea and mobile ICBMs deployed in the field. Whether 170 effective weapons are sufficient for deterrence in peacetime (i.e., on day-to-day alert) only Russian leaders can determine. But this relatively small surviving arsenal does illustrate why some Russian leaders talk about LUA options on day-to-day alert because launching vulnerable silo-based ICBMs, mobile ICBMs in garrison, and some fraction of their SLBMs in port prior to the incoming attack significantly increases the size of the Russian effective retaliation (fourfold, in this analysis, to approximately 675 effective weapons, as illustrated in Figure 9.3). Hence, to Russian leaders, LUA, a tactic long embraced in Soviet, and now Russian, military writings, is likely to appear as an inexpensive way to ensure an effective retaliatory force at low day-to-day alert levels, despite the risks associated with an accidental nuclear war. On generated alert, approximately 900 effective weapons would survive a U.S. attack. With LUA, this number increases to approximately 1,150 effective weapons. Hence, deterrence under these scenarios is quite robust.

If Russian leaders believed that the United States has an effective antisubmarine warfare capability that could threaten their SSBNs at sea or a capability to threaten their mobile ICBMs deployed in the field, they might become extremely concerned about the adequacy of their strategic nuclear retaliatory deterrent at low day-to-day alert levels, again prompting them to consider LUA to address such a perceived vulnerability. Possible attacks against Russian strategic nuclear command and control nodes, although not included in this analysis, would add to the Russian sense of vulnerability. Finally, one should recall that Russia may wish to withhold some weapons for a secure reserve force to deter other possible threats from China, France, and/or Great Britain. The strategic nuclear weapons available for retaliation against the United States are, therefore, necessarily less than the number of effective weapons illustrated in Figure 9.3 in any given scenario.

The Impact of a Limited U.S. Nationwide Ballistic Missile Defense

Interest in how ballistic missile defense has affected U.S.-Russian strategic stability had been put to rest in 1972 with the ABM Treaty but was reawakened with President Ronald Reagan's 1983 "Star Wars" speech, which posited the goal of a nationwide defense that could handle large Russian ballistic missile attacks. However, his successor, George H. W. Bush, recognized by the early 1990s that President Reagan's Star Wars vision was impractical. Instead, the Bush administration committed itself to developing and fielding a limited ballistic missile defense of the U.S. homeland against accidental or unauthorized launches from Russia or China and from small, deliberate third-country ballistic missile attacks, although this "GPALS" system still called for both space-based interceptors and several hundred ground-based interceptors (GBIs). In addition, the Bush administration planned to develop and field theater ballistic missile defenses to protect U.S. troops overseas, as well as U.S. friends and allies.

The Clinton administration further adjusted U.S. priorities for missile defense by placing greater emphasis on theater missile defense and committing to develop, but not necessarily deploy, a much more limited national missile defense. By the mid-1990s, plans for developing space-based weapons for missile defense had all but disappeared. Development efforts focused instead on ground-based and sea-based interceptors for both regional and national missile defense utilizing "kill vehicles" designed to destroy their targets by the kinetic energy of impact from a direct collision.

In 2002, President George W. Bush reemphasized homeland defense, committing the United States to deploy a limited homeland defense by 2004, withdrawing from the ABM Treaty in the process. Today, the United States has deployed a limited, nationwide ballistic missile defense consisting of 30 GBIs, 26 of which are located at Fort Greely, Alaska, and four at Vandenberg Air Force Base, California, to be expanded to 44 GBIs by 2017 in response to North Korean nuclear weapon and ICBM development efforts, along with a series of political provocations in spring 2013.

The same drawdown curve methodology can be used to examine how thin ballistic missile defenses affect strategic stability. Until now, the only defenses included in this analysis were U.S. and Russian strategic air defenses, captured by the aircraft penetration rates given in Table 9.2 (air-delivered weapons cannot be used in counterforce attacks because they are slow). This section focuses only on the effects of a U.S. nationwide ballistic missile defense because only the United States is currently pursuing such a defense. The effects of Russia's antiballistic missile defense system have not been included because it protects only the region around Moscow. For the purpose of this analysis, we examine a U.S. homeland missile defense consisting of 100 GBIs, even though current plans call for only 44 GBIs by 2017.

Calculating the effects of a nationwide U.S. ballistic missile defense is complicated by the fact that one must decide how the defense operates in light of the structure of the adversary attack. For example, if Russia launches its retaliatory strike in multiple waves, the first wave presumably would be used to saturate the defense, with subsequent waves getting a free ride because a limited U.S. homeland missile defense would be exhausted. The defense may act to defend certain targets preferentially, i.e., defending some high-value assets more heavily, while leaving others undefended, which complicates Russian attack planning, or may simply subtract a limited number of Russian warheads randomly from a large attack. For this analysis, I assume that Russian surviving ICBMs and SLBMs are launched in one large wave and that the U.S. missile defense protects SSBN and bomber bases preferentially but otherwise simply subtracts warheads randomly from the incoming attack until the defense runs out of interceptors. Each GBI is assumed to have an 80-percent chance of shooting down a Russian warhead—an assumption that will appear to some as rather optimistic in light of recent GBI test failures. I ignore Russia's highly sophisticated ballistic missile defense countermeasures, an assumption that greatly exaggerates the effectiveness of the U.S. defense, to illustrate worst-case Russian thinking, whether this is valid or not. Hence, this analysis tries to capture Russian worst-case fears about how a limited (100 interceptor) U.S. homeland missile defense system will affect Russia's strategic nuclear deterrent.

U.S. missile defense affects the previous analysis of U.S. and Russian strategic missile exchanges in two ways. First, it interferes with a Russian counterforce first strike and, second, it interferes with a Russian retaliatory strike in scenarios in which the United States strikes first. The latter is the principal Russian concern. The first effect is illustrated in Figure 9.4. Comparing this figure with Figure 9.2 reveals that the U.S. missile defense compels Russia to expend approximately ten times more warheads (although this is still a relatively small number) to attack SSBNs in port and bombers at their bases, under the assumption that these bases would be highly defended and that Russian planners want at least one warhead to land on each base. The attack against ICBM silos is also less effective because the arrival probability for Russian warheads targeted at Minuteman silos is reduced by the remaining GBIs. The net effect is that a few more U.S. effective weapons survive (655 in this analysis) in the defended case than in the undefended case (648), but it takes a Russian attack with approximately 70 more weapons to ensure this effect. Hence, fewer Russian effective weapons remain after their counterforce attack (approximately 350 compared to 420 in the absence of a 100 GBI defense). Again, these numbers are illustrative because the attack has not been optimized to penetrate the defense.

The second and far more important impact of a U.S. homeland missile defense is to negate a certain number of Russian retaliatory weapons if the United States attacks

Figure 9.4
Russian Counterforce First-Strike Scenarios Against Varying U.S. Strategic Offensive Force Postures with a Limited U.S. Homeland Missile Defense

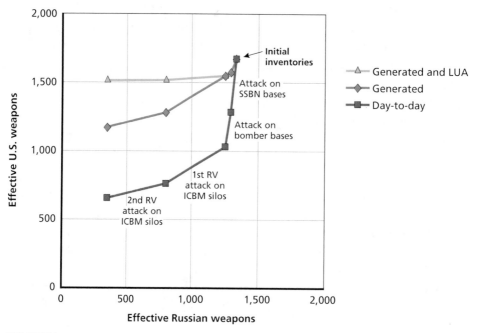

first, assumed here to be a subtraction of 80 warheads, i.e., 100 warheads each engaged with a single GBI, leaving only 20 of these warheads unscathed to give the assumed 0.80 single-shot kill probability for a GBI. If the surviving Russian strategic nuclear arsenal is already relatively small, limited U.S. missile defenses may be able to significantly limit damage from the Russian retaliation. This second effect for the day-to-day posture case is illustrated in Figure 9.5 where, by assumption, Russia has no defense to protect its nuclear forces, so the U.S. drawdown curve is identical to that in Figure 9.3. However, the U.S. missile defense subtracts 80 weapons from the size of the Russian retaliation (since, by assumption, no bomber weapons survive on day-to-day alert). Therefore, the drawdown curve moves closer to the y-axis in the effective weapon domain.

With 100 GBIs, the hypothetical Russian retaliation now consists of only approximately 90 ballistic missile warheads. That is, of the 170 effective weapons illustrated in Figure 9.3, only 90 would be expected to get through a 100-interceptor U.S. homeland missile defense. If the United States deployed 200 GBIs and if Russian countermeasures are assumed to be completely ineffective, which is not likely to be the case, the Russian secure second strike under day-to-day alert conditions would largely vanish—a scenario that would greatly concern Russian political and military leaders. It is important to note, however, that this vulnerability is due far more to the low alert

Figure 9.5
U.S. Counterforce First-Strike Scenarios Against Varying Russian Strategic Postures and Response Options with a Limited U.S. Homeland Missile Defense

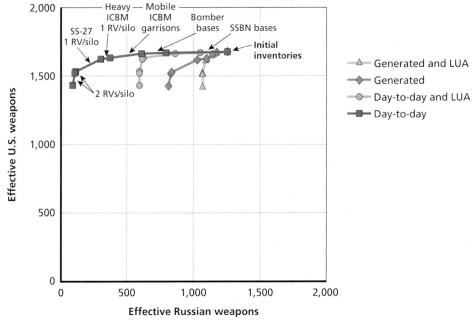

rate assumed for Russian forces under routine peacetime day-to-day alert conditions than to the effectiveness of a U.S. limited homeland missile defense. If Russia chooses to launch its vulnerable ballistic missiles out from under a U.S. counterforce attack on day-to-day alert, the size of the Russian secure second strike increases from 90 to almost 600 effective weapons. Hence, some Russian leaders and planners might favor this approach as a necessary counter to U.S. missile defenses, despite concerns about accidental or unauthorized Russian missile launches (which are used sometimes to justify U.S. missile defense deployments).

Generating Russian forces without opting for LUA increases the retaliatory potential to approximately 810 effective weapons after taking U.S. homeland missile defense into account. Therefore, if one believes that U.S. and Russian forces will be fully generated in an intense crisis, deterrence appears to be quite robust, even in the presence of a limited U.S. nationwide ballistic missile defense. However, the transition from peacetime to generated alert postures might be problematic during a crisis if rapid Russian force generation is interpreted by the United States as a prelude to a Russian first strike and not as a defensive measure taken to ensure the robustness of the Russian deterrent. This "mobilization instability" may become the principal threat to strategic stability if the United States continues to deploy a limited homeland ballistic missile defense and if Russia maintains low day-to-day alert levels. This is so because potential misperceptions of Russia's intent when it begins to generate its strategic nuclear forces may make future crises more difficult to control.

Obviously, U.S. leaders are less concerned about the retaliatory effectiveness of Russia's deterrent force than about that of the United States. However, this perspective ignores the strategic interaction between these two nuclear powers. Undermining Russia's deterrent would adversely affect political relations between the two countries, might stimulate another arms race as Russia attempts to shore up its strategic deterrent, and might create mobilization instabilities if Russia continues to maintain a low peacetime alert posture. If Russian leaders opt for the less-expensive option of preparing to launch a large fraction of their vulnerable missiles out from under a U.S. first strike upon warning that such an attack is under way, the United States (and Russia) will have to live with the risks this tactic entails.

Of course, the Russian strategic vulnerability illustrated here can easily be avoided if Russia deploys highly effective ballistic missile defense countermeasures to help overwhelm a limited U.S. defense and/or keeps a higher fraction of its strategic nuclear forces on alert in peacetime. This would entail additional expense, but with matters this grave, the money would be well spent—unless, of course, Russian leaders believe that the prospect of conflict with the United States is truly remote, in which case they should not be so concerned about the effectiveness of a limited U.S. homeland missile defense in the first place. Alternately, Russian leaders could try to generate political pressure to limit the size of any U.S. homeland defense. Currently, this appears to be their preferred approach.

A similar drawdown analysis can be carried out for any hypothetical U.S. or Russian strategic nuclear force posture but, in particular, for force levels as they are reduced along the path to eliminating all nuclear weapons. In general, such drawdown curves will look very similar to the ones presented here, but with the axes scaled proportionately to the total size of each country's arsenal, assuming the fraction of each side's forces on alert remains approximately the same. Consequently, one can conclude that, if offensive forces are reduced gradually on the path to zero, even the most limited homeland missile defense will, at some point, undermine strategic stability. Therefore, if zero is the ultimate goal and if limited defenses exist, offensive force reductions must, at some point, halt until agreement is reached to rapidly eliminate them altogether, thereby passing through the point of greatest instability quickly and moving into a regime of "defense dominance," i.e., a strategic relationship in which operational nuclear arsenals no longer exist and in which air and ballistic missile defenses provide insurance against cheating and nuclear breakout.[5]

Concluding Observations

The United States and Russia cannot arbitrarily reduce the sizes of their strategic nuclear arsenals, reduce the day-to-day alert rates associated with these forces in peacetime, and deploy limited nationwide ballistic missile defenses without running a serious risk of undermining mutual deterrence between the United States and Russia.

Nationwide ballistic missile defense, even one of relatively limited size, has two different effects on strategic stability between the United States and Russia. First, such a defense can strengthen deterrence by complicating Russia's counterforce first strikes and denying Russian limited attack options (to the extent they are part of Russian war plans). Second, they can weaken Russia's nuclear deterrent by reducing the size of its secure second strike. This second effect is the principal concern that Russian officials have cited repeatedly regarding a limited U.S. homeland ballistic missile defense. Under New START strategic offensive force levels, relatively low levels of U.S. nationwide missile defense could potentially undermine deterrence if Russia continues to maintain low peacetime alert rates for its forces and if its sophisticated missile defense countermeasures prove ineffective. Russia has three options for redressing this potential vulnerability—preparing to launch vulnerable missiles out from under an incoming missile attack, maintaining a higher fraction of its vulnerable missile forces in a more survivable mode by putting more SSBNs at sea and deploying more mobile ICBMs in the field during peacetime, and increasing the effectiveness of its missile defense countermeasures. The United States clearly prefers that Russia change its peacetime day-to-

---

5   See Dean Wilkening, "Nuclear Zero and Ballistic Missile Defense," *Survival: Global Politics and Strategy*, Vol. 52, No. 6, December 2010.

day alert posture and/or improve its missile defense countermeasures but would not like to see Russians increase their reliance on LUA because of the dangers associated with such a policy. The Russians have indicated that they would like the United States to agree to strict limits, preferably legally binding, on the size and character of the U.S. homeland missile defense to avoid this problem in the first place.

With no resolution of these differing preferences and perspectives in sight, the instability that could develop as both the United States and Russia reduce their strategic nuclear forces, with low peacetime alert rates for the Russian strategic force, is "mobilization instability." This would occur if Russia feels pressure to generate its strategic forces quickly during a crisis to strengthen its deterrent posture while the United States misperceives this action as an offensive rather than defensive move, thus making future crises more difficult to control. If Russian leaders rely instead on LUA options to redress perceived Russian vulnerabilities, accidental or unauthorized nuclear attacks become more likely—an unattractive prospect for both countries.

Regardless of where one comes out on this debate, the tools that Ted Warner and others helped develop and popularize to assess the stability of the strategic nuclear balance during the Cold War remain very relevant today.

References

Kent, Glenn A., Randall J. DeValk, and Edward L. Warner, *A New Approach to Arms Control*, Santa Monica, Calif.: RAND Corporation, R-3140-FF/RC, 1984. As of January 10, 2014: http://www.rand.org/pubs/reports/R3140.html

Warner, Edward L., Glenn A. Kent, and Randall J. DeValk, "Key Issues for the Strategic Offensive Force Reduction Portion of the Nuclear and Space Talks in Geneva," Santa Monica, Calif.: RAND Corporation, N-2348-1-AF, 1985. As of January 10, 2014: http://www.rand.org/pubs/notes/N2348-1.html

Wilkening, Dean, "Nuclear Zero and Ballistic Missile Defense," *Survival: Global Politics and Strategy*, Vol. 52, No. 6, December 2010.

Wohlstetter, Albert, "The Delicate Balance of Terror," Santa Monica, Calif.: RAND Corporation, P-1472, November 6, 1958. As of January 22, 2014: http://www.rand.org/about/history/wohlstetter/P1472/P1472.html

CHAPTER TEN

The Need for Limited Nuclear Options

Elbridge A. Colby

I first met Ted Warner in the spring of 2009. I was about to graduate from Yale Law School and had been awarded a fellowship to work for a year in the government on nuclear policy issues. Ted had been tapped by Secretary of Defense Robert Gates to lead the department's team for the follow-on to the expiring Strategic Arms Reduction Treaty (START). David Ochmanek, whom I'd known from my adjunct work at RAND, recommended I talk to Ted, and he gave me a spot on the team.

For the next year, I worked closely with Ted, first on the delegation to the treaty negotiations in Geneva and then on the effort to gain Senate advice and consent to ratification. During this period, I learned a tremendous amount from Ted—about nuclear and conventional forces policy, Cold War strategy, Russia, the Department of Defense, and beyond. Following the end of my fellowship, I left the Pentagon but kept in close touch with Ted and continued to benefit from his sage advice and comments on my work as well as from his generous mentorship.

❧

What should the long-term policy of the United States be regarding the role and guidelines for the potential employment of its nuclear weapons? Whatever one thinks of the merits of the project to abolish nuclear weapons, we find ourselves still very far from the realization of its goal, despite the endeavor's recent rise to the top of the international security agenda and its embrace by large numbers of distinguished political and military figures. Given that the reasons that have impelled almost a dozen nation-states to obtain and maintain nuclear weapons remain potent today, it seems clear that nuclear weapons will remain an important part of the international security landscape for as far into the future as the eye can see. It is therefore important for the United States to prepare its nuclear policy and forces for the long haul.

On what lasting conceptual foundations, then, should the United States form its nuclear force structure and posture, decide about the appropriate criteria for using or threatening to use its nuclear weapons, and determine what measures it is prepared to undertake in terms of the restraint and control of these arms? Which attributes of U.S. nuclear capability should be privileged and which disfavored? Which strategic, military, and political ends should U.S. nuclear policy seek to serve? And how should the current U.S. nuclear policy, forces, and day-to-day posture differ from the nuclear policy and posture inherited from the closing years of the Cold War?

The short answer is that the long-term U.S. nuclear policy, force, and posture should not differ substantially in their basic form from those that exist today. The nuclear arsenal and the policies that governed its possible use that emerged from the Cold War and that have come down to us today, albeit with a smaller arsenal and with somewhat more-restrictive guidelines for use, reflect the astute and sensible perception that the U.S. nuclear force should combine the ability to wreak devastating damage on an opponent with efforts to minimize the degree to which that very capability spurs or exacerbates tensions. The goal is thus both effective deterrence and a high degree of stability. Like this force, then, a long-term U.S. nuclear policy for the 21st century should ensure that the U.S. nuclear deterrent can deter aggression against vital U.S. and allied interests, is sized and shaped according to what is needed to deter (and, to a lesser but important degree, to what is needed to assure allies and partners), ensures that the United States maintains a devastating second-strike capability even under the most stressing conditions, provides for technical redundancy and a reserve capacity should geopolitical conditions deteriorate or the worst-case scenario come to pass, and minimizes its own destabilizing aspects.[1] Needless to say, any of these objectives might be more perfectly achieved than they have been in the past, but these are well established and relatively uncontroversial principles to guide U.S. nuclear policy and the posturing and development of the force.[2]

But in other respects, the U.S. nuclear force that emerged from the final years of the Cold War—and thus, to a considerable degree, the nuclear force that exists today in much the same basic form, albeit in significantly smaller numbers—is not well suited to the emerging international security environment. The late Cold War U.S. nuclear force was a product of the fear of titanic global nuclear war with the Soviet Union and the consequent overriding concern with deterring that eventuality by being able to deliver a massive, devastating retaliatory blow against the Soviet Union under any conceivable circumstances. Concerns for the survivability of U.S. strategic nuclear forces in the face of a possible counterforce attack, for the ability to penetrate enemy strategic air and missile defenses, and for other attributes connected to that cornerstone ability of being able to unleash an annihilating counterblow therefore overrode interests in developing a nuclear force capable of more-limited, tailored application. Recognition of the importance of and thus interest in controlling escalation and consequently in creating a force capable of more-discriminating employment grew sub-

---

[1] For the author's views on the overall principles that should guide the U.S. nuclear force, see Elbridge A. Colby, "Guiding Principles for the New Nuclear Guidance," *New Paradigms Forum*, April 11, 2011.

[2] See, for instance, U.S. Department of Defense, *Nuclear Posture Review Report*, Washington, D.C.: U.S. Government Printing Office, 2010, especially pp. 19–30, and U.S. Department of Defense, "Report on Nuclear Employment Strategy of the United States Specified in Section 491 of 10 U.S.C.," June 12, 2013.

stantially over the course of the Cold War, especially once the Soviets began to field a large and survivable strategic force of their own. The U.S. nuclear force that existed by the end of the Cold War, however, still reflected the overwhelming priority of ensuring the ability to deliver a massive, devastating blow.[3] Capabilities for control of escalation in a nuclear conflict were recognized and acknowledged but only unevenly and imperfectly realized in practice.[4] Because today's U.S. nuclear policy and force structure are essentially modestly revised and smaller versions of those of the late Cold War, they too remain suited far less for discrimination and control than for carrying out devastating nuclear retaliation.

---

[3]   Interest in greater flexibility began tentatively under the Eisenhower administration, peaked in the early Kennedy administration, and then came to fruition in the Nixon, Ford, Carter, and Reagan administrations. For a historical treatment, see Elbridge A. Colby, "The United States and Discriminate Nuclear Options in the Cold War," in J. Larsen and K. Kartchner, eds., *Limited Nuclear War*, Palo Alto, Calif.: Stanford University Press, 2014. See also Terry Terriff, *The Nixon Administration and the Making of U.S. Nuclear Strategy*, Ithaca, N.Y.: Cornell University Press, 1995; Scott Sagan, *Moving Targets: Nuclear Strategy and National Security*, Princeton, N.J.: Princeton University Press, 1989; and Janne E. Nolan, *Guardians of the Arsenal: The Politics of Nuclear Strategy*, New York, Basic Books, 1989. For contemporary official treatments of the problem, see National Security Study Memorandum 169, "U.S. Nuclear Policy," February 13, 1973; National Security Study Memorandum 169 Summary Report, June 8, 1973; National Security Decision Memorandum 242, "Policy for Planning the Employment of Nuclear Weapons," January 17, 1974; Major General John A. Wickham, Jr., memorandum to Major General Brent Scowcroft, "Policy Guidance for the Employment of Nuclear Weapons [NUWEP]," April 3, 1974; Secretary of Defense James R. Schlesinger, *Annual Defense Department Report for FY1975*, Washington, D.C.: U.S. Government Printing Office, 1974; "Nuclear Targeting Policy Review," November 1978; Presidential Directive 59, "Nuclear Weapons Employment Policy," July 25, 1980; U.S. Department of Defense, "Policy Guidance for the Employment of Nuclear Weapons (NUWEP)," October 1980; Secretary of Defense Harold Brown, remarks delivered at the Convocation Ceremonies for the Naval War College, Newport, Rhode Island, August 20, 1980, in Philip Bobbitt, Lawrence Freedman, and Gregory F. Treverton, eds., *U.S. Nuclear Strategy: A Reader*, New York: New York University Press, 1989; Secretary of Defense Harold Brown, *Department of Defense Annual Report for FY1981*, Washington, D.C.: U.S. Government Printing Office, 1980; Walter B. Slocombe, "The Countervailing Strategy," *International Security*, Vol. 5, No. 4, Spring 1981; and Caspar W. Weinberger, "U.S. Defense Strategy," *Foreign Affairs*, Spring 1986. For influential nongovernmental works from the time, see, for instance, Desmond Ball, *Déjà Vu: The Return to Counterforce in the Nixon Administration*, California Seminar on Arms Control and Foreign Policy, 1974; Lynn Davis, *Limited Nuclear Options: Deterrence and the New American Doctrine*, Adelphi Paper 121, 1976; Benjamin S. Lambeth, *Selective Nuclear Options in American and Soviet Strategic Policy*, Santa Monica, Calif.: RAND Corporation, R-2043-DDRE, 1976; Sidney Drell and Frank von Hippel, "Limited Nuclear War," *Scientific American*, November 1976; Desmond Ball, *Can Nuclear War Be Controlled?* Adelphi Paper 169, 1981; Colin Gray, "Nuclear Strategy: The Case for a Theory of Victory," *International Security*, 1979; and Michael Howard, "On Fighting a Nuclear War," *International Security*, Spring 1981. The Soviets were also interested in developing capabilities. See, for instance, Edward L. Warner, *Soviet Concepts and Capabilities for Limited Nuclear War: What We Know and How We Know It*, Santa Monica, Calif.: RAND Corporation, N-2769-AF, 1989.

[4]   Attempts to integrate greater discrimination and flexibility into U.S. nuclear war plans and the U.S. nuclear posture were retarded and hobbled by bureaucratic inertia; changes in leadership; concerns about the potential for such changes to have destabilizing implications; and, perhaps above all, by the formidable technical, organizational, and other difficulties of building and planning for a realistic limited nuclear warfare capability. For a discussion of this problem, see Colby, 2014. See also William E. Odom, "The Origins and Design of Presidential Decision-59: A Memoir," in Henry D. Sokolski, ed., *Getting MAD: Nuclear Mutual Assured Destruction, Its Origins and Practice*, Carlisle, Pa.: Strategic Studies Institute, 2004.

This is a problem, given the nature of the emerging international security environment to which U.S. nuclear policy should be adapted. The threat of a massive nuclear attack on the United States remains a possibility and, thus, so too does the threat of such a large-scale strike being used for coercive purposes. The likelihoods of both, however, are dramatically lower than their Cold War heights. Russia remains the only country with a nuclear arsenal comparable in size and sophistication to that of the United States, yet Moscow's strategic nuclear force today is both far smaller and more perceptibly oriented to retaliation than it was during the Cold War. While conflict between the United States and Russia remains plausible, the likelihood of war between the two countries is much lower, and the chances that a war would escalate to apocalyptic levels are far more modest as well. Meanwhile, China, probably the most serious military-strategic challenge for the United States in the coming decades, appears, at least for the present, to be eschewing the buildup of a nuclear force on par with those of the two Cold War superpowers. Beijing is focusing instead on the development and deployment of high-end conventional capabilities designed to blunt U.S. power projection in East Asia and of a medium-sized, modern, and sophisticated strategic nuclear force able to provide a reliable but relatively modest second-strike capability in the event of an attempted U.S. disarming first strike.[5]

Taken together, these assessments of Russia and China strongly suggest that the probability of cataclysmic nuclear war is considerably smaller than it was during the Cold War. Of course, it is still only prudent to prepare and posture U.S. strategic nuclear forces for the possibility of such a conflict and to continue to be able to escalate to such a level of devastation—by maintaining substantial numbers of our strategic ballistic missile submarines at sea and our silo-based intercontinental ballistic missiles (ICBMs) on day-to-day alert, for instance. The prospect of such a war need not and should not, however, receive the same priority in U.S. national policy and force planning and procurement that it did during the 1970s and 1980s.

But while massive nuclear war appears exceedingly unlikely, serious conflict at lower levels of destructiveness *does* appear possible and, in some respects, may be becoming increasingly so.[6] Needless to say, the United States has an interest in deter-

---

[5]   See U.S. Department of Defense, *Annual Report to Congress: Military and Security Developments Involving the People's Republic of China, 2013*, Washington, D.C.: Government Printing Office, 2013.

[6]   Several factors point toward the continued, albeit thankfully lower, possibility of major war. While contemporary politics lack the ideological intensity that characterized the 75-year period that followed World War I, disputes between other major powers (and their allies or clients) do remain—over territory, as in the East and South China Seas; over the treatment of favored minorities, as with ethnic Russian groups in nations now independent of Moscow's suzerainty; over influence and the control of policy, as on the Korean Peninsula; and over the proper boundaries of forceful intervention, as in Syria, Libya, and Kosovo. Moreover, structural developments in the international arena suggest that the possibility of conflict remains and may be growing. The nearly hegemonic power structure that typified the immediate post–Cold War era, one of almost untrammeled American influence, is passing, and hegemonic systems are often seen to be more conducive to stability than multipolar systems. (See, for instance, Robert Gilpin, *War and Change in World Politics*, Cambridge, UK: Cambridge University Press,

ring and, if necessary, prevailing in such contingencies. Moreover, the United States has an interest not only in preventing actual war but also in deterring the effective use of the *threat* of military force for political leverage—that is, deterring future instances of Hitler's remilitarization of the Rhineland and seizure of Czechoslovakia. Yet the use of military capabilities for coercive purposes appears alive and well, most notably in the waters of the western Pacific and South China Sea and in the Middle East. Therefore, for its own security, and more immediately because of its explicit and implicit extended deterrent commitments in Europe, Asia, and the Middle East, the United States is going to need to be prepared to resist attempts at coercion against itself and its allies and, should war break out, to meet or at least tolerably satisfy its strategic-political requirements. In concert with nonnuclear U.S. military capabilities, the U.S. nuclear deterrent should help the United States achieve these objectives of deterring more-limited wars and assaults on its vital interests, not least because the most plausible route to general nuclear war lies through a war that begins at a lower level of armed conflict.

Given this strategic landscape, what should the United States' nuclear force posture and policy be? An answer to this question must be derived from an estimate of the likely strategic landscape the United States will face because any sensible method for determining what a military capability—and thus the U.S. nuclear force—should look like ought to proceed from an assessment of the plausible serious threats and types of major conflicts the United States will likely face. Broadly speaking, these are likely to fall into two categories: first, conflicts with rogue states, such as North Korea and Iran, potentially armed with much smaller but still significant arsenals of nuclear weapons and long-range delivery systems, and, second, conflicts with large, near-peer adversaries, namely China and Russia, capable of mounting daunting challenges to the United States at the conventional level (especially in their neighboring regions) and possessing very serious nuclear capabilities (more advanced and far larger in the Russian case). Each of these scenarios introduces a decidedly novel factor into a U.S. defense planning accustomed to escalation dominance since the collapse of the Soviet Union: in the first case, the existence of plausibly survivable and iteratively usable nuclear forces on

---

1981.) Even as predictions of American decline seem grossly exaggerated, it does seem evident that the emerging international security environment will involve at least one power—China—with a comparable amount of national strategic power, as well as others that can play the role of major secondary powers, such as Russia. This suggests that the international system will lack the clarity and efficiency characteristic of hegemonic systems, promising more in the way of confusion, defensive behavior, and miscalculation. Also, while views on the utility and morality of war have clearly grown more negative, any evolution of mores away from the acceptance of war must be regarded as uneven and at least somewhat contingent. While Europeans seem sick and tired of war, views on the advisability and justifiability of war appear considerably different in Asia and the Middle East, not to mention North America. Finally, it must be reckoned that the recession of the influence of nuclear weapons from international politics has removed some caution from nations' calculations. U.S. decisions about assertive military intervention in the Middle East are no longer shadowed as they were in 1973 and even in 1990 by the restraining possibility of inadvertently coming into conflict with the Soviet Union. For a fuller exposition of this argument, see Elbridge A. Colby, "Is Nuclear Deterrence Still Relevant," in Adam B. Lowther, ed., *Deterrence: Rising Powers, Rogue Regimes, and Terrorism in the 21st Century*, New York: Palgrave MacMillan, 2012, pp. 49–74.

the part of small states hostile to U.S. interests and, in the second, considerably more fearsome conventional capabilities and a clearly assured (in the case of Russia) or practically near-assured (in that of China) second-strike nuclear capability.

In the event of armed conflict in either or both of these categories, the U.S. war effort would have to pursue two objectives to be justifiable: seeking to achieve important U.S. politico-military aims and, at the same time, limiting damage and risk to U.S. and allied interests, most importantly including the avoidance of nuclear attacks against our cities or those of our allies. Thus, in any conflict with adversaries who possess survivable nuclear arsenals of any significant size, the United States will want to navigate between the opposing perils of defeat or surrender of its stakes in the conflict on the one hand and unrestrained war on the other.

The United States is therefore going to need to be prepared to fight *limited* wars—wars characterized *both* by the pursuit of its military-political ends *and* by serious efforts to control or at least limit the likelihood of escalation.[7] One of the most obvious ways of limiting such wars is by fighting them solely with conventional weapons, and there is a growing amount of thought as to how to conduct major but limited conventional wars with both significant powers and rogue states.[8] Efforts to improve the ability of U.S. conventional forces to wage such wars, such as through the creation of and efforts to implement the Air-Sea Battle Concept, sensibly occupy the forefront of attempts to address the challenges that both rogue state adversaries and near peers pose.[9] For numerous reasons, conventional forces are and indisputably must be the preferred means of military response for the United States, above all because the clearest firebreak against catastrophic nuclear use is simply avoiding any nuclear use whatsoever.

---

[7]   For some signal studies of the nature and complexities of limited war and escalation, see, among others, Robert E. Osgood, *Limited War: The Challenge to American Strategy*, Chicago: University of Chicago Press, 1957; Robert E. Osgood, "The Reappraisal of Limited War," The Adelphi Papers, special issue, *Problems of Modern Strategy: Part I*, Vol. 9, No. 54, pp. 41–54; Bernard Brodie, *Strategy in the Missile Age*, Princeton, N.J.: Princeton University Press, 1959; Klaus E. Knorr and Thornton Reed, eds., *Limited Strategic War*, New York: Frederick A. Praeger, 1962; Herman Kahn, *On Thermonuclear War*, Princeton, N.J.: Princeton University Press, 1961; Herman Kahn, *On Escalation: Metaphors and Scenarios*, New York: Frederick A. Praeger, 1965; Thomas C. Schelling, *Arms and Influence*, New Haven, Conn.: Yale University Press, 1965; Henry A. Kissinger, *Nuclear Weapons and Foreign Policy*, New York: Harper Brothers, 1957; Morton H. Halperin, *Limited War in the Nuclear Age*, New York: John Wiley & Sons, 1965; and Richard Smoke, *War: Controlling Escalation*, Cambridge, Mass.: Harvard University Press, 1977.

[8]   See, for instance, Forrest E. Morgan, Karl P. Mueller, Evan S. Medeiros, Kevin L. Pollpeter, and Roger Cliff, *Dangerous Thresholds: Managing Escalation in the 21st Century*, Santa Monica, Calif.: RAND Corporation, MG-614-AF, 2008; Forrest E. Morgan, *Dancing with the Bear: Managing Escalation in a Conflict with Russia*, Paris: Institute Français des Relations Internationales, 2012; and Keir A. Lieber and Daryl G. Press, *Coercive Nuclear Campaigns in the 21st Century: Understanding Adversary Incentives and Options for Nuclear Escalation*, Monterey, Calif.: U.S. Naval Postgraduate School, 2013.

[9]   General Norton A. Schwartz and Admiral Jonathan W. Greenert, "AirSea Battle: Promoting Stability in an Era of Uncertainty," *The American Interest*, February 20, 2012.

But because some prospective U.S. adversaries have nuclear weapons (or might have them before long) and because the United States and its allies cannot forever guarantee conventional superiority in every scenario about which they care, U.S. nuclear weapons must also be part of the equation when planning for possible armed conflicts with both smaller hostile rogue states and with larger near peers. Moreover, there are political reasons for considering U.S. nuclear weapons in these contexts, not least because U.S. allies strongly insist that U.S. willingness and preparedness to use nuclear weapons remain at the core of the U.S. extended deterrence posture.[10] Thus, the United States also needs to grapple with the problem of how to conduct and manage a limited war in which nuclear weapons play a critical part. This means undertaking the thinking and planning required to wage limited nuclear war and developing the capabilities needed to do so effectively.

It is important to emphasize that the major rationale for planning for the possibility of limited nuclear war is to prevent war—including large-scale nuclear war—from breaking out in the first place. Deterrence—including specifically nuclear deterrence—of both the war prevention and intrawar escalation avoidance varieties is much more powerful and effective to the extent that U.S. military—again, including nuclear—capabilities are more practically employable and thus their potential use much more credible. This is because, to the extent such capabilities are credibly employable, potential adversaries will have to weigh the prospect of suffering the brunt of U.S. military—including nuclear—strikes more heavily, which in turn will add to their incentives for restraint. For this reason, the United States should want to make its nuclear forces more usable and its threats credible.[11] If, on the other hand, U.S. nuclear weapons can be used only in an unrestrained, massive fashion, their actual use in any contingency short of the apocalyptic would be wholly irrational—and thus incredible to U.S. adversaries.[12] And if their use would be incredible in any scenario short of the very worst, their deterrent effects would also be seriously reduced, as any rational opponent would sensibly reckon that the United States would not actually use them. We need not lean on the theoretical to believe that actual political actors would take advantage of the strategic space opened by what they perceive to be incredible or even simply implausible threats—we have solid evidence from the Cold War of just that.[13] Thus, the United

---

[10] See, for instance, Joel Gehrke, "Obama to South Korea: Our 'Nuclear Umbrella' Is Protecting You," *Washington Examiner*, February 12, 2013, and "Hagel Vows Defense Commitments to Japan Including Nuclear Umbrella," *Japan Times*, April 30, 2013.

[11] This interest needs to be carefully traded off against the potential risks of fielding such capabilities, including their destabilizing aspects. Effective trade-offs can be achieved, however, through measures such as careful attention to minimizing the strategic counterforce characteristics of such capabilities.

[12] No one has made this argument more pointedly than Herman Kahn. For instance, see *On Thermonuclear War* (Kahn, 1961).

[13] For an excellent exposition of this point, see Francis Gavin, "Politics, History and the Ivory Tower–Policy Gap in the Nuclear Proliferation Debate," *Journal of Strategic Studies*, Vol. 35, No. 4, August 29, 2012, pp. 573–600.

States will want to be able to use and credibly threaten to use its nuclear weapons in a discriminate and very limited fashion.

This is not to deny or belittle the profound and, in some cases, possibly insuperable difficulties of limiting escalation once the nuclear threshold has been crossed. But how can our nuclear weapons be strategically persuasive to an opponent if he knows that our using them would result in a spasm of almost inconceivable destruction wholly out of proportion to the stakes we have in a conflict? This is what a policy that does not provide control and discrimination in the use of nuclear weapons must logically entail. Of course, the possibility, however remote, that the United States would use nuclear weapons even in a manifestly irrational way is bound to induce some caution, but it can hardly be argued that this prospect would have as potent a deterrent effect as a nuclear force that could be employed in ways short of massive use would.[14]

The problems of an inflexible U.S. nuclear force are particularly acute in the context of American extended deterrence commitments. Are we going to deliberately invite nuclear strikes against our homeland over an armed conflict involving a Baltic state NATO ally? Or Taiwan? Or even for longer-standing allies, especially now that political conflict has lost the Manichean ideological character that typified international politics from the 1930s until 1991? As Henry Kissinger is supposed to have sagely observed, "Great powers do not commit suicide for allies"—or, it should hardly need to be added, *should* they.[15] Yet neither our allies nor our adversaries are likely to be so credulous or foolish as to allow us to rest our deterrent threats on bluffs in the event of a serious crisis or armed conflict without altering their behavior accordingly in ways we might well not much like—on the part of our allies by, for instance, becoming more accommodating toward our strategic rivals and, on the part of our adversaries, by behaving more aggressively against our interests.

But even if this all might be theoretically true, some object that nuclear war simply cannot be restrained. Given that nuclear weapons have not been used since 1945, it must be said that it remains highly speculative whether a nuclear war could remain limited. Of course, even the slight danger of an apocalyptic outcome must counsel the greatest caution in testing this proposition. But while the possibilities of escalation across the nuclear threshold must be considered with the most somber gravity, the notion that *any* nuclear use would *necessarily* lead to Armageddon strains credulity. Ultimately, *no one* in a conflict between adversaries with survivable nuclear forces would have an interest in a large-scale exchange of nuclear weapons, a fact that would provide immensely strong incentives for restraint that must not be ignored even as we must pay heed to the very real impetuses toward escalation that would exist but that

---

[14] For a contrary view, see Kenneth N. Waltz, "Nuclear Myths and Political Realities," *American Political Science Review*, Vol. 84, No. 3, pp. 731–745.

[15] Quoted in William Pfaff, "Why Georgia Does Not Belong in NATO," *International Herald Tribune*, August 13, 2008.

are already widely and amply acknowledged. Is it therefore reasonable to conclude that, because a nuclear weapon has been used, the factors that we normally understand as determining the likelihood of escalation, restraint, and de-escalation—factors such as the type and location of the targets attacked, the scale of destructiveness inflicted, the military effect achieved, and the proposed terms for ending the war—would become irrelevant? Perhaps their relative weighting would change—but would they be irrelevant? Certainly, exacerbating factors of fear, confusion, and pride would intensify in the event of crisis, and even more so in war, but would the crossing of the nuclear threshold mean the end of rational calculation and attempts to exercise restraint? It seems not.[16]

It is equally important to emphasize that the ability to execute such options would *not necessitate* their implementation. Rather, in the event that the fortunes of war pressed the United States to consider options for serious escalation, U.S. leaders might well and reasonably choose other options—including vertical or horizontal escalation with conventional weapons or, conversely, partial or even full retreat; the stakes simply might not justify the grave risks such dramatic forms of escalation would entail. But U.S. leaders equally might well decide that escalation *is* needed and justified and that conventional options are insufficient or too escalatory. It is therefore important that the United States have these limited nuclear options. In any case, it should be emphasized that the United States would—or at the very least *should*—only seriously consider the employment of nuclear weapons under the most "extreme circumstances," as the 2010 Nuclear Posture Review Report aptly put it.[17] No one should be suggesting that we use nuclear weapons (or seriously threaten to use them) in anything short of the most serious and grave contingencies.[18]

The United States will therefore want to have ways of credibly threatening to employ its nuclear weapons—and, if need be, of actually employing them—that are potent but that also have limited escalatory implications. In particular, it should be able to use these weapons in ways that are rationally correlated to the provocation or aggression—ways that are neither feckless nor suicidal. The purpose of such options would be to help persuade the enemy that it is better to terminate or at least de-escalate the conflict on a basis acceptable to the United States and its allies rather than to continue along the path he has embarked on.

U.S. nuclear weapons can reasonably serve two more specific roles in this context. First, they can be used to deter escalation by an adversary. Above all, of course,

---

[16] For a similar view, see Herman Kahn, *Thinking the Unthinkable in the 1980s*, Washington, D.C.: Hudson Institute, 1984, p. 37.

[17] U.S. Department of Defense, 2010, p. 16.

[18] Circumstances that might justifiably provoke a U.S. nuclear response might, in the foreseeable future, include (although not exclusively) the use of nuclear weapons or the initiation of nonnuclear attacks causing massive loss of life against the United States, its forces, or its allies. These would be the only kinds of circumstances in which it would be morally defensible to run such risks.

this means deterring an adversary's escalation to the use of nuclear weapons, especially against U.S. or allied population centers. But their role need not and should not be limited only to deterring an enemy's nuclear escalation. Rather, U.S. nuclear weapons can and should be used to deter a broader range of attacks, for instance large-scale biological or "existential" cyber attacks.[19] That said, in arenas in which the United States and its allies enjoy conventional superiority, the practical focus of nuclear deterrence would most reasonably be on enabling U.S. and allied conventional forces to achieve their objectives while deterring the opponent from introducing nuclear weapons or some other mechanism of catastrophic destruction or disruption into the struggle. U.S. nuclear weapons' basic purpose, in this context, would be to "keep the fight clean." This role already has utility in the case of Russia and China and would become increasingly important if North Korea continues to expand and improve its nuclear weapons and delivery systems or if Iran achieves a nuclear weapon capability.

The second purpose of nuclear weapons in the emerging strategic environment is quite different, however. This would be for the United States to use its nuclear weapons or the threat of their use to redress serious, and perhaps fatal, disadvantages in the balance of conventional military capabilities. It is fortunately true that U.S. conventional forces appear to hold the promise of remaining broadly superior to those of any competitor for the foreseeable future. Nonetheless, this second purpose could become more salient for two reasons. One is that the United States and its allies may not enjoy conventional superiority *within the realistic political-strategic boundaries of a given conflict scenario*. That is, within the confines of a given limited conflict, U.S. and allied conventional forces might be overmatched by an adversary's forces to such a degree that, to avoid defeat within the boundaries of the conflict, the United States and its allies might feel pressed to escalate—but doing so with available conventional forces might entail risks unacceptable to U.S. or allied political leadership, negating the relevance of overall U.S. conventional superiority.[20] For instance, the United States might fall behind in the military-technological competition with China over the western Pacific, and China might gain the ability to achieve local military objectives, the frustration of which would require the United States to substantially broaden or intensify a conflict with the People's Republic in ways that would be exceedingly unpalatable because of

---

[19] The scope of things that the United States has actively sought to deter with its nuclear weapons has varied over time, but it would seem reasonable that the boundaries of such deterrence could include any attack of catastrophic consequence. For the utility of relying on the U.S. nuclear deterrent to ward off "catastrophic" cyberattacks, see Defense Science Board, *Resilient Military Systems and the Advanced Cyber Threat*, Washington, D.C.: Office of the Under Secretary of Defense for Acquisition, Technology and Logistics, January 2013.

[20] A classic instance of this was the Vietnam War, in which the United States clearly outmatched North Vietnam in overall military terms but was unwilling to bring that conventional superiority to bear in ways that would be decisive because of the fear of intervention from China or the Soviet Union. Of course the same logic applied to the employment of nuclear weapons, which were briefly but never very seriously considered for use during the conflict in Vietnam.

China's own ability to match those escalatory steps.[21] Such hazardous conventional steps might include broadening the geographical scope of a conflict or hitting more-important and -valued targets, such as leadership or command and control facilities. For instance, the U.S. position in a conventional conflict might appear to be so dire and "extreme" that the only realistic options for deterring further adversary progress would be through conventional attacks on key enemy leadership elements, their strategic forces and command and control, or other among their most highly valued assets—or, on the other hand, through limited nuclear strikes. To a U.S. decisionmaker, especially one facing an adversary with survivable nuclear forces, conducting distinctly *limited* nuclear strikes might well seem *less* escalatory than mounting what an adversary might reasonably see as *unrestrained* conventional strikes.[22] In the context of such a conflict, it is therefore not impossible that some types of escalation to the nuclear level, especially if confined *within the conflict's existing geographical and other boundaries of escalation*, would be more effective and yet in important respects more restrained than dramatically widening or intensifying the war solely with conventional arms.[23]

But the second role of limited nuclear options is also important because it cannot be ruled out that the United States may lose at least some important elements of its wider conventional superiority in the coming decades, given the high demands placed on U.S. military capabilities by its far-flung extended deterrence commitments, the

---

[21] While this situation does not appear yet to have developed, Chinese progress in its anti-access and area-denial capabilities and the vulnerability of U.S. forces and especially striking power in the western Pacific, in part due to their concentration in and on a few bases and naval vessels, poses a worrying and, in some respects, intensifying problem.

[22] Indeed, the very shock of nuclear use would likely actually substitute, to some degree, for the value of the targets struck, allowing limited nuclear strikes to aim for somewhat *less* valued adversary targets, thus minimizing at least some of the escalatory and destabilizing aspects of such strikes.

[23] A historical example may help illustrate this point. The Yom Kippur War is probably the relevant historical conflict for contemporary consideration of limited nuclear options; it is the one example of a major war that was distinctly limited and that included the participation (albeit largely indirect) of multiple nuclear-armed states. There is substantial evidence that Israel at least considered employing the nuclear weapons it was alleged to have possessed during the 1973 war, especially if the military situation had continued to deteriorate and the Syrians in particular had made further advances into the Golan Heights and even into the Galilee and Israel proper. Discussions in senior Israeli political and military circles at this time included consideration of a number of severe forms of escalation in the event that the military situation continued to worsen, including not only nuclear employment but also strikes against Soviet aircraft supplying the Arab forces, a step that would have risked drawing the Soviet Union—and thus likely the United States as well—into the conflict. Had the Arabs advanced beyond the borders of pre-1967 Israel, these options would have been used to demonstrate to the Arabs and the Soviets the depth of Israeli resolve and to make clear that they had transgressed a genuine Israeli "red line." Had this scenario come to pass, there is substantial reason to think that a *limited* and primarily demonstrative Israeli use of a nuclear weapon—for instance either away from the battlefield or against Arab military units on the battlefield—could well have been *less* escalatory and *more* effective in achieving Israel's aims of repelling the Arab assault, restoring deterrence, and avoiding Soviet intervention than undertaking large-scale attacks on Soviet aircraft and/or against key Arab leadership or national targets. For more on this issue, see Elbridge A. Colby, Avner Cohen, William McCants, Bradley Morris, and William Rosenau, *The Israeli "Nuclear Alert" of 1973: Deterrence and Signaling in Crisis*, Alexandria, Va.: Center for Naval Analyses, 2013.

proliferation of advanced military technology (conventional and nuclear), the growth of Chinese power, and the impact of sequestration and budget tightening on the U.S. military. It was only a generation ago, after all, that it was considered settled wisdom that Warsaw Pact forces seriously overmatched NATO forces in Europe. This is not to say that such a deterioration of U.S. conventional advantage is inevitable, let alone advisable—it is neither and definitively not the latter—but simply that we cannot practically rule out the possibility that U.S. conventional superiority may significantly erode over the decades-long time frame over which serious nuclear policy decisions must be made. Should this come to pass, U.S. nuclear forces could reasonably be relied on to plug major holes in the overall U.S. defense posture, as they did during the Cold War.

Under either role, however—as a deterrent to nuclear escalation on the part of the adversary or to rectify local or general conventional inferiority—the best way to use nuclear weapons would be *discriminately*. Such use should be tailored in its nature or effects in such a way as to combine coercive impact with very evident limitation. In particular, such capabilities for limitation should afford the United States the ability to threaten harm to an adversary—and, more to the point, *further* harm if the adversary refuses to relent—while clearly avoiding endangering or damaging assets the endangerment or damaging of which would be most likely to provoke a spasmodic or full-blown nuclear retaliation from the adversary. The central idea is to demonstrate U.S. resolve and ability to employ nuclear weapons in ways that are perceptibly well short of large-scale and unrestrained use but that nevertheless pose a credible threat of increasing escalation and damage to the adversary. An adversary using nuclear weapons first would at best see the abundant foolhardiness or at least the exceeding dangers of further nuclear use; if it was the United States that felt compelled to use nuclear weapons first to stave off conventional disaster, the enemy would see the grave perils of continuing the assault.

The optimal way to make such limited nuclear use effectively coercive would be for the United States to enjoy escalation advantage against its enemy in a contest of its limited nuclear capabilities. Escalation advantage or superiority, the position in which one can escalate more effectively, controllably, and decisively than one's opponent, is crucial for determining who will come out ahead in a limited conflict. This is intuitive—the one who is in a position in which an intensification of the conflict will improve his position in some meaningful military or political way will have coercive leverage over his adversary. If the enemy can retaliate with a nuclear response of his own that negates the strategic effect of one's own nuclear strike or even worsens the situation, a limited nuclear deterrent's effectiveness is substantially reduced—especially if the enemy has deeper stakes in the conflict, since that should give him the advantage in a straight contest of resolve. Thus, the United States and its allies are better off if the United States possesses escalation advantage in the conduct of a limited nuclear war, just as they are better off if the United States is superior in the conduct of a limited conventional war.[24]

The large and diverse U.S. nuclear arsenal is, of course, a natural source of potential escalation advantage. The sources of such superiority do not, however, lie solely in preponderance of force, which the U.S. nuclear arsenal provides over every opponent save Russia. Having greater military capability than an enemy but not being realistically able to use it because of political or other constraints largely if not entirely nullifies the advantages that derive from such superiority in capability. This was the quandary the United States faced in Vietnam. Rather, one is only in a position of genuine escalation advantage if one has ways of using one's military forces that improve one's military or political position vis-à-vis one's adversary *and* that one can realistically and sensibly employ in such a context.

This is why the ideal for the U.S. nuclear posture (and for the U.S. defense posture more broadly) is to provide capabilities that can be employed in a manner that is not only efficacious in attaining military objectives but also tailored. Tailoring—whether through limiting a weapon's destructiveness, shaping its physical effects, manipulating its trajectory, or otherwise controlling its nature, course, or consequences—is effectively equivalent to limiting the strategic consequences of a weapon's use.[25] And limiting the consequences of a weapon enables the United States to use it more precisely and thus to employ force more readily and effectively by reducing the military and political risks and collateral effects attendant to such use, above all by reducing the need to wage war in such a way that an enemy will see the U.S. way of war as akin to a life or death struggle.[26] By being able to wage war more discriminately, the United States can achieve at least some of its objectives, then, without prompting an adversary (most importantly a nuclear-armed one) to think that the United States is trying to destroy him, in turn reducing (although assuredly not eliminating) the risks of waging war against such an opponent.

This is particularly valuable in the emerging strategic environment, in which it is practically certain that Russia and probably China will have significant survivable nuclear forces and quite possible that rogue states, such as North Korea, will also gain

---

[24] The Department of Defense AirSea Battle document commendably notes the importance of retaining "escalation advantage," but the AirSea Battle effort appears focused on the conventional level of war. The document, for instance, refers to nuclear weapons only once, in reference to other missions of the U.S. armed forces. U.S. Department of Defense, AirSea Battle Office, *Air-Sea Battle: Service Collaboration to Address Anti-Access and Area Denial Challenges*, June 2013, p. i.

[25] For a related but broader discussion of the importance of tailoring deterrence, see M. Elaine Bunn, "Can Deterrence Be Tailored?" *Strategic Forum*, No. 225, January 2007, pp. 1–8.

[26] So, for instance, the U.S. military has made giant strides in reducing the likelihood of collateral damage by improving the accuracy of its missiles and bombs. More-developed U.S. command and control and intelligence, surveillance, and reconnaissance capabilities, meanwhile, allow a President to conduct more iterative, disaggregated military campaigns that are better adapted to particular political circumstances, rather than having to choose between launching an all-out attack or doing nothing at all.

survivable nuclear forces of their own (albeit smaller, less-sophisticated versions)—nuclear forces whose use the United States would very much want to avoid, especially against its own or ally's cities.[27]

But how can the United States seek to thread this needle between being able to use its nuclear weapons for meaningful effect and also limiting the escalatory impetus of such employment? The way for the United States most intelligently to employ nuclear weapons in a limited fashion in the case of either of the two types of conflicts would be to use the dramatic nature of even a limited employment of such weapons to place searing pressure on an opponent to de-escalate while avoiding triggering a major nuclear response on his part. The actual mechanics of effective limited nuclear use cannot be precisely anticipated in advance, naturally, given that any such use would need to be adapted to the particular constellation of political and military circumstances of a given conflict.

Broadly speaking, however, sensible limited nuclear use should seek to telegraph the dangers to the enemy of further escalation in the most visceral fashion. Such strikes should vehemently communicate (not least simply by the actual military use of a nuclear weapon) the clear message to the enemy that he had crossed a genuine red line, testify to the firm resolve to protect U.S. interests, threaten the possibility of further harm if the enemy refused to de-escalate, and clearly and credibly demonstrate restraint and the willingness to de-escalate should the enemy be willing to cooperate on terms that are acceptable to the United States and its allies. The purpose of such strikes would be, colloquially, to "shake the collar" of the adversary, making it clear to him in the most concrete way that he had crossed a red line and that further such actions on his part would very seriously risk further nuclear escalation while at the same time offering him a tolerable way down the metaphorical escalation ladder.[28]

A useful focus for U.S. limited nuclear use in such contests that would also impose a natural limiting factor would be to orient such capabilities toward contributing to gaining the upper hand or prevailing in the conflict that had provoked the nuclear escalation, for instance against enemy general-purpose forces engaged in combat with U.S. or allied forces in a confined theater of conflict, preferably away from the enemy's capital, leadership redoubts, and strategic forces and command and control assets. That is, such nuclear use would be integrated with the objectives and the conduct of the limited conventional war that had led to nuclear use in the first place. This would both advance the original objectives the United States was pursuing while linking U.S. nuclear use to an intuitive limiting logic—prevailing in the original conventional

---

[27] It is important to point out that the fact that the enemy has survivable nuclear forces does not obviate the utility or benefits of escalation advantages. It does change them, however, by imposing constraints on what can be targeted and how far it is sensible to go in terms of attacking the enemy, but escalation advantages can still be exploited.

[28] For a similar view, see Henry A. Kissinger, *White House Years*, Boston: Little, Brown and Company, 1979, p. 622.

conflict.[29] If the United States possessed advantages in this kind of limited nuclear-conventional war, the unfolding advantage that would proceed from iterative U.S. nuclear use would impose intense (and ideally anticipatory) pressure on an adversary to come to terms. It would be especially useful in extended deterrence scenarios, since it can be presumed that, in such instances, the United States would want to rely on superior capabilities rather than on its greater will and firmer resolve, if at all possible.

Limited nuclear options, to be sensibly employable, would not only have to be capable of achieving meaningful military goals, however, but would also have to be able to exhibit qualities of restraint in a very noticeable fashion. Strikes might be limited, for instance, in terms of their destructiveness, the type of targets attacked, their number, and the geographic boundaries within which the attacks were carried out. A particularly logical way to limit collateral damage would be to confine any nuclear strikes, at least initially, to the geographical boundaries of the original conflict and to focus solely on military targets. And, to avoid triggering the enemy's use of his own survivable nuclear forces, strikes would clearly need to avoid the most valued assets of the adversary, again at least initially, such as leadership facilities and strategic forces and command and control. An absolutely essential constituent part of any such limited nuclear use would be to communicate as clearly and credibly as possible with the adversary, both to make clear the nature of the attack (both its effect and its limits) and to propose the conditions of de-escalation. Needless to say, such strikes would, by their very nature, require a coherent and practical political strategy to accompany them, one designed to entice the adversary to step back from his ongoing course of action by offering plausibly acceptable terms for settlement or, at the least, for de-escalation—a dignified way out.[30]

In the ideal, then, the capability to execute a range of tailored, discriminate, limited nuclear strikes should provide the United States with the ability to use its nuclear weapons iteratively, in a precisely controlled fashion, in ways that increasingly improve the U.S. position vis-à-vis an adversary—particularly with reference to the critical conventional conflict that provoked the escalation to the nuclear level in the first place.

---

[29] It is assumed that limited nuclear use would only realistically arise as a serious and plausible option out of an existing conventional war. While it is theoretically possible that the United States could employ its nuclear forces in a limited fashion without a serious war first having broken out, it is exceedingly difficult to see how this could ever be a reasonable or rational decision.

[30] Veteran *New York Times* correspondent Richard Halloran likened this all-important element of allowing one's adversary a dignified way out to the Japanese kabuki function of the *hana-michi*. As Halloran put it,

> The Japanese have a ritual called "hana-michi," which literally means "path of flowers" and in practice means to allow a defeated adversary to make a graceful exit. The term comes from the kabuki theatre. A trounced opponent, whether in a sword fight or social conflict, is permitted to dash down a ramp called the "hana-michi" running through the audience, to stop to flourish his sword or hands in defiance, and to disappear out the door.

See Richard Halloran, "Hanamichi," *Real Clear Politics*, January 17, 2010.

What kinds of scenarios would these capabilities be useful for? Obviously, we cannot predict the future with clarity or confidence, but, based on the above discussion, these scenarios might reasonably be grouped into three categories of increasing gravity: first, a conflict in which a nuclear-armed rogue state, such as North Korea (or, should efforts to prevent Tehran's acquisition of a nuclear weapon fail, possibly Iran), attempted to use a portion of its nuclear forces as a way of disabling superior U.S. capabilities or of short-circuiting such superiority by holding allied or U.S. cities hostage; second, a conflict with a major nuclear-armed power, such as China or Russia, in which the adversary sought to resort to limited nuclear use of its own to frustrate or diminish U.S. and allied conventional superiority; and, third, a conflict with a major nuclear-armed power, again such as China or Russia, in which the adversary was able to achieve at least local conventional superiority and in which it was the United States that wanted to use its nuclear forces to stave off conventional collapse or defeat.

The first category of scenario is probably the most plausible in the near term, given North Korea's advancing nuclear weapons and missile delivery capabilities and its consistently belligerent behavior. A scenario like this could unfold if a large-scale war were to break out between the United States and South Korea (and perhaps Japan and others) on one side and North Korea on the other. Assume that North Korea's strategic capabilities had developed to such an extent that it fielded something in the vicinity of two dozen or more nuclear missiles on mobile transporter erector launchers and possessed a resilient ability to control and operate them in a reasonably survivable fashion.

In such a context, the tide of conventional conflict would almost certainly turn in the favor of the United States and its allies, given their vastly superior capabilities, a fact of which the North Korean regime would be fully aware. In light of this, North Korea might well seek to use its nuclear weapons for coercive or deterrent purposes in the midst of the conflict, either for compellent effect, to achieve its ambitions in the conflict, or for more defensive purposes, such as to stave off defeat or even an attempt at regime change by the United States and South Korea.[31] For instance, on the offensive side, North Korea might seek to force an end to the conflict on grounds unfavorable to the U.S.–Republic of Korea (ROK) side by threatening to launch limited but damaging nuclear strikes; on the more defensive end, North Korea might threaten to use or might actually use its nuclear weapons if U.S. and ROK forces approached Pyongyang or leadership redoubts or if the United States launched major strike campaigns against leadership targets and/or North Korean nuclear forces.[32]

---

[31] Fears that the United States was pursuing regime change would not be irrational, given the historical propensity of U.S. military campaigns to seek such a goal in conflicts with rogue states, for instance in Iraq and Libya and, to a lesser degree, Serbia. The United States thus needs to be prepared for hostile rogue states (and perhaps even major powers) to assess that it is pursuing regime change even in conflicts it may want to limit.

[32] For a similar analysis, see Lieber and Press, 2013.

In all cases, North Korea's operational approach would presumably be to launch or to threaten to launch a small number of nuclear attacks while withholding a sufficient number of controlled transporter erector launchers as an escalation reserve if the United States refused to relent or attempted a disarming strike. North Korea might start out by conducting nuclear strikes against military targets, particularly targets that would be lucrative in strengthening its position in the conventional war.[33] North Korea might also seek to drive a wedge in the coalition arrayed against it, for instance by targeting specifically U.S. rather than ROK forces and/or by shooting at targets in Japan (either U.S. or Japanese); natural targets could include bases on Okinawa and on the Home Islands (such as Yokosuka and Atsugi).

If the allies refused to come to terms or back down in the event of a first barrage of nuclear strikes or attempted to disarm North Korea's remaining nuclear capability, North Korea could prepare to launch at least a portion of its remaining nuclear forces against more highly valued targets, for instance, civilian areas in South Korean, Japanese, or even U.S. territory, such as Guam. A final, last-ditch capability could be reserved for a "Samson Option" for unrestrained use against the U.S. homeland.[34]

In this context, the United States *might* want to launch an attempt to destroy the North Korean regime—but it very well might not, given North Korea's possession of remaining survivable nuclear forces and the consequent huge risks and real possibility of great damage such an effort would entail. Rather, the United States would likely want to respond strongly to North Korea's actions but to do so in a way that kept the war limited. This is why the United States would profit substantially from having effective limited nuclear capabilities in this scenario. While it cannot be assumed that the United States would *actually* want to respond to North Korean nuclear use with a nuclear strike of its own, it is clear that it would want and indeed need to have the serious option to do so. Discriminate nuclear options would give the United States the ability to respond with vastly greater force than conventional options would offer and—of particular importance—to retaliate *in kind* to North Korean threats and/ or use. The ability to respond in kind while also seeking to limit the destructiveness and escalatory aspects of nuclear use would be particularly valuable because it is near

---

[33] These could include U.S. and/or ROK ground formations advancing in, into, or toward North Korea; U.S. or ROK air bases in South Korea; and/or U.S. naval vessels, especially aircraft carriers, in the waters around the peninsula, although the last would prove far more difficult for North Korea, given the targeting challenges.

[34] Brad Roberts rightly points out that an especially useful focus for U.S. missile defense is to make this strategy of iterative, controlled strikes against the United States more difficult. For an adversary like North Korea, missile defenses raise the bar for entry into this kind of strategic face-off considerably. See Brad Roberts, "Extended Deterrence and Strategic Stability in Northeast Asia," Tokyo: National Institute for Defense Studies, Visiting Scholar Paper Series No. 1, August 9, 2013, p. 11. Given the technological challenges missile defense efforts face even against less-sophisticated adversaries, such as North Korea, however, it would be imprudent to rely on them to eliminate this problem. Conventional disarming strikes, meanwhile, both risk triggering the very thing the United States would wish to avoid and have a distinctly uneven, if not poor, record in eliminating the threat from mobile missiles.

certain that North Korea, U.S. allies, countries likely to be indirectly involved or considering involvement (namely China), and indeed the world at large would be looking intently to see if the United States exhibited the resolve to respond to a nuclear attack against its forces, its allies, and perhaps even itself with a nuclear strike of its own. In particular, the United States would want to have nuclear options that it could exercise against North Korea in ways that would be seriously harmful to the North Korean regime but would also be credibly limited, since the United States would want to avoid triggering North Korean use of its "back pocket" ICBM capabilities. Such discriminate U.S. strikes could be launched against important bunkers holding valued regime assets, key military targets, and symbols of the North Korean regime while avoiding known leadership redoubts and strategic command and control; these strikes would be coupled with a strategic messaging campaign designed to persuade North Korea to settle on terms acceptable to Washington, Seoul, and Tokyo.

The second scenario, of a conflict with a major nuclear-armed power that sought to use its nuclear forces to counter U.S. conventional superiority in a regional contingency, would present a challenge for the United States in many respects similar to the one the first scenario posed but would make the utility of limited nuclear options even more clear. This is because the tantalizing option of attempting to disarm the adversary of his nuclear forces, while almost certainly too dangerous even in the parameters sketched out in the first scenario, would be positively foolish in the context of the second category, in which the United States was facing off against an adversary possessed of first-rate and survivable nuclear forces, like Russia or China. Response to limited nuclear use on the part of Russia or China would thus have to take the form of a limited strike rather than an attempt to disarm the opponent.

While the precise starting point of a war with a major power, such as China or Russia, cannot be predicted in advance and might change considerably as the strategic environment evolves in the coming decades, a scenario like this could unfold if the United States came to blows with China, for instance starting from a dispute over Taiwan or territorial claims in the western Pacific, or with Russia, for instance stemming from a fight over an Eastern European NATO member. Let us focus on the Chinese possibility. In the context of such a conflict, dynamics similar to the North Korean scenario could arise, in which U.S. conventional superiority could appear to be leading to a limited but still decisive and substantial U.S. victory, for instance over the autonomy of Taiwan or in a contest involving other territorial disputes in the western Pacific or South China Sea. The Chinese Communist Party might perceive such a defeat as jeopardizing its hold on power, especially in the Taiwan case, given the enormous investment of the regime's legitimacy in incorporating Taiwan into the People's Republic, or if Japan were perceived as having defeated China, given deep anti-Japanese sentiments among the Chinese populace.

In such a scenario, China might decide to attempt to use its nuclear forces to turn the tide of the conventional conflict by conducting a limited nuclear strike using a strategy similar to that of North Korea in the first scenario—first threatening U.S., Japanese, and/or other allied or partner military forces or assets; then threatening allied or U.S. broader and possibly civilian areas in the western Pacific; and finally holding back survivable ICBM (and possibly submarine-launched ballistic missile) forces for strikes against the U.S. homeland.[35] Facing this threat, the United States would not have the practical option of disarming the Chinese capability to conduct such a limited strike plan, given both the sophistication and survivability of the Chinese nuclear force and the extreme escalatory risks such an attempt would pose.[36]

U.S. leaders would therefore most logically look to options that could deter China from embarking on this course or could persuade China to halt such a campaign while also minimizing the risks of escalation. Assuredly, the United States would look to conventional options to help address this need and might well include them in any retaliatory strike package. But conventional-only options might not be able to achieve the required degree of potency, given formidable Chinese air and missile defenses, and also might not be practical, especially if China used its limited nuclear strikes to disrupt the ability of U.S. conventional forces to operate effectively by striking key U.S. nodes in the western Pacific, such as Okinawa or Guam. Moreover, only looking to conventional options in the face of Chinese nuclear use would risk appearing irresolute and timorous. This, in turn, not only would risk inviting subsequent Chinese attempts to gain advantage from further nuclear use or threats of use but also would risk persuading allies (including allies also involved in the conflict itself) of the same thing, allies that might deem such a failure to resort to nuclear use as a failure of will and thus grounds for pursuing a separate course of action, including independent military steps or, conversely, concluding a separate peace with Beijing.

The best response for the United States might well then be to retaliate against Chinese limited nuclear use with limited nuclear use of its own. Such use would be most effective if it not only demonstrated the U.S. resolve to respond in kind to nuclear strikes against itself or its allies but also contributed to restoring the conventional advantages in theater that U.S. forces had earned through the conventional conflict and demonstrated that a further nuclear duel would be increasingly unfavorable to China—all while making clear to the Chinese that such nuclear use was *not* intended to disarm or decapitate them and, thus, that they had great incentives for restraint.[37] Logical targets for such U.S. strikes would be valuable theater-level command and con-

---

[35] For similar speculation, see Barry Watts, *Nuclear-Conventional Firebreaks and the Nuclear Taboo*, Washington, D.C.: Center for Strategic and Budgetary Assessments, 2013, p. 65.

[36] Doing so in the Russian case would be practically impossible, given the much greater size and superior sophistication of the Russian force.

[37] These objectives would be far harder to meet in the case of Russia, whose nuclear forces match those of the United States not only in size but also in sophistication. Here, U.S. objectives *in a nuclear exchange* would have to be more modest because the United States could not expect to gain as much from the relative balance of capabilities.

trol facilities, military formations or bases, strike platforms, naval forces, and the like. Again, this approach would logically need to be accompanied by a political outreach designed to seek to persuade Beijing to settle the conflict on acceptable terms or, at the very least, to forswear further employment of its nuclear arms.

The third category, that in which it is the United States that would want to use its nuclear forces to halt a serious deterioration of its position in a conventional fight, is currently the least probable of the scenarios. Nonetheless, it could well become more plausible with respect to China should the conventional military balance in the western Pacific continue to shift in Beijing's favor, whether due simply to the "catch-up" and geographical advantages an increasingly rich China enjoys in the competition for military superiority in the region; to a weakening of U.S. military power in the western Pacific stemming from serious cuts to the defense budget, malinvestment, and/or continued U.S. focus on other regions and missions (for instance on counterinsurgency operations in the Middle East); or to both. While such a dramatic shift in the conventional balance in the western Pacific is unlikely to happen in the near term, it is a realistic medium and certainly a long-term possibility—which are the time frames around which U.S. nuclear policy and posture should be formulated.[38] In the event such a shift came to pass and assuming the United States would want to maintain its strategic posture and alliance network in the Asia-Pacific region, the United States would naturally then want to consider the role of limited nuclear options in deterring potential Chinese exploitation of its conventional military advantages in the region. (It is worth noting that this would essentially be a reprise of the U.S.-NATO posture against the conventionally superior Soviet Union–Warsaw Pact during the Cold War.[39])

An actual conflict falling into this category might, then, come to pass along lines similar to those discussed with respect to China in the second category—but with China, rather than the United States, gaining the upper hand in the conventional conflict. In a war, China might, for instance, be able to break down the U.S. "battle

---

[38] For a measured but sobering discussion of this possibility, see Robert O. Work and Shawn Brimley, *20YY: Preparing for War in the Robotic Age*, Washington, D.C.: Center for a New American Security, 2014.

[39] For the classic official statement of this posture, see NATO's "Flexible Response" statement: North Atlantic Military Committee, "Final Decision on MC 14/3: A Report by the Military Committee to the Defence Planning Committee on Overall Strategic Concept for the Defense of the North Atlantic Treaty Organization Area," January 16, 1968. The argument in this chapter mirrors this strategy in many respects—for instance, pp. 10–11:

> Deliberate Escalation. Deliberate escalation seeks to defend aggression by deliberately raising but where possible controlling, the scope and intensity of combat, making the cost and the risk disproportionate to the aggressor's objectives and the threat of nuclear response progressively more imminent. It does not solely depend on the ability to defeat the enemy's aggression as such; rather, it weakens his will to continue the conflict. Depending on the level at which the aggression starts, the time needed for each escalatory action and reaction and the rate of success, escalatory steps might be selected from among the following examples provided they have not previously been used as part of a direct defensive system: (1) broadening or intensifying a nonnuclear engagement, possibly by opening another front or initiating action at sea in response to low intensity aggression; (2) use of nuclear defence and denial weapons; (3) demonstrative use of nuclear weapons; (4) selective nuclear strikes on interdiction targets; (5) selective nuclear strikes against other suitable military targets.

network" in the western Pacific by using its conventional strike forces (missile, air, and naval) and other capabilities to degrade or destroy key U.S. nodes, for instance, on Guam and Okinawa and at sea.[40] At the very least, such victories would indicate that the post-1945 U.S. supremacy in the Pacific had been decisively broken, with difficult-to-calculate but surely pernicious implications for the U.S. alliance posture and the regional order it has underwritten in the region. Furthermore, such Chinese military successes might enable Beijing to coerce U.S. allies and partners in the region, even to employ direct military force, including power projection capabilities, against them and against U.S. territories in the region. In this context, the United States might not have realistic or timely options for conventional response, particularly if U.S. military reserves and the underlying defense industrial base were not adequately funded and prepared beforehand. Meanwhile, some conventional options to escalate the conflict and convey that Beijing has transgressed U.S. red lines—for instance attacks against leadership targets in Beijing—might seem unduly escalatory.[41]

In this scenario, the United States would clearly want to have the option to resort to limited nuclear use to stem the advance of Chinese power. (Even more, it would want to have credible nuclear options available *before* the outbreak of war to impose a limiting influence on Chinese objectives and to reassure U.S. allies and partners that would likely be considering independent courses of action in the face of an increasingly powerful People's Republic of China.) Such discriminate options would be designed to demonstrate U.S. resolve; threaten further escalation; and, ideally, frustrate the advance of Chinese forces or the ability of China to use its military forces to attack and coerce U.S. allies and partners. The last objective would be a natural focus for U.S. nuclear strikes, since it would both contribute to improving the U.S. situation in the conventional conflict while also constituting a natural limiting factor on U.S. nuclear use. The strategic purpose of such strikes would be not to achieve an elusive "victory" but rather to persuade Beijing to terminate the war on grounds tolerable to the United States. U.S. strikes would best be accompanied by the clear enunciation of a set of conditions that would lead to the cessation of U.S. nuclear use.

What implications does this all have for the current U.S. nuclear force? All things being equal, the more discrimination and tailoring potential the U.S. nuclear force provides, the more effective it should prove to be in a limited war scenario. And since the actual parameters of a scenario in which limited nuclear options would be a plausible option cannot be precisely anticipated, it makes sense for the nuclear force to provide as much discrimination and control as possible in terms of such criteria as

---

[40] For discussions of the concept of a "battle network" and the challenge posed to U.S. mastery of this vein of conflict, see, among others, Barry D. Watts, *Six Decades of Guided Munitions and Battle Networks: Progress and Prospects*, Washington, D.C.: Center for Strategic and Budgetary Assessments, 2007, and Andrew F. Krepinevich, Jr., "The Pentagon's Wasting Assets," *Foreign Affairs*, July/August 2009.

[41] This would be a context in which limited nuclear use might seem less escalatory than major conventional escalation options.

destructiveness, accuracy, radioactive release, utility against various targets, and redundancy. Such versatility in the effects available from its nuclear force would give the United States a greater ability to employ these forces to gain escalation advantage over an opponent. In blunter terms, it would enable the United States to be *better* at limited nuclear war than our adversaries, in turn giving us the strategic-political upper hand.

The current U.S. nuclear force can provide a substantial degree of discrimination and control, and thus a potential for escalation advantage, in most plausible scenarios Washington cares about. The problem, however, is that technological and military developments are moving in directions that could undermine the U.S. force's ability to provide these attributes. For instance, the ability to carry out highly discriminate strikes would be significantly weakened if advances in potential adversary air defenses make the bomber leg of the U.S. strategic triad a less reliable means of attack or if the Air Force is unable to fund and procure a next-generation nuclear-capable bomber, given the particular value of the bomber force in providing discriminate options. In addition, an aging U.S. command and control infrastructure risks making the precise control and application of U.S. nuclear forces in the circumstances of a limited nuclear conflict indelicate at best and self-defeating at worst.[42]

What then might be done to improve this situation, especially over the longer term? While the pursuit of the attributes required to conduct limited, discriminate attacks needs to be weighed against the benefits of other attributes that cannot always be simultaneously served to the same degree, there are steps the United States can sensibly take to sustain and improve its potential to execute limited nuclear options. Procuring a nuclear-capable, next-generation bomber that can deliver a newly developed B-61-12 nuclear bomb against the most sophisticated adversary air defense networks is a logical step, despite the expense entailed in doing so. The United States could also remove the secondary component of the nuclear warheads mounted on one or two of the Trident II D5 submarine-launched ballistic missiles carried on each *Ohio*-class nuclear submarine (and its successor) to provide a lower-yield strike option on a U.S. strategic ballistic missile. The long-range standoff option missile, the replacement for the nuclear air-launched cruise missile, could also be given a lower-yield option or options. More controversially, the United States could develop a more-effective nuclear "bunker buster"—that is, a nuclear weapon specially designed to neutralize hardened and deeply buried facilities. Perhaps most important, however, the United States should modernize its nuclear command and control system such that it can allow national leaders to employ U.S. nuclear forces with a satisfactory degree of control, precision, and restraint while also providing the capability to communicate reliably with allies and adversaries, even in the midst of war and in the face of cutting-edge

---

[42] For a (necessarily oblique) discussion of the need to modernize the nuclear command and control system, including to effectively control nuclear forces in conflict, see John R. Harvey, Principal Deputy Assistant Secretary of Defense for Nuclear, Chemical, and Biological Defense Programs, statement before the House Armed Services Committee Strategic Forces Subcommittee, May 9, 2013, especially pp. 6–7.

cyber and other threats. Specific weapons and weapon delivery capabilities would help improve the U.S. ability to wage a limited nuclear war—but it would absolutely require a refined command and control system. These improved capabilities for discriminate nuclear use can then be demonstrated—both to potential adversaries and to allies and partners—via command post exercises and occasional deployments, coupled with focused strategic messaging campaigns.

Beyond changes to hardware, however, the U.S. government can also strengthen its capabilities for adaptive and short-notice planning for nuclear scenarios, since effective limited nuclear warfighting absolutely depends on the intelligent and discriminate application of nuclear force. The U.S. government could also actively encourage a greater focus on the problems associated with the conduct of limited nuclear conflict among civilian and military defense officials and analysts and seek more concretely to integrate consideration of such problems into the tasking, development, and review of contingency plans for major theater conflicts, into U.S. military doctrine, and into the military requirements for delivery systems and nuclear weapons. Elements of the U.S. government beyond the Department of Defense should be included in efforts to try to anticipate the political aspects of a conflict in which highly limited nuclear strikes might be employed and how these political constraints would affect the conduct of such a war. Conclusions from such analyses should inform development and procurement of relevant systems, as well as nuclear force posture decisions. The basic point is that the U.S. government should begin to take the requirement to prepare itself for the very significant military capability and policy problems associated with planning for and conducting a limited nuclear war more seriously.

It should hardly need saying that care must be taken that such efforts not lead the U.S. government or, for that matter, any other government to look too sanguinely on the feasibility of controlling a limited nuclear war or the advisability of embarking on one. No one can know what that fateful crossing of the nuclear threshold—a threshold that has held, despite numerous adverse predictions, for almost 70 years—would entail, but we do know that the consequences could be disastrous, and quite possibly horrendous. As no less an authority on things military and strategic as Dwight Eisenhower pointedly observed,

> Now, nothing can be precluded in a military thing. Remember this: when you resort to force as the arbiter of human difficulty, you don't know where you are going; but, generally speaking, if you get deeper, there is just no limit except what is imposed by limitations of force itself.[43]

The utmost caution should therefore be observed should the use of such a limited nuclear war posture ever be contemplated.

---

[43] Dwight D. Eisenhower, "The President's News Conference," January 12, 1955.

But we must contemplate and prepare for limited nuclear war because, while nuclear weapons have chilled, they have not killed strategy. Nations and groups continue to seek advantage and gain in the manipulation of strength, weakness, risk, fear, and resolve. Strategies are therefore needed to ensure that the United States is on the favorable side of such encounters. And nuclear weapons, while they seem in their grotesque destructiveness the very antithesis of calculation, are nonetheless not immune from strategy either. To use them or to threaten with them successfully therefore requires that we do so strategically—in essence, that their use or threatened use be subject to some plausible rationality. And such rationality necessitates that they can be used in some way proportionate to the nature and scale of the contest—contemplated or actual. This is why it is important to plan for something as uncertain and menacing as a limited nuclear war.

Ultimately, however, both the point and the moral justification of preparing for limited nuclear use lie in the conviction that such readiness stands the best chance of convincing prospective adversaries that they stand little to gain and very much to lose if they truly cross the United States and that convincing them of that proposition is in turn the best way to avoid the great and very possibly catastrophic clash that would result if they were to test it. The point and justification for preparing for limited nuclear use lie, in other words, in the pursuit of the fulfillment of another of Eisenhower's dicta, that "the only way to win World War III is to prevent it."[44]

References

Ball, Desmond, *Déjà Vu: The Return to Counterforce in the Nixon Administration*, California Seminar on Arms Control and Foreign Policy, 1974.

———, *Can Nuclear War Be Controlled?* Adelphi Paper 169, 1981.

Brodie, Bernard, *Strategy in the Missile Age*, Princeton, N.J.: Princeton University Press, 1959.

Brown, Harold, *Department of Defense Annual Report for FY1981*, Washington, D.C.: U.S. Government Printing Office, 1980.

———, remarks delivered at the Convocation Ceremonies for the Naval War College, Newport, Rhode Island, August 20, 1980, in Philip Bobbitt, Lawrence Freedman, and Gregory F. Treverton, eds., *U.S. Nuclear Strategy: A Reader*, New York: New York University Press, 1989.

Bunn, M. Elaine, "Can Deterrence Be Tailored?" *Strategic Forum*, No. 225, January 2007, pp. 1–8.

Colby, Elbridge A., "Guiding Principles for the New Nuclear Guidance," *New Paradigms Forum*, April 11, 2011. As of January 10, 2013:
http://www.newparadigmsforum.com/NPFtestsite/?p=810

———, "Is Nuclear Deterrence Still Relevant," in Adam B. Lowther, ed., *Deterrence: Rising Powers, Rogue Regimes, and Terrorism in the 21st Century*, New York: Palgrave MacMillan, 2012, pp. 49–74.

---

[44] Dwight D. Eisenhower, "Radio and Television Address Opening the President's Campaign for Re-Election," September 19, 1956.

————, "The United States and Discriminate Nuclear Options in the Cold War," in Jeffrey A. Larsen and Kerry M. Kartchner, eds., *On Limited Nuclear War in the 21st Century*, Palo Alto, Calif.: Stanford University Press, 2014.

Colby, Elbridge A., Avner Cohen, William McCants, Bradley Morris, and William Rosenau, *The Israeli "Nuclear Alert" of 1973: Deterrence and Signaling in Crisis*, Alexandria, Va.: Center for Naval Analyses, 2013.

Davis, Lynn, *Limited Nuclear Options: Deterrence and the New American Doctrine*, Adelphi Paper 121, 1976.

Defense Science Board, *Resilient Military Systems and the Advanced Cyber Threat*, Washington, D.C.: Office of the Under Secretary of Defense for Acquisition, Technology and Logistics, January 2013. As of January 10, 2014:
http://www.acq.osd.mil/dsb/reports/ResilientMilitarySystems.CyberThreat.pdf

Drell, Sidney, and Frank von Hippel, "Limited Nuclear War," *Scientific American*, November 1976.

Eisenhower, Dwight D., "The President's News Conference," January 12, 1955. As of January 10, 2014:
http://www.presidency.ucsb.edu/ws/?pid=10232

————, "Radio and Television Address Opening the President's Campaign for Re-Election," September 19, 1956. As of January 10, 2014:
http://www.presidency.ucsb.edu/ws/?pid=10606

Gavin, Francis, "Politics, History and the Ivory Tower–Policy Gap in the Nuclear Proliferation Debate," *Journal of Strategic Studies*, Vol. 35, No. 4, August 29, 2012, pp. 573–600.

Gehrke, Joel, "Obama to South Korea: Our 'Nuclear Umbrella' Is Protecting You," *Washington Examiner*, February 12, 2013. As of January 10, 2014:
http://washingtonexaminer.com/obama-to-south-korea-our-nuclear-umbrella-is-protecting-you/article/2521300?custom_click=rss

Gilpin, Robert, *War and Change in World Politics*, Cambridge, UK: Cambridge University Press, 1981.

Gray, Colin, "Nuclear Strategy: The Case for a Theory of Victory," *International Security*, 1979.

"Hagel Vows Defense Commitments to Japan Including Nuclear Umbrella," *Japan Times*, April 30, 2013. As of January 10, 2014:
http://www.japantimes.co.jp/news/2013/04/30/national/hagel-vows-defense-commitments-to-japan-including-nuclear-umbrella/#.UkA80Yakpip

Halloran, Richard, "Hanamichi," *Real Clear Politics*, January 17, 2010. As of January 9, 2014:
http://www.realclearpolitics.com/articles/2010/01/17/hanamichi_99932.html

Halperin, Morton H., *Limited War in the Nuclear Age*, New York: John Wiley & Sons, 1965.

Harvey, John R., Principal Deputy Assistant Secretary of Defense for Nuclear, Chemical, and Biological Defense Programs, Statement before the House Armed Services Committee Strategic Forces Subcommittee, May 9, 2013. As of January 9, 2014:
http://docs.house.gov/meetings/AS/AS29/20130509/100558/HHRG-113-AS29-Wstate-HarveyJ-20130509.pdf

Howard, Michael, "On Fighting a Nuclear War," *International Security*, Spring 1981.

Kahn, Herman, *On Thermonuclear War*, Princeton, N.J.: Princeton University Press, 1961.

————, *On Escalation: Metaphors and Scenarios*, New York: Frederick A. Praeger, 1965.

———, *Thinking the Unthinkable in the 1980s*, Washington, D.C.: Hudson Institute, 1984.

Kissinger, Henry A., *Nuclear Weapons and Foreign Policy*, New York: Harper Brothers, 1957.

———, *White House Years*, Boston: Little, Brown and Company, 1979.

Knorr, Klaus E., and Thornton Reed, eds., *Limited Strategic War*, New York: Frederick A. Praeger, 1962.

Krepinevich, Jr., Andrew F., "The Pentagon's Wasting Assets," *Foreign Affairs*, July/August 2009.

Lambeth, Benjamin S., *Selective Nuclear Options in American and Soviet Strategic Policy*, Santa Monica, Calif.: RAND Corporation, R-2043-DDRE, 1976. As of January 9, 2014:
http://www.rand.org/pubs/reports/R2034.html

Lieber, Keir A., and Daryl G. Press, *Coercive Nuclear Campaigns in the 21st Century: Understanding Adversary Incentives and Options for Nuclear Escalation*, Monterey, Calif.: U.S. Naval Postgraduate School, 2013.

Morgan, Forrest E., *Dancing with the Bear: Managing Escalation in a Conflict with Russia*, Paris: Institute Français des Relations Internationales, 2012.

Morgan, Forrest E., Karl P. Mueller, Evan S. Medeiros, Kevin L. Pollpeter, and Roger Cliff, *Dangerous Thresholds: Managing Escalation in the 21st Century*, Santa Monica, Calif.: RAND Corporation, MG-614-AF, 2008. As of January 9, 2014:
http://www.rand.org/pubs/monographs/MG614.html

National Security Decision Memorandum 242, "Policy for Planning the Employment of Nuclear Weapons," January 17, 1974. As of January 9, 2014:
http://nixon.archives.gov/virtuallibrary/documents/nsdm/nsdm_242.pdf

National Security Study Memorandum 169, "U.S. Nuclear Policy," February 13, 1973. As of January 9, 2014:
http://nixon.archives.gov/virtuallibrary/documents/nssm/nssm_169.pdf

National Security Study Memorandum 169 Summary Report, June 8, 1973. As of January 9, 2014:
http://www.gwu.edu/~nsarchiv/NSAEBB/NSAEBB173/SIOP-21.pdf

Nolan, Janne E., *Guardians of the Arsenal: The Politics of Nuclear Strategy*, New York, Basic Books, 1989.

North Atlantic Military Committee, "Final Decision on MC 14/3: A Report by the Military Committee to the Defence Planning Committee on Overall Strategic Concept for the Defense of the North Atlantic Treaty Organization Area," January 16, 1968. As of January 9, 2014:
http://www.nato.int/docu/stratdoc/eng/a680116a.pdf

"Nuclear Targeting Policy Review," November 1978. As of January 9, 2014:
http://www.gwu.edu/~nsarchiv/nukevault/ebb390/docs/11-1-78%20policy%20review%20summary.pdf

Odom, William E., "The Origins and Design of Presidential Decision-59: A Memoir," in Henry D. Sokolski, ed., *Getting MAD: Nuclear Mutual Assured Destruction, Its Origins and Practice*, Carlisle, Pa.: Strategic Studies Institute, 2004.

Osgood, Robert E., *Limited War: The Challenge to American Strategy*, Chicago: University of Chicago Press, 1957.

———, "The Reappraisal of Limited War," The Adelphi Papers, special issue, *Problems of Modern Strategy: Part I*, Vol. 9, No. 54, 1969, pp. 41–54.

Pfaff, William, "Why Georgia Does Not Belong in NATO," *International Herald Tribune*, August 13, 2008. As of January 9, 2014:
http://www.williampfaff.com/modules/news/print.php?storyid=334&PHPSESSID=999365a153d199 3501b3986f3352b897

Presidential Directive 59, "Nuclear Weapons Employment Policy," July 25, 1980. As of January 14, 2014:
http://www.jimmycarterlibrary.gov/documents/pddirectives/pd59.pdf

Roberts, Brad, "Extended Deterrence and Strategic Stability in Northeast Asia," Tokyo: National Institute for Defense Studies, Visiting Scholar Paper Series No. 1, August 9, 2013.

Sagan, Scott, *Moving Targets: Nuclear Strategy and National Security*, Princeton, N.J.: Princeton University Press, 1989.

Schelling, Thomas C., *Arms and Influence*, New Haven, Conn.: Yale University Press, 1965.

Schlesinger, James R., Secretary of Defense, *Annual Defense Department Report for FY1975*, Washington, D.C.: U.S. Government Printing Office, 1974.

Schwartz, Norton A., and Jonathan W. Greenert, "AirSea Battle: Promoting Stability in an Era of Uncertainty," *The American Interest*, February 20, 2012.

Slocombe, Walter B., "The Countervailing Strategy," *International Security*, Vol. 5, No. 4, Spring 1981.

Smoke, Richard, *War: Controlling Escalation*. Cambridge, Mass.: Harvard University Press, 1977.

Terriff, Terry, *The Nixon Administration and the Making of U.S. Nuclear Strategy*, Ithaca, N.Y.: Cornell University Press, 1995.

U.S. Department of Defense, "Policy Guidance for the Employment of Nuclear Weapons (NUWEP)," October 1980. As of January 9, 2014:
http://www.gwu.edu/~nsarchiv/nukevault/ebb390/docs/10-24-80%20nuclear%20weapons%20 employment%20policy.pdf

———, *Nuclear Posture Review Report*, Washington, D.C.: U.S. Government Printing Office, 2010.

———, *Annual Report to Congress: Military and Security Developments Involving the People's Republic of China, 2013*, Washington, D.C.: Government Printing Office, 2013.

———, AirSea Battle Office, *Air-Sea Battle: Service Collaboration to Address Anti-Access & Area Denial Challenges*, June 2013. As of January 9, 2014:
http://navylive.dodlive.mil/files/2013/06/ASB-26-June-2013.pdf

———, "Report on Nuclear Employment Strategy of the United States Specified in Section 491 of 10 U.S.C.," June 12, 2013. As of January 10, 2014:
http://www.defense.gov/pubs/ReporttoCongressonUSNuclearEmploymentStrategy_Section491.pdf

Waltz, Kenneth N., "Nuclear Myths and Political Realities," *American Political Science Review*, Vol. 84, No. 3, pp. 731–745.

Warner, Edward L., *Soviet Concepts and Capabilities for Limited Nuclear War: What We Know and How We Know It*, Santa Monica, Calif.: RAND Corporation, N-2769-AF, 1989. As of January 9, 2014:
http://www.rand.org/pubs/notes/N2769.html

Watts, Barry D., *Six Decades of Guided Munitions and Battle Networks: Progress and Prospects*, Washington, D.C.: Center for Strategic and Budgetary Assessments, 2007.

————, *Nuclear-Conventional Firebreaks and the Nuclear Taboo*, Washington, D.C.: Center for Strategic and Budgetary Assessments, 2013.

Weinberger, Caspar W., "U.S. Defense Strategy," *Foreign Affairs*, Spring 1986.

Wickham, John A., Jr., memorandum to Brent Scowcroft, "Policy Guidance for the Employment of Nuclear Weapons [NUWEP]," April 3, 1974. As of January 9, 2014:
http://www.gwu.edu/~nsarchiv/NSAEBB/NSAEBB173/SIOP-25.pdf

Work, Robert O., and Shawn Brimley, *20YY: Preparing for War in the Robotic Age*, Washington, D.C.: Center for a New American Security, 2014.

CHAPTER ELEVEN

The Development and Ratification of New START

Rose E. Gottemoeller

This is not an analysis or commentary on nuclear weapon policy, but homage to a respected colleague and dear friend. I first got to know Ted Warner when he and I worked together at the RAND Corporation in the 1980s. We were both in the orbit of Tom Wolfe, who had been the air attaché in Moscow in the Khrushchev era, when he helped to dispel the bomber gap. In those days, Tom was the senior analyst of Soviet strategic doctrine and force structure at RAND and an expert on arms control policy. I was Tom's research assistant, and Ted was himself a former assistant air attaché recently returned from Moscow with an insider's knowledge of the strategic rocket forces and long-range aviation.

Ted and I were colleagues for many years, coming to be neighbors in the offices at 2100 M Street that were the Washington outpost of RAND in the 1970s, 1980s, and early 1990s. We shared a much loved and respected assistant, Rosalie Fonoroff, whom I liked to scare with my babies. On one occasion in the mid-80s, I left my son Daniel sleeping on a quilt on the floor of Ted's office—he was out of town—between pediatrician appointments. Rosalie was petrified, but Dan survived the experience. He is now thirty years old and an expert on information systems. As far as I know, Ted never heard that his office had served as a nursery.

❦

Since Ted and I worked together at RAND, our paths have crossed many times—sometimes in government, sometimes out. Never was that crossing more fortuitous than in April 2009, when Jim Miller—then Principal Deputy Under Secretary of Defense for Policy—told me that he would like Ted to serve as the representative of the Secretary of Defense to the planned strategic arms reduction negotiations with the Russians.

The negotiations unfolded in record time, producing by April 2010 the treaty that we now call the New Strategic Arms Reduction Treaty (New START). Many factors affected the speed of the negotiations—the impending expiration of START in December 2009 was an important spur, as was the prevalent mood of U.S.-Russian relations—the famed but short-lived "reset." The accumulated joint experience of four decades of nuclear arms limitation and reduction was another important influence—both we and the Russians understood how to do on-site inspections, for example, and many of the established procedures did not have to be laboriously renegotiated. Finally, the advent of electronic communications sped the process up in ways that I could not have predicted when I was a junior member of the original START delegation in 1990.

The most critical influence on the pace of progress, however, was the quality of the negotiating teams on both sides of the table—a mixture of experienced "gray-beards," who knew the START and Cold War diplomacy, and young Turks, who did not know diplomacy but knew the strategic nuclear systems inside and out. Although he never sported much hair, he did have a beard, and I can say that Ted Warner, one of my two deputy heads of the U.S. delegation, was the preeminent graybeard on the New START delegation. For that reason, I knew he could be trusted with the complex task of negotiating the Inspection Activities portion of the Protocol and the Inspection Activities Annex of New START. That decision did not emerge immediately, but Ted *was* present at the creation. On April 24, 2009, a small triumvirate of Ted, George Look—then Senior Director for Arms Control on the National Security Council Staff—and I met with a small team on the Russian side, let by Anatoly Antonov, the Russian chief negotiator and head of the Arms Control and Nonproliferation Directorate in the Ministry of Foreign Affairs. Our first meeting was in the palazzo that houses the American Embassy in Rome. The room was an enormous red and gold-gilt ballroom, and our small discussion table was dwarfed at one end of it—an impressive but overwhelming environment to begin our talks.

Anatoly, a canny negotiator who—he tells me—loves to play games, immediately tried to knock me off stride by being rude, in the old-timey style of Soviet diplomacy. I responded with a light touch, and Ted and George both helped push past his opening gambit by keeping the focus on substance. It was immediately clear, however, that we had a different view of what the new treaty should look like. The Russian side had in mind a kind of "START Lite:" further reductions but a very weak verification regime—essentially a transparency program. We had in mind a kind of replay of START with new reduction numbers and a new approach to counting.

The intervening weeks to the Moscow Summit of July 2009 did not resolve this difference of views but brought it into sharper focus. Ted was instrumental in explaining the U.S. position with regard to the START attribution counting rules, which held that a delivery vehicle would be counted as carrying the maximum number of reentry vehicles (warheads) with which it had been tested. This rule had disadvantaged the United States during the life of START, once the Air Force and Navy began downloading intercontinental ballistic missiles (ICBMs) and submarine launched ballistic missiles (SLBMs) to numbers of reentry vehicles lower than those with which they had been tested.

In explaining this issue to the Russian delegation, Ted showed not only his deep knowledge of both the U.S. and Russian strategic nuclear forces, but also his power of explanation. The first of many Warner sketches on yellow foolscap emerged at our first Moscow meeting in May. They became both famous and dreaded on the Russian side of the table. "No, no more pictures!" was a common Russian cry by the end of the negotiations a year later. I have to say that I had to make similar comments sometimes in delegation meetings, or we never would have gotten out of there. Ted's pictures, however, brought the issues alive for many on both sides of the table.

The July 2009 Moscow Summit created some basic agreement on numbers; it also provided invaluable Presidential guidance to the negotiating teams. However, we remained far apart on the concept for the treaty. When we met to present our first treaty drafts in September 2009, one Russian delegation member said point blank that Ted Warner was "crazy" for presenting a detailed verification regime. The Russian side was still stuck on a "lite" approach, favoring a transparency regime over anything that would resemble intrusive verification.

It was at this point that we entered the period of greatest creativity for the U.S. negotiating team, and Ted was right at the center of it. He approached me as we were wrapping up our September session and said he thought it would be worthwhile to leave a team of technical experts in Geneva in early October, to scrub through our verification proposals and develop concepts better suited to the new counting approach that we were proposing and also designed to be more economical to implement.

Already, rumblings of impending budget austerity were causing treaty implementers in the Air Force, Navy, and Department of Defense to urge us to look for more-efficient but still-effective methods of verification. We needed to look for means that would cost less but still give us what we needed in terms of confidence and predictability. Similar rumblings were coming from the Russian side. Although the Russians do have a general allergy to intrusiveness, they also were experiencing budget cutbacks in the Ministry of Defense that were affecting their own treaty implementers.

So it came about that the delegation's "young Turks" stayed in Geneva for an intensive early October work project that created the basic concept of the New START verification regime. The graybeards returned to Washington to work the issues with the administration leadership. Keen interest at the top in the White House ensured that we were explaining the rationale for our proposals at every step of the way. Ted, along with Mike Elliott, the experienced Joint Staff representative, and Kurt Siemon and Dick Trout, who taught me everything I know during the START negotiations in 1990, were the connective tissue to the technical team in Geneva. We all spent a lot of time on secure telephone and email lines to Geneva during the opening weeks of that month.

The result was an effective verification regime well-suited to U.S. interests: fewer types of inspections, but ones that addressed the particular demands of the treaty. The inspections also would become multifunctional, covering multiple tasks—such as data updating—that had previously taken place as separate inspection events. The rationale behind that approach was to save money in the implementation process by consolidating the inspection trips that each side would be taking and also by cutting down on the interruptions that inspections cause to operations at the bases where the weapons are deployed.

The most important innovation of the new regime was the Type One inspection, which came about because of the necessity of accounting for warheads actually mounted on delivery vehicles. No longer would it be sufficient to use an attribution counting rule based on the test history of a particular missile. Instead, the approach would be based on confirming the number of warheads declared to be mounted on individual ICBMs and SLBMs.

This approach was developed as a response to the counting "penalty" that emerged in START as ICBMs and SLBMs were downloaded. The D5 SLBM, for example, always had to be counted as carrying eight operational warheads, despite the fact that it came to be carrying consistently fewer. As the concept developed, however, it became that clear the notion of confirming the number of warheads declared on individual missiles would also have a forward-looking purpose. Future arms control treaties would focus not only on large items of account—launchers and delivery vehicles—but also on smaller items of account—warheads. These are less easy to account for because they cannot be monitored by national technical means in the same way that an ICBM silo or bomber can. The Type One concept thus was the first step in the direction of accounting for individual warheads and inspecting to confirm that accounting.

Ted Warner was at the intellectual heart of this new concept. When the senior team returned to Geneva late in October 2009, he had gotten there early to go over the new ideas that the technical experts had generated, to critique them as only Ted can, and to prepare to present them to the rest of us. We worked hard in Geneva and with Washington to hone these proposals to be ready to present to the Russians, then began the hard slog to negotiate the measures and turn them into treaty language.

At this point, the Inspection Activities Working Group began to take shape, and I asked Ted to chair it. It was one of the soundest decisions I made in the negotiating process, and it had wide support both in Washington and on the team in Geneva. Along with his Russian counterpart, Colonel Yevgeny Il'in, and experts on both sides of the table, the working group made a huge contribution to the success of New START. By the end of the negotiations, the two sides had gotten thoroughly sick of each other, but the hard work and great knowledge and diplomatic skills of both teams generated a lot of mutual respect between them.

There is much more that I could say about Ted Warner's contribution to the negotiations, but I would like to fast forward to the next challenge to get the treaty entered into force—the ratification process in the U.S. Senate. From the day when New START was signed—April 8, 2010—until the day the Senate voted to give its advice and consent to its ratification—December 22, 2011—Ted was a principal member of the team that explained the treaty to the American public; the media; the expert community; and, ultimately, to the Senate. From the moment the treaty was signed, Ted was at the center of efforts to promote it.

On April 8, the five senior members of the negotiating team—Marcie Ries and Ted, my deputies, and Mike Elliott, Kurt Siemon, and Dick Trout—had joined me at

Prague Castle when President Obama signed the treaty with Russian President Medvedev. We had a chance to shake hands with the President prior to the signing ceremony, but there was no champagne afterward.[1] We were hustled away immediately for a press conference, to begin explaining the details of the treaty to the media. It was an odd setting, inside a kind of tent affair that I imagine served as a sound buffer for the broadcast microphones. For those not used to the press, it would have been nonplussing, but Ted immediately dove in, explaining the technical details and how they fit together.

It was the first of many sessions before the press and public and especially before the U.S. Senate. During the course of the ratification process, we did 21 hearings or briefings before Senate members or staff, often in closed sessions where the senators could dig deep concerning the technical details of the treaty. We also paid many calls on individual senators, and here, Ted's knowledge and experience, as well as his great reputation, paid off. He took charge of explaining the new Inspection Activities portions of the treaty—their innovative aspects proved to be one of the areas that the Senate focused on during the ratification debate, wondering why it had to be different from START.

This process was deliberate and highly detailed, but, eventually, we were able to build up the case that the new verification regime is in the interests of U.S. national security. During the course of the ratification debate, we answered more than 1,000 questions for the record, and many of them addressed the technical aspects of the verification regime. Because Ted had been in at the creation and every step of the way, he could explain, as no one else could, the need to tackle a new monitoring task—accounting for warheads rather than using an attribution counting rule—and point out how this new approach could save money for the Air Force, Navy, and Department of Defense overall. His contribution, therefore, was critical to the success of the ratification effort.

Another of Ted's lines of expertise that came in handy was his knowledge of the vagaries of Cold War era nuclear doctrine and strategy—mutual deterrence, warfighting, the offense-defense relationship, and other aspects. In the years since the Senate had given its advice and consent to START in 1992, many new members had arrived, and several generations of staffers had turned over. Those who remembered the debates of the Reagan-Gorbachev era and earlier years were few. When questions came up about the history of U.S. nuclear weapon policy and the Cold War, Ted was able to answer clearly and succinctly—and at great length. I sometimes thought the senators heard more about history than they had in mind, but they always had more questions, and we welcomed the chance to answer them.

In reflecting on New START ratification, I have concluded that one of the reasons for its success was this serious, patient, iterative process. For good reason, the sena-

---

[1] There were beer and sausage that night and toasts among the six of us in Prague and pizza and beer with toasts among the U.S. team left back in Geneva—a night of great happiness and satisfaction for us all.

tors and their staffs had a lot of questions: It had been twenty years since the Senate had wrestled with a major nuclear arms reduction treaty, and in that time, the Cold War had ended; the Warsaw Pact had gone away; and our relationship with the Russian Federation had altered—not in the direction of a perfect bilateral relationship, but in serious ways nevertheless. What would nuclear arms reduction mean in this environment? What would its importance be? And how would it relate both to the previous era and to the future? These questions had not only policy implications but also intertwining budgetary and technical ones. Questions about the modernization of the U.S. nuclear weapon infrastructure were just one example of how the New START debate took on larger meaning in Washington.

I always have believed that wrestling with such questions is at the heart of a good policy process, wherein skeptics and proponents have a chance to dig deep into issues, try to understand them, and eventually agree on a path forward. Some will never agree: In today's Washington, a tendency to shun compromise runs in some circles. For those willing to work the issues, however, patience, seriousness, experience, and whip-smart knowledge seem to make a difference. At least that's the lesson that I took from the debate over New START.

And no one exemplifies these qualities better than Ted Warner. In thirty years of working together, he often has been patient with me—and we often have had our arguments. But he has also been a great mentor, as he was for a couple of generations of young people on the New START delegation, at RAND, and throughout the Pentagon. That willingness to be generous with his time and experience is a gift that Ted has given again and again.

Ted Warner's influence on national policy has been evident throughout his career, but it is most vivid to me in the story of New START. His contribution was unique, both in negotiating the treaty and in its ratification process. Looking forward, to advance any complex national security policy, whether in Washington or with foreign partners, I would like to have Ted in my corner. He would field questions with calm expertise, keep returning to an issue as many times as was needed, and maybe draw some pictures on yellow foolscap. In the end, he would wear everyone down—in the interests of U.S. national security, and international peace and stability.

I am glad I have had him as a colleague and friend.

CHAPTER TWELVE

Multilateral Nuclear Disarmament: Are We Ready to Open the Box of Pandora?

Alexei G. Arbatov

My wife Nadia and I have been friends with Edward Warner and his family for almost a quarter of a century. We first met Ted and his wife, Pam, in the late 1980s at an Aspin Institute conference on international security and arms control, organized under the leadership of former Senator Dick Clark, at an exotic and luxurious resort in Jamaica. Since that time, we have developed a lasting friendship, which at some point included my daughter, Katherine, and his daughter, Erika.

It is quite possible, though, that I had met Ted even earlier at some of many conferences on arms control and strategic relations that proliferated in the 1970s and 1980s, but neither of us can remember it now with certainty, since it happened in the previous century.

Since the early 1990s, we have seen one another regularly at various seminars and conferences in the United States and Russia, more often in a bilateral format (Ted and myself), but sometimes all four of us. When I and my family stayed for a few months in Washington, Santa Monica, or Boston in the 1990s, we visited each other and spent wonderful time together.

While Ted was working as Assistant Secretary of Defense and I was a deputy chairman of the Defense Committee of Russian Parliament (State Duma) during the 1990s, we always met when I visited Washington, which happened several times a year (and Pam often joined us). A couple of years ago, after a considerable interval, Ted and Pam visited Nadia and me in Moscow, and we had a warm reunion as very old and dear friends.

Ted is a great professional, warm, and witty human being, and so are Pam and his daughter Erika (and certainly so is their other daughter Kelly, although I do not know her so well). During the quarter century of our friendship, we developed a close relationship—almost like relatives, not just good friends. I have a lot of American friends and colleagues, but this relationship is one of a few unique cases.

Ted has made a distinguished career as a military officer and then an expert and civil servant in the fields of international security, strategic studies, arms control, and U.S. defense policy. I believe the peak of his professional ascent was the successful negotiation of the U.S.-Russian New Strategic Arms Reduction Treaty (New START), which he negotiated along with Rose Gottemoeller and their Russian counterparts in 2009–2010. According to Russian participants, many of whom I know personally (e.g., Ambassador Anatoly Antonov, the lead Russian negotiator, who is presently a deputy minister of defense), Ted was a tough negotiator, but he earned respect and sympathy among the Russian team, since he had been friendly, straightforward, and knowledgeable and always kept his word.

During the many years that we have been interacting, we have developed professional mutual understanding and respect, even when we have disagreed on various esoteric issues of nuclear deterrence and arms control. Ted is a very positive person, and it is gratifying to find agreement with him, as well as to clarify the points of disagreement.

Most recently, both of us have participated in Carnegie Endowment's project on U.S.-Russian-Chinese trilateral strategic relationship. It has been fascinating to see how, on various issues of nuclear deterrence and arms control, two of the three parties united against the third in shifting, kaleidoscopic combinations.

That is why I have decided to dedicate to Ted a portion of my most recent research, which represents further elaboration of a philosophy of multilateral arms control and explores the prospects of its expansion from a bilateral format to an even broader scope.

ℰℛ

Multilateral Idealism

At a roundtable in the Russian Federal Nuclear Center in the city of Sarov on February 24, 2012, Russian presidential candidate Vladimir Putin told a gathering of Russian specialists on defense and arms control matters that he had convened: "We will not disarm unilaterally. ... All nuclear powers should participate in the process. We cannot disarm while other nuclear powers are building up their arms."[1] Since that time, he has repeated this idea in various speeches, and it has become an integral part of Russian official foreign policy documents.

Many politicians and experts in the United States and Russia intuitively share this stance. This is one of few points of agreement of the two parties, and, hence, it deserves most careful examination, especially in the context of another, hopefully temporary, impasse in bilateral U.S.-Russian nuclear disarmament.

Comparing the strategic nuclear forces of the two leading powers, as they will be reduced under New START (see Figure 12.1), and the nuclear arsenals of the other seven nuclear weapon states, this position appears to be quite convincing. It is possible that it is this particular picture that military advisors demonstrate to their respective state leaderships.

Nevertheless, this generally sensible political position does not remove the need for scientific scrutiny. A systemic assessment requires a thought-through answer to a number of substantive questions and may lead to quite unexpected conclusions. It does not look like the bureaucracies of the two leading nuclear states have done this job or have even started doing it—to say nothing of reporting such analysis to their presidents.

---

[1] Vladimir Putin met with experts in Sarov, February 24, 2012 ("Prime Minister Vladimir Putin Meets with Experts in Sarov to Discuss Global Threats to National Security, Strengthening Russia's Defences and Enhancing the Combat Readiness of Its Armed Forces," Working Day web archive, February 24, 2012.

Figure 12.1
Russia, the United States, and the Other Nuclear-Weapon States

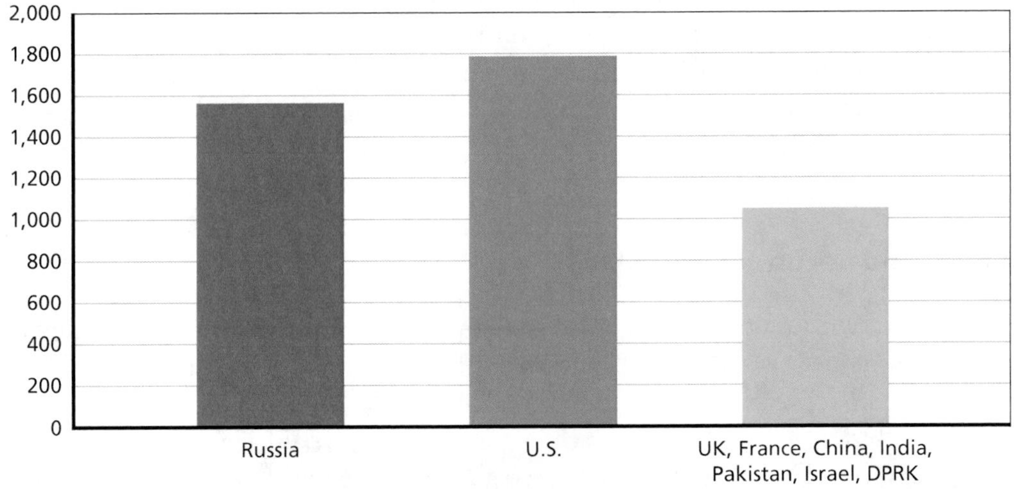

SOURCES: Stockholm International Peace Research Institute (SIPRI), *SIPRI Yearbook 2011: Armaments, Disarmament and International Security*, New York: Oxford University Press, 2011, pp. 319–353; U.S. Department of State, "New START Treaty Aggregate Numbers of Strategic Offensive Arms," web page, April 6, 2012; Federation of American Scientists, "Status of World Nuclear Forces," web page, May 7, 2012.
RAND *CP765-12.1*

First and foremost, it should be demonstrated that the time has really come to engage additional countries in the process of nuclear disarmament. Why exactly now and not before now or later? What countries should be engaged, in what sequence, and which nuclear weapons should be limited? What would serve as a conceptual basis—parity, stability, status quo, allocation of quotas—for their involvement, and on what counting rules should it be based? Finally, what opportunities will emerge for exchanging relevant military and technical information, and what capabilities will be required to verify arms limitations by "third" nuclear-weapon states?

Declarations by and political pressure from Russia and the United States regarding broadened participation in the nuclear disarmament process would hardly be enough to bring these countries to the negotiating table; the world is becoming more polycentric, and other global and regional centers of power are becoming increasingly independent and self-assertive. The rest of the nuclear club members invariably and uniformly respond to the calls for their inclusion in the disarmament process from the two leading nuclear powers by stating that they will join only if and when Russia and the United States further reduce their nuclear arsenals down to a level at least comparable to those of other nuclear-weapon states. All parties refer to the Article VI of the Treaty on the Non-Proliferation of Nuclear Weapons (NPT) in this regard but have unfortunately failed to shift from mere political rhetoric to indicating any willingness to enter substantive negotiations.

Usually, the models and options for engaging other nuclear-weapon states in nuclear disarmament are considered as steps on the way to a nuclear-weapon-free world. While sharing this vision on moral and philosophical grounds, this chapter presents a somewhat different perspective on the problem for the foreseeable future. It is based on pragmatic political, military-strategic, and technical perspectives, which may be more relevant to the practical policies of states than the idealistic wording of Article VI of the NPT is.

Political and Security Context

Russia has every reason to be more insistent than the United States in its urge to make nuclear disarmament a multilateral endeavor. Russia's territory lies within reach of the nuclear weapon delivery means of all the remaining seven nuclear-weapon states (and the eighth candidate for the nuclear club—Iran), none of which is Russia's formal military-political ally. By contrast, U.S. territory is presently vulnerable to a hypothetical nuclear attack from only two states: Russia and China. The other six nuclear-weapon states are either allied to the United States (the United Kingdom and France) or have no delivery means of a sufficient range (North Korea, India, Pakistan, and Israel). Moreover, most of the latter have also been U.S. partners (Israel, for a long time, and in recent years also India and Pakistan, despite Pakistan's growing reservations).

Nevertheless, there are political considerations that cast doubt on the notion of third countries' "joining" the process of nuclear disarmament, either on an individual basis, or in groups, for example, of the "European two" (the United Kingdom and France), "the NPT five" (the United States, Russia, China, the United Kingdom, and France), or the "non-NPT four" (India, Pakistan, Israel, and North Korea) nuclear-weapon states. Such models appear to be too excessively "mechanical" to be implemented. The political and military relations among the nine nuclear-weapon states are too variable to solve the extremely complicated task of incorporating them into the nuclear arms limitation process based on such formal criteria.

Russia's strategic relations with the United Kingdom and France, as North Atlantic Treaty Organization (NATO) members, are determined by its relations with the United States. The two European nuclear powers are rather open regarding the size of their nuclear forces, have recently considerably reduced them, and have stated that they plan further nuclear arms reductions in the future. These two states, in reality, present no serious independent or additional threat to Russia; neither can they tangibly affect the projected U.S.-Russian nuclear balance, at least as long as the U.S. and Russia's operationally deployed strategic nuclear forces remain above or at the New START levels (700 deployed strategic missile launchers and heavy bombers and 1,550 strategic warheads).

India has long been Russia's close partner, while Russia and Israel have established a partnership in recent decades. Russia's relations with these two countries are most likely to remain stable, and if there is a mutual deterrence relationship between Russia and Israel, it is latent and remains far in the background of their political relations. In terms of *realpolitik*, engaging these two countries in nuclear disarmament is not a matter of paramount importance or urgency in terms of Russian national security interests and concerns.

In contrast to that situation, Russia should look with concern primarily at its relations with Pakistan and the Democratic People's Republic of Korea (DPRK) as being those that could be drastically destabilized in the event of radical changes in their domestic situations or foreign policies, which are beyond Russia's influence. There is another unpredictable country, Iran, whose capabilities may cross the "nuclear threshold" and cause an outbreak of war in the region and/or a chain reaction of further nuclear and missile proliferation in the vicinity of Russia's borders. Both contingencies would be highly detrimental to Russian security. Although an important first step in peaceful resolution of the Iranian problem was made in the Geneva interim agreement in November 2013, reaching a comprehensive deal is a long way ahead and in no way assured.

Although China, a new superpower in the 21st century with which Russia is building a strategic partnership, should not in any sense be placed in the same group with the three countries cited immediately above, the possibility of drastic changes in China's domestic and foreign policy cannot be ruled out. Alongside China's growing economic and military potential, including its expanding nuclear-armed strategic missile forces, such changes could, in a foreseeable future, have a direct bearing on the security of Russia and other countries, fundamentally altering the strategic landscape of the world.

For this reason, limiting the nuclear weapons of China and Pakistan, achieving the nuclear disarmament of the DPRK, and preventing Iran from acquiring nuclear weapons are certainly in Russia's most basic security interest. Interestingly enough, this, in principle, coincides with likely U.S. priorities, although this fact has not received much attention from either the general public or the political communities of the two nations. The reason is that strategic rationality often gives way to political biases, and for this reason, Russia tends to understate the security problems China, Iran, and North Korea pose, while the U.S. plays down the issue of Pakistan.

However, in each case, it will take the creation of an adequate format and the right moment to convince each of these countries to join a nuclear disarmament process—not just appealing to obligations set forth in Article VI of the NPT or placing the states noted above in formal groups and asserting that they will need to join the nuclear disarmament process at a particular time as members of these groups.

No doubt, it would be most convenient for the two superpowers to formalize the existing balance of nuclear forces by first limiting, at the present levels, the nuclear arms of the other three NPT nuclear-weapon states, then extending such freeze-in-place limitations to the remaining four nuclear-weapon states. Another option would involve establishing an aggregate ceiling of about 1,000 nuclear warheads for the nuclear arsenal of all seven remaining countries, which may be close to the present overall number of their warheads today, and letting them develop individual quotas among themselves or create quotas that allocate them according to their actual current proportion. However, both these and other, similar artificial options seem totally unfeasible.

It should be kept in mind that, just like Russia and the United States, each nuclear-arms state has pursued its own national security interests by acquiring nuclear weapons. These interests include deterring conventional, nuclear, and other weapons of mass destruction attacks; exerting political pressure on adversaries; securing increased political status and prestige; and acquiring bargaining chips for use in negotiations with other powers. More often than not, these nuclear-weapon states do not measure their nuclear capabilities by comparing them with those of the two superpowers or of the majority of other nuclear-weapon states. Hence, they would not agree to either an aggregate ceiling for the seven or individual quotas divided among them according to any set ratio.

Strategic Balances

Keeping in mind that third nuclear-weapon states are likely to refuse in principle to be included in one or several groups for comparison with the two superpowers regarding the size of nuclear forces, it would be convenient to divide the nine nuclear-weapon states into three relatively simple and purely formal categories to assess the military balance. The first grouping is made up of the two leading superpowers, Russia and the United States. The second comprises the three other NPT nuclear-weapon states, which also happen to hold permanent seats in the United Nations Security Council: the United Kingdom, France, and China. The third grouping consists of the four non-NPT nuclear-arms states: Israel, India, Pakistan, and North Korea.

For the sake of objectivity, the full range of types of nuclear weapons should be considered, not just the strategic nuclear arms of Russia and the United States, which are limited under New START, when comparisons are made with the total nuclear arsenals of the rest of the nuclear-weapon states.

Hence, nuclear forces of the groups of three and four nuclear-weapon states noted above (of which, only the United Kingdom and France have made information on the size of their nuclear arsenals publicly available) should be compared to total nuclear arsenals of Russia and the United States, rather than merely their strategic nuclear forces. These forces include strategic and nonstrategic (operational-tactical) nuclear weapons, including both those that are operationally deployed, that is, mounted day-to-day on their delivery vehicles, and those kept in secure storage in different technical conditions and for different purposes. This is logical, since all or a large portion of the nuclear weapons of China, India, Pakistan, and Israel are reportedly nondeployed and kept at a level of reduced readiness; in particular, nuclear warheads are stored separately from their missile delivery systems and nuclear bombs separate from the aircraft that would deliver them. Regarding North Korea, it is not even clear whether its six to eight nuclear explosive devices have been adapted for delivery by ballistic missiles because due to their big size packing them in gravity bombs for delivery by combat aircraft might be at present a more feasible option.

In this case, the balance of forces between either of the two superpowers, on the one hand, and the aggregate number of nuclear warheads in possession of "the NPT three" and "the non-NPT four," on the other hand, appears much more asymmetrical, leaning heavily in favor of the two superpowers, the United States and Russia (see Figure 12.2). The uncertainty arises mainly with regard to the estimates of China's nuclear forces because China has never publicly released any information regarding the size of its nuclear arsenal or provided any explanation regarding the intended use of the enormous complex of underground tunnels reportedly built by its Second Artillery Corps (the equivalent of Russia's Strategic Missile Forces). If these tunnels are being used to store nuclear-armed, mobile, theater-range and intercontinental ballistic missiles, the number of its missiles and warheads may reach many hundreds, as the aggregate length of the tunnels reportedly stands at approximately 5,000 km.

Figure 12.2
Global Stockpiles of Nuclear Weapons (Strategic, Nonstrategic, and Those Kept in Storage, Including Those Awaiting Disposal)

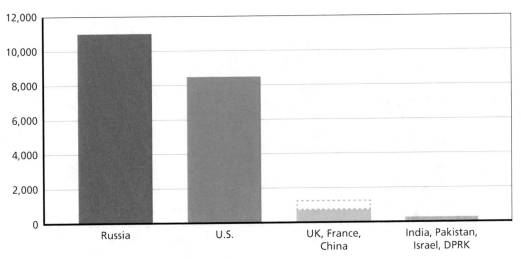

SOURCES: SIPRI, 2011, pp. 319–353; U.S. Department of State, 2012; Federation of American Scientists, 2012.

RAND *CP765-12.2*

Comparing the nuclear arsenals of "the NPT three" and "the non-NPT four" that can be regarded to be strategic by the New START counting rules shifts the ratio of the number of aggregate warheads of the third world weapon states to that of the two biggest powers from 5 percent to about 11 to 17 percent (see Figure 12.3). Still, U.S. and Russian forces vastly outnumber the others.

Therefore, in terms of the balance of comparable categories of nuclear arms, Russia and the United States, even after they implement the New START reductions that are to be completed by February 2018, will retain a huge advantage over the nuclear forces of seven other nuclear-weapon states taken together, to say nothing of comparison with individual nuclear-weapon states. Moreover, each of them views itself as an individual nuclear-weapon state, not as a member of a group of such states, which is similar to the way the United States and Russia think of themselves. The only uncertainty relates to the size of the Chinese nuclear arsenal and the possible presence of nuclear weapons in its secret tunnels, as well as the very large military production capacity China possesses for building up its nuclear-weapon stockpile.

In addition, in view of the existing and projected balance of nuclear forces, there is no urgent need to involve third-country nuclear-weapon states in arms reductions at this time. This is true of the situation after the United States and Russia implement New START and also if they conclude a follow-on treaty to limit their strategic nuclear forces at approximately 1,000 strategic warheads, which would be reached after 2020. Here again, the only exception is related to China, for the reasons mentioned above.

Figure 12.3
Nuclear-Weapon Stockpiles as Counted Under the 2010 New START

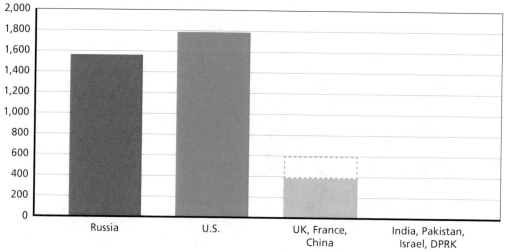

SOURCES: SIPRI, 2011, pp. 319–353; U.S. Department of State, 2012; Federation of American Scientists, 2012.
RAND CP765-12.3

Strategic Relations in a Multilateral Format

Substantive negotiations on nuclear arms limitation are a pivotal element of military strategic relations among the nations, as has been the case of the relations between the United States and the Union of Soviet Socialist Republics (USSR), now Russia, for the past 45 years. Therefore, in line with the only practical experience available to us, for substantive arms limitation treaties to be concluded, the strategic relations between the nuclear states should involve a mutually recognized state of mutual nuclear deterrence, like that which exists between the United States and Russia and previously existed between the United States and the USSR. In this case, one of the states may limit its forces and military programs in exchange for similar limitations on the part of the other. This has been and remains the essence of substantive nuclear arms limitations and reductions, in contrast to political posturing and appeals to Article VI of the NPT.

Of the present nine nuclear-weapon states, some have indeed developed relations of more or less symmetrical mutual nuclear deterrence with other adversary nuclear-weapon states, which strategically and technically provides the optimum basis for negotiations. Another set of states has asymmetrical nuclear deterrence, with one having a decided numerical advantage over the other, although both are likely to be subject to devastating retaliation from the other should they strike first, which makes arms limitation agreements much more difficult to reach. The third set of countries could technically deliver a nuclear strike against each other, but for political reasons, nuclear deterrence is not a key element of their relations, or alternatively, it may have a latent nature, which does not provide a clear foundation for negotiations. Finally, the fourth and fifth varieties of nations do not have relations of mutual deterrence at all, either for military-technical reasons (i.e., if they are out of reach of each other's forces) or in view of their friendly political relationship.

Hence, the world system of nuclear relations among nuclear-weapon states consists of at least five different paradigms, some of which are conducive to arms control talks and some not, but neither suggests a possibility of participation on the "welcome to the club" principle. Existing world strategic relationships are not sufficiently uniform to provide a universal foundation of multilateral nuclear arms limitation, despite the fact that a "get on the bandwagon" model is most commonly discussed at formal political and expert forums.

The United Kingdom and France are two nuclear-weapon states located within range of each other's nuclear weapons. However, their relationship is not characterized by nuclear deterrence because they are allies in NATO and the European Union. They relatively recently concluded an agreement on cooperation in the military-nuclear field, and they have no incentive to negotiate a mutual reduction of nuclear forces with each other. The same is true for the relations of these two powers with the United States; they are all members of NATO.

Similarly, there are no grounds for negotiations on mutual nuclear arms limitations between China and the United Kingdom or China and France. China is mostly beyond the range of the nuclear arms of the United Kingdom and France, and so—despite some recent declarations by Paris to the contrary—they do not have relationships with China based on mutual deterrence.

For the same reason, the three mentioned powers have no incentives for joining subsequent U.S.-Russian START negotiations. The size and specifications of Beijing's nuclear capability are not strategically linked in any way to the forces and programs of Paris or London, and the three countries have no common ground for agreeing on mutual arms limitations, although all three belong to the five NPT "legitimate" nuclear-weapon states. In particular, Beijing may always claim that it is entitled to many more nuclear weapons than the European states because China is not allied with any other nuclear-weapon state; has no security assurances from any other power; and has mutual deterrence relationships with three other nuclear-weapon states, the United States, India, and latently Russia.

Mutual nuclear deterrence is also absent in the relations of the United States, France, and the United Kingdom with Israel, India, and Pakistan. A highly asymmetrical nuclear deterrence relationship between the United States and the DPRK (North Korea), with the latter striving to target both the United States and U.S. allies, excludes any hope for mutual U.S.-DPRK arms limitations.

There is also no trace of nuclear deterrence between Russia and India, although they are not formal allies. Russia's nuclear relations with Israel, Pakistan, and the DPRK are quite uncertain. Even if there is a weak case of latent nuclear deterrence in these relationships, it hardly provides a tangible foundation for mutual arms limitations.

Similarly, China's security relations with Israel, Pakistan, and the DPRK do not follow a nuclear deterrence pattern; Israel and China remain out of range of each other, while the DPRK and Pakistan are correspondingly de jure and de facto allies of China.

In contrast to the above assessments, the relations between the United Kingdom and France, on one hand, and Russia, on the other, do feature mutual nuclear deterrence at their core. In recent years, these two NATO countries have reportedly also targeted their nuclear arms against the "rogue states," such as Iran, while Russia allegedly targets only a small part of its nuclear force against these two European states. Nevertheless, theoretically, there is some strategic basis for negotiations, although the quantitative balance is highly asymmetrical in the favor of Russia in both cases.

No doubt, there is also a relationship of asymmetrical nuclear deterrence between the United States and China, and implicitly and latently between China and Russia, with each of the three countries having various levels of assured retaliatory capabilities vis-à-vis the others. However, this "triangle" is far from equilateral, in terms of both nuclear forces and political distances among the powers. While there may be some strategic ground for negotiations between the United States and China, there is much more uncertainty as to the possibility of Russian-Chinese dialogue. In any case, trilateral negotiations and agreements on the nuclear force limitations or reductions are most unlikely in the foreseeable future. There are no established pillars for negotiations of the kind that have served as the foundation of 45 years of U.S.-Russian arms control, such as unequivocal mutual nuclear deterrence, rough quantitative and qualitative parity in nuclear capabilities, and strategic stability on the basis of each possessing assured nuclear second-strike capability against the other.

From this perspective, mutual deterrence and approximate parity exist between New Delhi and Islamabad, so negotiations on nuclear weapon limitations or reductions are possible between India and Pakistan, as well as (although with less certainty) between India and China. However, in this case, trilateral negotiations are hardly feasible, from both strategic and technical perspectives.

Finally, there are two unacknowledged nuclear-weapon states at two opposite ends of Eurasia, Israel and the DPRK, and these two states can hardly take part in any formal arms-control talks with anyone. If their nuclear assets are ever covered by any agreements, those will most probably be linked to resolving difficult regional security issues, limiting conventional armed forces, and settling external and internal political conflicts in the framework of an enhanced NPT regime, rather than following the traditional mutual nuclear arms reduction pattern with any other nuclear-weapon states.

On the whole, the nuclear forces of third country nuclear-weapon states are intertwined much deeper within regional contexts as compared to the strategic nuclear forces of Russia and the United States. In the case of the third states, the prospects for nuclear arms limitation will be much more affected by regional and local territorial, ethnic, and political issues. This is very evident, in particular, with regard to the relations between India and Pakistan, China and India, most of the countries of the Middle East and in the Persian Gulf region, and the two Korean states. The regional balance of general-purpose forces will have a much stronger influence on the prospects for nuclear disarmament in these areas than that balance has on U.S.-Russian START negotiations.

Furthermore, considering the relatively small size and, in many cases, inferior qualitative characteristics of third countries' nuclear forces, the issues of their sufficiency and the possibility of their limitation would be much more affected by rapidly developing regional and global missile defense systems and the potential counterforce threat posed by long-range, high-precision conventional weapons.

Options for Multilateral Nuclear Arms Control

There are presently some multilateral nuclear disarmament agreements—the treaty on the nonproliferation of nuclear weapons, the prohibition on deploying weapons of mass destruction in outer space, the Comprehensive Test Ban Treaty, and potentially on a fissile material cutoff treaty. However, there is no treaty explicitly limiting nuclear arms in a multilateral format, and no such negotiations have been proposed by any of the nuclear-weapon states.

The main conclusion of this chapter is that multilateral nuclear arms control will never happen according to the modes commonly imagined and presently discussed at the P-5 forums: "joining the club" or "getting on the bandwagon."

If such multilateral negotiations are ever to happen, they will probably take the form of separate negotiations in several specific bilateral or limited multilateral forums: the United Kingdom/France with Russia, the United States with China, China with India, and India with Pakistan. The nuclear weapons of Israel and the DPRK may eventually be addressed within appropriate regional security and nonproliferation formats.

Conducting such talks, should they take place, will be much more difficult than the 45 years of experience of U.S.-Soviet/Russian strategic arms limitations and negotiations talks demonstrated—as difficult as they were. The third nuclear-weapon states will never be able to formally join a U.S.-Russian strategic arms reduction dialogue; instead, they will have to elaborate their own paradigms. Conceivably, in some cases, the third nuclear-weapon states will be able to rely on procedures and technical means of verification developed either by Russia and the United States or by international organizations like the United Nations special commissions or the International Atomic Energy Agency.

Encouraging the creation of these new forums and coordinating among them might be the greatest challenge and the most significant achievement of the joint efforts and cooperative diplomacy undertaken by Moscow and Washington in the field of nuclear disarmament and nonproliferation in the 21st century.

References

Federation of American Scientists, "Status of World Nuclear Forces," web page, May 7, 2012. As of January 16, 2014:
http://www.fas.org/programs/ssp/nukes/nuclearweapons/nukestatus.html

"Prime Minister Vladimir Putin Meets with Experts in Sarov to Discuss Global Threats to National Security, Strengthening Russia's Defences and Enhancing the Combat Readiness of Its Armed Forces," Working Day web archive, February 24, 2012. As of March 4, 2014:
http://archive.premier.gov.ru/eng/events/news/18248/

Stockholm International Peace Research Institute, *SIPRI Yearbook 2011: Armaments, Disarmament and International Security*, New York: Oxford University Press, 2011.

U.S. Department of State, "New START Treaty Aggregate Numbers of Strategic Offensive Arms," web page, April 6, 2012. As of January 16, 2014:
http://www.state.gov/t/avc/rls/178058.htm

Afterword

Michèle A. Flournoy and James N. Miller

It is not uncommon to find books written as tributes to the extraordinary contributions of extraordinary people. This book is indeed a tribute to the remarkable contributions and influence of Edward L. Warner III on U.S. defense and national security policy over the last 50 years—from his time as an intelligence officer in the U.S. Air Force, to his time as a leading strategic thinker and analyst at the RAND Corporation, to his time as a policymaker in the Pentagon. But it is also more than that. This is also a collection of deeply personal tributes from many of those who have worked most closely with Ted and whose lives have been meaningfully changed as a result. In that sense, this book is more than an accounting of Ted's remarkable professional achievements; it is also a labor of love.

A wise mentor once said, "Choose the boss, not the job." No matter how appealing a job description might be, the character traits and leadership style of the person you work for will ultimately determine the quality of your experience in a particular position. Sage advice—and advice we both followed in choosing to work for Ted Warner when he served as Assistant Secretary of Defense for Strategy and Requirements, and later as Assistant Secretary of Defense for Strategy and Threat Reduction, in the Clinton administration.

By that point in his career, Ted had already earned a reputation as an exceptional mentor to those who worked for him (as well as many others who did not). Perhaps it was his experience as an assistant professor at the Air Force Academy. Perhaps it was his experience working with younger colleagues at RAND. Or perhaps it was just who he was. In any case, Ted had become known not only as someone who developed smart, new ideas on defense and national security policy but also someone who helped to grow smart, new policy analysts, practitioners, and leaders.

Michèle first met Ted when he called her up out of the blue when she was working for the Arms Control Association. He had read an article she wrote in *Arms Control Today* about the implications of the soon-to-be-ratified Strategic Arms Reduction Treaty for U.S. strategic force posture. He introduced himself, told her he was impressed with her analysis, and invited her to RAND for lunch. Soon after that first meeting, Michèle began receiving invitations to speak at international conferences and write articles for other publications, all courtesy of Ted's marketing efforts behind the scenes. Little did she know that this was just the beginning of 30 plus years of mentorship.

As for Jim, he first met Ted when Jim was working for then Chairman of the House Armed Services Committee Les Aspin. Jim had read Ted's insightful work on the Soviet Union and nuclear weapons, and arranged to meet with him. Immediately impressed, Jim asked Ted to testify to the committee. Soon thereafter, in August 1989, Ted joined Les Aspin, Jim, Rudy de Leon, and others on a two-week-long trip around military bases in the Soviet Union, at the invitation of the Soviet military. Ted and Jim stayed in close touch over the years. In early 1997, as Jim and his wife Adele were enjoying a late dinner in Durham, North Carolina, where Jim was teaching, Ted called. Getting straight to the point as usual, Ted asked Jim to come back to Washington to work in the Pentagon. Notwithstanding the comforts of academia, working for Ted was an opportunity not to be missed. A few months later, Jim had left academia and was working for Ted in the Department of Defense.

Working for Ted in the Pentagon was a seminal experience for both of us. As a boss, he was demanding yet empowering, tough but supportive, all about the mission yet willing to do anything for his people.

As a leader, Ted exhibited several traits that made working for him a life-changing experience for many of his staff. All of these have been touched on in the foregoing chapters, but we summarize them here:

A fierce and incisive intellect. Ted was never one to skim the surface of things. If he is going to deal with an issue, he will seek to understand it deeply and in detail, to master the subject matter. Not surprisingly, Ted would often bypass his deputy assistant secretaries and office directors to engage and learn from the real experts on his staff. For young action officers, facing "the Warner inquisition" on an issue could be a daunting yet exhilarating experience. Ted would rarely get beyond the first slide of a briefing before peppering the briefer with queries, questioning his or her assumptions and analysis, or interrupting with exclamations of disbelief or editorial commentary. But for all the intellectual fireworks, he would listen, and he would learn. He treated his staff as his intellectual equals and his partners in developing policy and moving the department forward.

A master architect of conceptual frameworks. Ted is a creative and conceptual thinker who often brings greater clarity to a subject by creating new conceptual frameworks. He has an uncanny ability to synthesize information, make connections that others miss, and create new ways of thinking about an issue. For example, Ted was perhaps the first person to bring to the Pentagon the notion of an explicitly defined end-to-end operational concept for describing how a given military capability would actually operate to achieve a desired effect. Ted's ability to conceptualize military operations was critical also to his role in leading the civilian review of war plans. His ability to define key phases of military operations and critical decision points for the deployment and employment of military forces ensured that, in the event of a conflict, the President and Secretary of Defense would have real options to shape the course of that conflict.

A boss committed to excellence. Ted has a passion for doing work of the highest quality and for getting it right. As assistant secretary, he set his standards high and then pushed his staff—and himself—to meet or exceed them. This often involved a significant amount of iteration as ideas were honed and concepts were refined. While this constant refining sometimes irked those responsible for revising version 102 of a briefing, we appreciated Ted's openness to incorporating new ideas and his drive toward excellence. Jim's first substantive engagement when working for Ted in 1997 was a memorable experience. Ted had asked for—and participated in—multiple rewrites of a report to Congress on new operational concepts for military missions, such as the attack of time-critical targets and joint suppression of enemy air defenses. Over the course of these revisions, not only the text but the operational concepts themselves were much improved.

A leader willing to take risks to do the right thing. Ted has always understood that, to serve well as a political appointee, one has to be willing to speak truth to power, even when it involves a degree of risk to one's career. While an assistant secretary, he demonstrated his willingness to do just that on any number of occasions. Perhaps even more important, he created a command climate in which his staff felt empowered to bring him news he did not necessarily want to hear and to express a different or dissenting view. Two examples stand out in memory.

The first was a controversial but consequential effort to capture the strategic lessons learned from Somalia after the battle of Mogadishu. Ted took the risk of supporting a clear-eyed and unvarnished assessment of the policies and operations leading up to that fateful event, even though doing so might cast several decisionmakers in the department and beyond in a less than favorable light. Ted was determined to get to the bottom of what happened and why and to ensure that the U.S. government learned from whatever mistakes were made so as not to repeat them in future operations. What's more, he insisted that the results be briefed not only to the Secretary of Defense and the Chairman of the Joint Chiefs but also to senior officials in other agencies and the White House. Once that was done, he spearheaded an effort to ensure that the lessons learned were institutionalized in a new Presidential Decision Directive (PDD-56), an interagency training program, and in the planning for subsequent operations, such as the U.S. interventions in Haiti and Bosnia.

A second example was Ted's willingness (along with then Under Secretary of Defense for Policy Walt Slocombe) to support his staff in writing the occasional "memo of conscience" to express dissent in advance of the Secretary of Defense making a particularly consequential decision. If a Deputy Assistant Secretary of Defense disagreed with the advice being provided up the chain and felt particularly strongly that the secretary was about to make the wrong decision on an issue or had not heard the strongest possible arguments for an alternative course of action, Ted (and Walt) would support us in sending a memo up to the secretary, even if he did not agree with our point of view. He believed that better decisions were made in an environment that enabled alternative viewpoints to be presented fairly and forcefully.

A master of navigating bureaucratic politics and translating policy into action. In contrast to many political appointees, Ted entered office understanding that crafting a good policy was just the first step—not the last—in having impact. Having previously served in the Pentagon, he understood the complex bureaucratic processes that had to be navigated to translate policy into programs and budgets and the web of stakeholders who needed to be brought on board to make any change stick. He regularly engaged his counterparts on the Joint Staff, the service staffs, and the combatant commander staffs to socialize ideas, get their buy-in, and get things done on behalf of the secretary. After the 1997 Quadrennial Defense Review identified the need to improve chemical and biological defenses of U.S. and allied forces as a top priority, Ted developed a close partnership with then U.S. Central Command commander General Tony Zinni—and ensured that this partnership led to tangible progress. Ted led a comprehensive effort first to improve understanding of the strategic and operational challenges associated with chemical and biological weapons and then to take systematic steps to improve U.S. and coalition capabilities to address these challenges. The Desert Breeze war-game series, supported by RAND's Bruce Bennett, provided new insights, which led to significant changes in operational planning, in training and equipping both U.S. and Gulf Cooperation Council forces, and in a series of coalition exercises.

A boss willing to showcase talent and put others forward. During his tenure as assistant secretary, Ted routinely displayed that rarest of qualities in Washington— a certain selflessness in putting his subordinates forward to present their work to his bosses, rather than seeking the spotlight and credit for himself. Perhaps the most striking example of this was the final strategy briefing of the 1997 Quadrennial Defense Review to the DoD leadership. Assembled in one room to hear the briefing were the Secretary of Defense, the Chairman of the Joint Chiefs, all the service chiefs, all of the service secretaries, all the combatant commanders and all the undersecretaries—a dream audience for any ambitious Assistant Secretary of Defense. But rather than do the briefing himself, Ted said to Michèle, who had led the development of the "Shape, Respond, Prepare" strategy, "You did the work, and you should present it. I will be there to kibitz." Seeing this as a professional development opportunity for one of his deputies rather than an opportunity to advance himself was quintessential Ted.

Taken together, Ted's leadership style and character traits made his office— Strategy and Resources and later Strategy and Threat Reduction—a talent magnet and *"the* place to work in Policy."

Fast forward to early 2009 and the beginning of the Obama administration. As we were privileged to take on leadership roles in Policy and began to assemble our team, it was impossible not to think of Ted and the extraordinary talent, expertise, and perspective he would bring to the table. But would he be willing to step out of the more sane life he had created for himself (including time with beloved grandchildren) and return to government service to work for two of his former deputies? When we popped the question, he did not hesitate. If there was a way in which he could help to advance the mission, he was all in. He didn't care about the title or status; he cared about advancing the ball and helping his former—and once again—teammates.

In Ted's most recent government role, as Senior Advisor for Arms Control and Strategic Stability during President Obama's first term, he provided daily advice not only to the two of us, but to assistant secretaries, deputy assistant secretaries, and fortunate action officers throughout OSD Policy. Ted provided mentoring, on an equal opportunity basis, to us all. In serving as senior Department of Defense member on the New Strategic Arms Reduction Treaty negotiating team, Ted capped a career of extraordinary achievement in national security by playing a central role both in the conclusion of the treaty with the Russians and in its ratification by the Senate.

The bulk of this book chronicles the enormous substantive contributions Ted Warner has made to the defense and security of the United States over many decades and the lasting impact he has had on the policies of multiple administrations. But perhaps his greatest and most enduring impact may be the hand he has had in developing the next generation of defense policy professionals and leaders. Not surprisingly, many of them jumped at the chance to contribute to this volume as a testament of their admiration, respect, gratitude, and affection for a truly remarkable public servant, leader, colleague, and friend.

Edward L. Warner III: Publications

"The Bureaucratic Politics of Weapons Acquisition," in Michael MccGwire, Ken Bush, and John McDonnell, eds., *Soviet Naval Policy: Objectives and Constraints*, New York: Praeger Publishers, 1975.

Comparative Defense Policy, with Frank B. Horton and Anthony Robertson, eds., Baltimore: Johns Hopkins University Press, 1975.

The Military in Contemporary Soviet Politics: An Institutional Analysis, New York: Praeger Publishers, 1977.

"The Defense Policy of the Soviet Union," in Douglas Murray and Paul Viotti, eds., *The Defense Policies of Nations: A Comparative Study,* 1st ed., Baltimore: Johns Hopkins University Press, 1981.

"A Framework for Planning the Employment of Air Power in Theater War," with Glenn A. Kent, Santa Monica, Calif.: RAND Corporation, N-2038-AF, 1984. As of March 5, 2014: http://www.rand.org/pubs/notes/N2038.html

A New Approach to Arms Control, with Glenn A. Kent and Randall J. DeValk, Santa Monica, Calif.: RAND Corporation, R-3140-FF/RC, 1984. As of March 5, 2014: http://www.rand.org/pubs/reports/R3140.html

"Defense Policymaking in the Soviet Union," in Robert J. Art, Vincent Davis, and Samuel P. Huntington, eds., *Reorganizing America's Defense: Leadership in War and Peace,* Washington D.C.: Pergamon-Brassey's, 1985.

"Key Issues for the Strategic Offensive Force Reduction Portion of the Nuclear and Space Talks in Geneva," with Glenn A. Kent and Randall J. DeValk, Santa Monica, Calif.: RAND Corporation, N-2348-1-AF, 1985. As of March 5, 2014: http://www.rand.org/pubs/notes/N2348-1.html

"U.S.-Soviet Nuclear Arms Control: The Next Phase," with Arnold L. Horelick, Santa Monica, Calif.: RAND Corporation, OPS-003-1, 1986. As of March 5, 2014: http://www.rand.org/pubs/occasional_papers-soviet/OPS003-1.html

"1986: The Year in Arms Control," with David Ochmanek, Santa Monica, Calif.: RAND Corporation, P-7277, 1987. As of March 5, 2014: http://www.rand.org/pubs/papers/P7277.html

"Key Personnel and Organizations of the Soviet Military High Command," with Josephine J. Bonan and Erma F. Packman, Santa Monica, Calif.: RAND Corporation, N-2567-AF, 1987. As of March 5, 2014: http://www.rand.org/pubs/notes/N2567.html

"Soviet Interests, Concerns, and Activities with Regard to Ballistic Missile Defense," Santa Monica, Calif.: RAND Corporation, P-7367, 1987. As of March 5, 2014: http://www.rand.org/pubs/papers/P7367.html

"SDI and the Existing Arms Control Regime," in Joseph S. Nye Jr. and James A. Schear, eds., *On the Defensive? The Future of SDI*, Lanham, Md.: University Press of America, 1988.

"Approaches to Conventional Arms Reductions," with David Ochmanek, in Robert D. Blackwill and F. Stephen Larrabee, eds., *Conventional Arms Control and East-West Security*, New York: Institute for East-West Security Studies, 1989.

"The Defense Policy of the Soviet Union," Santa Monica, Calif.: RAND Corporation, N-2771-AF, 1989. As of March 5, 2014:
http://www.rand.org/pubs/notes/N2771.html

Next Moves: An Arms Control Agenda for the 1990s, with David Ochmanek, New York: Council on Foreign Relations, 1989.

"The Rise of the Institutchiki," *Defense and Disarmament Alternatives*, Vol. 2, No. 1, January 1989.

"Soviet Concepts and Capabilities for Limited Nuclear War: What We Know and How We Know It," Santa Monica, Calif.: RAND Corporation, N-2769-AF, 1989. As of March 5, 2014:
http://www.rand.org/pubs/notes/N2769.html

"Soviet Military Doctrine: New Thinking and Old Realities in Soviet Defence Policy," *Survival*, Vol. 31, No. 1, January–February 1989.

"The Decline of the Soviet Military: Downsizing, Fragmentation, and Possible Disintegration," Santa Monica, Calif.: RAND Corporation, P-7762, 1992. As of March 5, 2014:
http://www.rand.org/pubs/papers/P7762.html

About the Authors

James M. Acton is a senior associate in the Nuclear Policy Program at the Carnegie Endowment for International Peace. His research spans the field of nuclear policy. He is the author of two Adelphi books, *Deterrence During Disarmament: Deep Nuclear Reductions and International Security* and *Abolishing Nuclear Weapons* (with George Perkovich). He wrote, with Mark Hibbs, *Why Fukushima Was Preventable*, a first-of-its-kind study into the accident's root causes. Dr. Acton is a member of the Trilateral Commission on Challenges to Deep Cuts and a former member of the International Panel on Fissile Materials. In 2010–2011, he cochaired the Next Generation Working Group on U.S.-Russia arms control. He has published in *Bulletin of the Atomic Scientists*, *Foreign Affairs*, *International Herald Tribune*, *Jane's Intelligence Review*, *New York Times*, *Nonproliferation Review*, *Survival*, and *Washington Quarterly*. He holds a Ph.D. in theoretical physics from the University of Cambridge.

Michael Albertson has worked in the Department of Defense since 2004, primarily as an analyst studying the capabilities and doctrine of foreign military forces. He is currently serving as a director for Russia and Central Asia on the National Security Staff. He worked in the Office of the Secretary of Defense as a policy advisor to Dr. Ted Warner, Senior Advisor for Arms Control and Strategic Stability to the Under Secretary of Defense (Policy). In this capacity, he served on the U.S. delegation in Geneva during negotiation of the New Strategic Arms Reduction Treaty and worked as part of the DoD team on treaty ratification and implementation efforts. His work involved assisting the senior advisor in dialogues on strategic stability issues involving the nuclear balance, emerging conventional long-range strike and missile defense systems, space/counterspace developments, and the impact of cyber capabilities. Mr. Albertson holds a B.A. from Claremont McKenna College in international relations and government, an M.S. in strategic intelligence from the National Defense Intelligence College, and an M.A. in security policy studies from George Washington University.

Alexei G. Arbatov is a scholar in residence with the Carnegie Moscow Center's Nonproliferation Program. Formerly, he was a member of the State Duma, vice chairman of the Russian United Democratic Party (Yabloko), and deputy chairman of the Duma Defense Committee. He is a member of the Russian Academy of Sciences. He leads the academy's Center for International Security at the Institute of World Economy and International Relations, where he was once a department head and a research fellow. He is a member of numerous boards and councils, including the research council of the Russian Ministry of Foreign Affairs, the board of directors of the Nuclear Threat Initiative, the governing board of the Center for Nonproliferation Studies at the Monterey Institute, and the Russian Council for Foreign and Defense Policy. Dr. Arbatov is author of several books and numerous articles and papers on issues of global security, strategic stability, disarmament, Russian military reform, and various current domestic and foreign political issues.

Elbridge A. Colby is the Robert M. Gates Fellow at the Center for a New American Security, where he focuses on strategic, deterrence, nuclear weapons, Asia-Pacific, and related issues and advises a number of U.S. government entities. He was previously a principal analyst and division lead for global strategic affairs at the Center for Naval Analysis. Prior to that, he served as policy advisor to Ted Warner when he was the Secretary of Defense's representative for the new Strategic Arms Reduction Treaty, as an expert advisor to the Congressional Strategic Posture Commission, and in a number of other government positions. He is the author of a number of book chapters and studies on strategic issues and was the coeditor of *Strategic Stability: Contending Interpretations*. Mr. Colby is a graduate of Harvard College and Yale Law School.

Michèle A. Flournoy is a senior advisor at the Boston Consulting Group. From 2009 to 2012, she served as the Under Secretary of Defense for Policy, the principal advisor to the Secretary of Defense in the formulation of national security and defense policy, oversight of military plans and operations, and in National Security Council deliberations. After the 2008 election, she co-led President Obama's transition team at DoD. In January 2007, she cofounded the Center for a New American Security (CNAS), a nonpartisan think tank dedicated to developing strong, pragmatic and principled national security policies, and served as CNAS' president. Previously, she was senior advisor at the Center for Strategic and International Studies and, prior to that, a distinguished research professor at the Institute for National Strategic Studies at the National Defense University. Ms. Flournoy served as the Principal Deputy Assistant Secretary of Defense for Strategy and Threat Reduction and Deputy Assistant Secretary of Defense for Strategy in the Office of the Secretary of Defense during the Clinton administration. She now serves on the boards of directors of both CNAS and the Atlantic Council. She is also a senior fellow at Harvard's Belfer Center for Science and International Affairs; a member of the Defense Policy Board; director of the Central Intelligence Agency's External Advisory Board; and a member of the Aspen Strategy Group, the Council on Foreign Relations, and Women in International Security.

Rose E. Gottemoeller has been Assistant Secretary of State for the Bureau of Arms Control, Verification, and Compliance since April 2009. She was the chief U.S. negotiator of the New Strategic Arms Reduction Treaty (New START) with the Russian Federation, which entered into force on February 5, 2011. In February 2012,

President Obama designated her as the Acting Under Secretary for Arms Control and International Security. Prior to joining the Department of State, in 2000, she became a senior associate with the Carnegie Endowment for International Peace, where she also served as the Director of the Carnegie Moscow Center (January 2006–December 2008). In 1998–2000, as Deputy Undersecretary of Energy for Defense Nuclear Non-proliferation and before that, Assistant Secretary of Energy for Nonproliferation and National Security, she was responsible for all nonproliferation cooperation with Russia and the Newly Independent States. Prior to her work at the Department of Energy, she served for three years as Deputy Director of the International Institute for Strategic Studies in London. From 1993 to 1994, she served on the National Security Council staff as director for Russia, Ukraine, and Eurasia Affairs, with responsibility for denu-clearization in Ukraine, Kazakhstan, and Belarus. Previously, she was a social scientist at the RAND Corporation and a Council on Foreign Relations International Affairs Fellow. She has taught on Soviet military policy and Russian security at Georgetown University. Ms. Gottemoeller received a B.S. from Georgetown University and an M.A. from George Washington University.

Andrew R. Hoehn is Senior Vice President for Research and Analysis at the RAND Corporation. He previously served at RAND as Vice President and Director of Project AIR FORCE (PAF), where he was responsible for overseeing research and analyses on strategy, force employment, personnel and training, and resource man-agement. He first joined RAND as director of PAF's Strategy and Doctrine program. Previously, he was the Deputy Assistant Secretary of Defense for Strategy and Princi-pal Director for Strategy and Director for Requirements in the Office of the Secretary of Defense. Prior to joining government, he was associate editor of the *Marine Corps Gazette*. He is professor of policy analysis at the Pardee RAND Graduate School and was adjunct professor of strategic studies at the Johns Hopkins School of Advanced International Studies. He is a member of the Council on Foreign Relations and the board of visitors at the University of Pittsburgh Graduate School of Public and Inter-national Affairs. Mr. Hoehn earned a bachelor's degree in political science from Baldwin-Wallace College and a master's degree in public and international affairs from the University of Pittsburgh.

Christopher J. Lamb is a Distinguished Research Fellow in and currently Deputy Director of the Institute for National Strategic Studies at National Defense University. His previous positions include Deputy Assistant Secretary of Defense for Resources and Plans in the Office of the Secretary of Defense; study director for the Project on National Security Reform's 2008 report, "Forging a New Shield"; Deputy Director for Military Development on the Department of State's Interagency Task Force for Military Stabilization in the Balkans; and Director of Policy Planning in the Office of the Assistant Secretary of Defense for Special Operations and Low-Intensity Conflict. From 1985 to 1992, he was a foreign service officer with service in Haiti, Ivory Coast, and Benin. Dr. Lamb received his doctorate in international relations from Georgetown University in 1986 and has been an adjunct professor in the university's national security program.

James N. Miller is President of Adaptive Strategies, LLC. He served as the Under Secretary of Defense for Policy from May 2012 to January 2014. In that role, he provided advice and assistance to the Secretary of Defense and Deputy Secretary of Defense on all matters concerning the formulation of national security and defense policy and the integration and oversight of DoD policy and plans to achieve national security objectives. From 2009 to 2012, he served as Principal Deputy Under Secretary of Defense for Policy. Previous positions include serving as Senior Vice President and Director of Studies at the Center for a New American Security (2007–2009); Senior Vice President (2003–2007) and Vice President (2000–2003) at Hicks and Associates, Inc.; Deputy Assistant Secretary of Defense for Requirements, Plans, and Counter-proliferation Policy (1997–2000); assistant professor at Duke University (1992–1997); and senior professional staff member for the House Armed Services Committee (1988–1992). A member of the International Institute for Strategic Studies, he has served as an advisor to the Combating WMD Panel of DoD's Threat Reduction Advisory Committee and the Defense Science Board; as senior associate at the Center for Strategic and International Studies; and as senior associate member at St. Antony's College, Oxford. He has received the Department of Defense's highest civilian award, the Medal for Distinguished Public Service, four times. Dr. Miller received a B.A. degree with honors in economics from Stanford University and master's and doctoral degrees in public policy from the John F. Kennedy School of Government at Harvard University.

David Ochmanek is the Deputy Assistant Secretary of Defense for Force Development. Prior to joining the Office of the Secretary of Defense, he was a senior defense analyst and director of the Strategy and Doctrine Program for Project AIR FORCE at the RAND Corporation, where he worked from 1985 until 1993, and again from 1995 until 2009. From 1993 until 1995, he served as Deputy Assistant Secretary of Defense for Strategy. Prior to joining RAND, he was a member of the Foreign Service of the United States, serving from 1980 to 1985. From 1973 to 1978, he was an officer in the U.S. Air Force. Mr. Ochmanek is a graduate of the U.S. Air Force Academy and Princeton University's Woodrow Wilson School of Public and International Affairs. He has been an adjunct professor at Georgetown and George Washington Universities.

Eugene Rumer is a senior associate and director of the Russia and Eurasia Program at the Carnegie Endowment for International Peace. From 2010 to 2014, he served as the National Intelligence Officer for Russia and Eurasia at the National Intelligence Council. From 2000 to 2010, he worked at the Institute for National Strategic Studies, National Defense University. Prior to that, he served on the National Security Council Staff and at the Policy Planning Staff at the Department of State. He began his professional career as an analyst of Soviet, then Russian, politics and defense policy at the RAND Corporation, where he worked from 1988 to 1996, including three years in Moscow as a resident RAND representative. Dr. Rumer holds degrees from Boston

University (B.A.), Georgetown University (M.A.), and the Massachusetts Institute of Technology (Ph.D.).

James A. Schear served as Deputy Assistant Secretary of Defense for Partnership Strategy and Stability Operations from April 2009 to June 2013. He led initiatives to help foreign partners build effective and accountable defense ministries, to reshape U.S. stability operations investments post-Afghanistan, and to provide lifesaving aid amid natural disasters and complex emergencies. His public service contributions span more than two decades, including support for United Nations missions in Cambodia and former Yugoslavia and serving as the Deputy Assistant Secretary of Defense for Peacekeeping and Humanitarian Affairs in the Office of the Secretary of Defense from 1997 until 2001. He has also held research appointments at Harvard University's Kennedy School, the Brookings Institution, the Carnegie Endowment, the International Institute for Strategic Studies, and the Stimson Center. Dr. Schear holds a doctorate from the London School of Economics and Political Science, a master's degree from Johns Hopkins' School of Advanced International Studies, and a bachelor's from American University's School of International Service.

Walter B. Slocombe is now a lawyer at the Washington, D.C., law firm of Caplin & Drysdale. His government positions included Under Secretary of Defense for Policy (1994–2001), Principal Deputy Under Secretary of Defense for Policy (1993–1994), Deputy Under Secretary for Policy Planning (1979–1981), Principal Deputy Assistant Secretary for International Security Affairs (1977–1979), member of the National Security Council's Program Analysis Staff (1969–1970), and law clerk to Supreme Court Justice Abe Fortas (1968–1969). In 2003, he was Senior Director for National Security and Defense in the Coalition Provisional Authority for Iraq. Mr. Slocombe was educated at Princeton University; Balliol College, Oxford; and Harvard Law School.

Michael Sulmeyer is currently senior policy advisor in the Office of the Deputy Assistant Secretary of Defense for Cyber Policy. Prior to this assignment, he served as policy advisor for Arms Control and Strategic Stability in the office of the Under Secretary of Defense for Policy. He is a graduate of Stanford Law School and received his doctorate in politics from Oxford University as a Marshall Scholar. His dissertation, "Money for Nothing: Understanding the Termination of U.S. Major Defense Acquisition Programs," was awarded the Political Studies Association's Sir Walter Bagehot Prize for Best Dissertation in Government and Public Administration. Dr. Sulmeyer earned his master's in war studies at King's College London and was a Zukerman Fellow at Stanford's Center for International Security and Cooperation. His academic research examines how civil-military relations and the constitutional principles of the separation of powers affect defense resource allocation and strategy.

Dean A. Wilkening is a physicist at the Lawrence Livermore National Laboratory (LLNL) currently on assignment to the Office of the Secretary of Defense as a special assistant to the Assistant Secretary of Defense for Global Security Affairs and the Under Secretary of Defense for Policy. Prior to joining LLNL, he worked at the

Center for International Security and Cooperation at Stanford University for 16 years as a senior scientist. From 1982 to 1995, he worked at the RAND Corporation in Santa Monica, California, where he held several management positions. His major research interests include nuclear strategy and policy, arms control, the proliferation of nuclear and biological weapons, bioterrorism, ballistic missile proliferation, and ballistic missile defense. His most recent research focuses on the technical viability of ballistic missile defense and its strategic impact in Northeast Asia and Europe, including the potential impact of U.S. missile defense on Russian and Chinese strategic nuclear forces. Prior work focused on the technical feasibility of airborne boost-phase ballistic missile defense. He has participated in several U.S. National Academy of Science committees on biological terrorism and recently was a member of the National Academy of Sciences study entitled "An Assessment of Concepts and Systems for U.S. Boost-Phase Missile Defense in Comparison to Other Alternatives." Dr. Wilkening received his Ph.D. in physics from Harvard University; is a fellow of the American Physical Society; and has published over 60 journal articles, book chapters, and monographs on a range of security topics.

Abbreviations

ABM	Anti-Ballistic Missile
AOR	area of responsibility
ATO	air tasking order
BUR	Bottom-Up Review
CIA	Central Intelligence Agency
CNAS	Center for a New American Security
CPG	Contingency Planning Guidance
D	Democrat
DoD	Department of Defense
DPG	Defense Planning Guidance
DPRK	Democratic People's Republic of Korea
FDO	flexible deterrent options
GBI	ground-based interceptor
ICBM	intercontinental ballistic missile
JSTARS	Joint Surveillance and Target Attack Radar System
LANTIRN	Low-Altitude Navigation and Targeting Infrared for Night
LLNL	Lawrence Livermore National Laboratory
LUA	launch under attack
MAD	mutually assured destruction
MIRV	multiple independently targeted reentry vehicle

MMIII	Minuteman III
MoD	Ministry of Defense
MRC	major regional conflict
NATO	North Atlantic Treaty Organization
NPT	Treaty on the Non-Proliferation of Nuclear Weapons
NSC	National Security Council
NSPD	National Security Presidential Directive
OSD	Office of the Secretary of Defense
PAF	Project AIR FORCE
PDD	Presidential Decision Directive
PGS	prompt global strike
pol-mil	political-military
R	Republican
ROK	Republic of Korea
RV	reentry vehicle
S/CRS	Department of State, Office of the Coordinator for Reconstruction and Stabilization
SALT	Strategic Arms Limitation Treaty
SAM	surface-to-air missile
SLBM	submarine-launched ballistic missile
SSBN	missile-carrying nuclear submarine
START	Strategic Arms Reduction Treaty
UN	United Nations
UNITAF	United Nations Task Force
USSR	Union of Soviet Socialist Republics
WMD	weapons of mass destruction